Chris Henderson

JUMP!

Deliver astonishing results by unleashing your Leadership Team

RedDoor

Every effort has been made to ensure attributions and references are correct. Please notify the publisher if any amendments should be made for subsequent print runs or editions.

Published by RedDoor
www.reddoorpublishing.com

© 2015 Chris Henderson

The right of Chris Henderson to be identified as author of this Work has been asserted by him in accordance with sections 77 and 78 of the Copyright, Designs and Patents Act 1988

ISBN 978-1-910453-24-7 paperback
ISBN 978-1-910453-06-3 hardback

A CIP catalogue record for this book is available from the British Library

Cover design: Gemma Wilson
Typesetting: Gemma Wilson

Printed in the UK by TJ International, Padstow, Cornwall

Picture credits
Images on pp. 32, 72, 80-1, 118-9, 134-5, 136, 156, 206, 208, 236 © Chris Henderson
Images on pp. 9, 18, 34, 61, 67, 80, 118 (top), 134 (top) ©iStock.com/shironosov
Image on p. 11 © yekophotostudio/depositphotos.com
Images on pp. 44, 154 (top) © minervastock/depositphotos.com
Image on p. 52 ©SergeyNivens/depositphotos.com
Image on p. 74 © karelnoppe/depositphotos.com
Images on pp. 100 (top), 180 (top), 219 © pressmaster/depositphotos.com
Image on p. 100-1 ©Photocreo/depositphotos.com
Image on p. 154-5 © Andaman/depositphotos.com
Image on p. 180-1 © Birute/depositphotos.com
Image on p. 215 © ml12nan/depositphotos.com
Cover images © Getty Images/Adam Jones (Maasai jumping) and © Getty Images/Arco Images/Lukasseck Frank

A powerful read? Who says so?

'★★★★★: Essential reading on leadership'

This book … will undoubtedly appeal to anyone who is interested in the dynamics of Leadership Team performance.

[It] provides a superb balance between leadership theory and common sense, as well as easily digestible, practical advice on how to facilitate these [Six Game Changing] conversations.

I found the tools and case studies particularly useful. The book even contains fascinating insights from the author's experience of the Kenyan Maasai people and how their collective approach to success has much to teach us in the Boardroom.

JUMP! acts as an important reminder to constantly think about how Leadership Teams can improve. It's essential reading for even the busiest executive.

HR Magazine

'★★★★★: Exceptional, a "must read" for any manager or leader'

Chris Henderson has designed a brilliant introduction specifically for busy leaders who need to quickly get to grips with their team.

Although this book rewards the 'quick dip' approach (with superb diagrams, well laid out boxed highlights and a comprehensive 'toolkit' annex) I'm deeply impressed with the quality and clarity of thinking in this book.

I'd recommend this book for busy leaders who want a simple framework to help them get to grips with their teams but also for those who are interested in a deeper read to support group coaching within organisations.

Chartered Management Institute

Book of the Month: November 2015

If you're [a] CEO/CXO and have the desire to really work your Leadership Team into shape for something better … you should start moving from (as Chris calls it) *silos of misery* to a cross-functional, intertwined Leadership Team setting strategy to work and delivering that elusive high performing executive promise that appeals to their own people, customers and shareholders alike.

HR Director Magazine

Feedback from leaders and developers of teams

'A really well-written and wise book. It is the first thing I've read that concisely gets to the beliefs and actions that I really think make the difference for Leadership Teams, and makes the case and tools for developing them. I can think of many people who I want to read this book and take action.'

'I read a lot of business books, and this is the one of the best I have read. I really appreciated the way it was put together, allowing me to dip in and out of it to pick out the parts that were most relevant, so that I didn't need to read it cover to cover to get the full benefit. That said, I enjoyed it so much that I have now read it all the way through!'

'A practical and well-created book… a source of inspiration to leaders and their teams.'

'A most engaging read… Engaging as it committed to text many of the experiences/ learnings that I have encountered – good, bad and ugly. I have no doubt that the sorts of approaches you outline make a real difference, without being rocket science.'

'I've now had a chance to read Jump! *and found it very rewarding.* The book is brimming with helpful insights, anecdotes and examples. The "Six Conversations" structure holds it all together very well and the tools provide a lot extra. I can imagine any Leadership Team, especially one struggling in difficult times, taking heart and inspiration from this book.'

Dedication

As befits the subject matter, this book, too, has been a huge team effort and I'd like to thank and dedicate it to all those who have played a part in its creation. Thank you to:

Helena, my wife, who humbles me with the strength of her care and support. Without her patience, forbearance and encouragement, this book, like so much else, would not have been possible.

My parents, who were the first team I ever knew and are the best one I'll ever see.

My daughters, Jocelyn and Tamsin, who have taught me every day for more than two decades about the value and meaning of love.

The development professionals who inspired me when I saw them in action, and whom I have been privileged to go on to work with. There are too many to mention but David Parton, Bridget Farrands, Nic Turner, John Scherer and Carol Daniels have been particularly influential.

The faculty on the Masters in Organisational Consulting at Ashridge Business School, who opened my eyes to how much else there was for me to learn, and transformed my practice from enthusiastic amateur to learning professional.

All of the writers and experts I have learned from, in disciplines from anthropology to team dynamics, from sociology to change and from philosophy to leadership. Most of these are acknowledged in the text, but I'm sure there will be others whose work I have unknowingly drawn from.

The friends and colleagues who have encouraged me and helped me so much in shaping this book: Charles Kingsmill, Lisa Beutler, Mark Evans, John Richards, Norman Usher, Ian Webster and David Parton.

Kakuta, and everyone in Merrueshi, for teaching me so much, sharing their extraordinary home with me and giving me inspiration and purpose. And John Scherer, who was my partner in making my first-ever visit there possible, for helping me tell the stories that illuminate the world of Leadership Teams.

My publishing team: Ian Shircore for helping turn my ideas into readable words, Gemma Wilson for the design that animates those words and Clare Christian at Red Door Publishing for turning all of that into the book you are now holding.

And last, but certainly not least, to my clients, who have given me the privilege of their trust, shared their journeys with me, helped me refine the thinking and approaches in this book and given me permission to share some of their stories.

Contents

SECTION FOUR

'Never doubt that a group of thoughtful and committed citizens could change the world. Indeed, it is the only thing that ever has'
Usually attributed to Margaret Mead – source unknown

FOREWORD

John Richards

Honorary Professor in Management Learning,
University of Nottingham

When I first met Chris Henderson, he was part of the management team at The Boots Company plc, in a profitable business but a turbulent environment. I worked with Chris and the rest of the executive team as they progressed through the many changes in strategy, structure and culture that needed to be made, and this experience probably marked the birth of his interest and expertise in helping top management teams. Chris brings to this work a piercing intellect, strategic insight, a strong theoretical base (he has, for example, taught Balanced Scorecard techniques at Nottingham University Business School) and a high degree of empathy with his clients.

Jump! is firmly grounded in a combination of experience, wide reading and systematic empirical research. Chris's commitment to working with the Maasai in Kenya has provided him with a powerful comparative metaphor that sheds light on many Western business practices, and the book gets to the heart of top management teamworking in its focus on the dialogues necessary for team effectiveness.

I believe *Jump!* adds real value to the current literature. David Hambrick, for example, is one of the key thinkers in this field, with his work on upper echelons theory. But even he puzzles over the difficulty of finding really effective top management teams:

> *Team? How do you define 'team'? When I think of a team, I think of interaction, give-and-take, and shared purpose. Here, we're a collection of strong players, but hardly a team. We rarely meet as a team – rarely see each other, in fact. We don't particularly share the*

same views. I wouldn't say we actually work at cross purposes, but a lot of self-centred behaviour occurs. Where's the 'team' in all this?

(Hambrick, 1997)

Senge, in his work on the learning organisation (Senge 2006), emphasises that achieving corporate aspirations depends on understanding the complexity of the external and internal environment, which can only be achieved through generative conversation. In his chapter on team learning, Senge argues: 'A team committed to learning must not only be committed to telling the truth about what's going on "out there" in their business reality, but also about what's going on "in here", within the team itself.'

The Harvard Negotiation Project has focused, like Chris, on effective conversations. In their book, *Difficult Conversations*, the Harvard team of Stone, Patton and Heen (Patten, Stone, & Heen, 2011) make the case for moving from what they call 'a battle of messages' to a learning conversation that addresses different perspectives on what happened and the emotions that were aroused, and calls for an open exploration of how the different parties all contributed to the situation.

Chris draws these two strands together in his unique model of the Six Game-Changing Conversations, with their specific focus on ambition, relationships, priorities, accountability, delivery and learning.

Above all, though, he gives practical advice on how to engage in and get the best out of these conversations.

Reading this book will encourage and inspire you to appraise the working of your own team and consider how best to harness its disparate talents, for the benefit of the business and the wellbeing of the team members. It will quite probably trigger a realisation that you need to make significant changes to how your team works, though this will thankfully be backed up by immediate practical advice on how to go about making them.

Maybe, too, there will be the realisation that you may need help to do all this. *Jump!* will provide you with an enormous amount of useful advice about what sort of help you'll need – and how to go about getting it.

John Richards
MA MBAS CPsychol
University of Nottingham

JUMP!
executive summary

Getting your Leadership Team right is quite possibly the largest single business opportunity available to you. You should know why, and what can be done to make your Leadership Team your organisation's greatest asset.

You don't have to read this book to benefit from it. If you're a member of a Leadership Team, you probably don't have time to read a book about them.

But take a moment to think about it. You know your team doesn't run at anything like full throttle. It doesn't make the most of the talents of the people involved – and it doesn't get the most out of the time you spend together.

Perhaps I'm wrong about your team. But if I'm wrong, your organisation is in that tiny minority where Leadership Teams are truly delivering the goods.

I have a lot to tell you about how you can improve this situation. But you don't have time to read.

So here's my proposition.

I have boiled down all the main points of the book into a six-page 'power-read' summary, starting overleaf, that you can take in without investing more than a few minutes of your time.

Read this first, and then, if you like, stop.

You'll have seen the headlines and the main messages. You'll be able to discuss these ideas with others. And maybe, later, you will want to come back, when you're on a long flight or on a beach somewhere, and fill yourself in on the details and the specific techniques.

For now, though, here's the summary. Getting your Leadership Team right is quite possibly the largest single business opportunity available to you. You should know why, and what can be done to make your Leadership Team your organisation's greatest asset.

Is this you?

- ▲ You're leading an organisation, or a significant part of one, but those around you think you are the only person with responsibility for the organisation as a whole.
- ▲ The team of bright but challenging people around you are not only too focused on their own areas but also aren't working together well enough, so you have to invest a lot of your time in bringing them, as well as the organisation, together.
- ▲ When you get your Leadership Team together, and despite huge and overcrowded agendas, you never fully manage to properly address the underlying issues so end up stuck in a cycle of firefighting.

What's in it for you?

- ▲ The unique role and influence of your Leadership Team means that turning it into a high performing team will have a huge impact on both your results and on your working experience.
- ▲ Not only is making this transition possible, it can happen much faster than you might think. You'll start to see real benefits in weeks rather than months.
- ▲ This book will help you to better understand your Leadership Team, tell you how to transform it and give you a complete toolkit for travelling the journey.

Why this book?

- ▲ Leaders I meet are working incredibly long hours but usually have, at best, only marginal improvements in results to show for all this effort. They yearn to make a bigger difference, but are frustrated by how hard it is to make real progress. It's clear that something is missing in our approach to leadership.
- ▲ This book brings together a wealth of research and best practice from psychology and sociology, our own research into Leadership Teams and years of experience of working with them.

▲ It also includes ideas and insights from time spent with a Maasai community over a period of more than ten years – collective endeavour is not, after all, a phenomenon only of late 20th and early 21st century management literature.

Why Leadership Teams?

▲ Academic research and organisational practice have become obsessed with individual leadership. This is an important subject, but it misses the equally important issue of how leaders work together in the boardroom.
▲ No individual leader has all the skills, knowledge and experience needed to drive a large organisation. Only a complete and effective Leadership Team can bring together the full set of all these attributes. Most Leadership Teams are at least ineffective and many are significantly dysfunctional with unproductive conflict, poor meetings and not enough genuine teamwork.
▲ All the biggest challenges in organisations are cross-functional in nature. High quality collaboration across boundaries is needed if we are to fully understand them, identify optimum solutions and implement changes.

What makes Leadership Teams different?

▲ Leadership Teams almost always report to a relatively remote owner, shareholder or parent board. This gives them a lot of autonomy for action, a high degree of pressure for bottom line results and little in the way of interest or support in how they are achieved.
▲ They are typically populated by people who are driven, have strong views and have reached their positions because of their functional expertise. They are used to leading their own teams, rather than being naturally collaborative or working as part of a team.
▲ While there are many teams of many types in organisations, the nature of the challenge facing Leadership Teams

is particularly difficult and ambiguous as they have to understand and address huge complexity, both in the external environment and within their own organisations.

The research

Given the lack of research and practice specifically on Leadership Teams, we have conducted our own research, which shows, among other findings:

▲ Leaders believe huge uplifts, between 45 per cent and 90 per cent, in bottom line performance would be realised if the team could work to its potential. In terms of the value at stake, that makes it the biggest single issue on most CEOs' agendas, and potentially the most rewarding.
▲ There are equally dramatic figures for the degree to which members find their Leadership Team demotivating and the degree to which they feel it hinders them rather than helping get results.
▲ Paradoxically, though, very few team members (only about 1 in 8 in high performing teams, and hardly any in average and underperforming teams) report that they have been involved in a serious and sustained effort to develop the team.

The Six Game-Changing Conversations

▲ Our research also identified a set of 'competencies', The Six Game-Changing Conversations that distinguish high performing Leadership Teams from those who underperform. While every team will mix them together in different ways (just as individual leaders have varied competency profiles), they provide a framework for the assessment and development of any team.
▲ Each of the Six Conversations has the potential to make a big difference, but when put together they have truly transformational power. All teams have these conversations to some degree. Few excel at many of them and even fewer are

consistently good at all of them.

▲ Each of the Six Conversations is quite different in nature and requires different skills, processes and disciplines.

What are the Six Conversations?

Ambition Conversations – In which teams create a powerful, energising goal that is big enough to require profound change and motivating enough to keep people striving towards it when the going gets tough.

Relationship Conversations – Which build the trust and confidence team members need for the robust and challenging discussions, on difficult and sometimes sensitive subjects, that are necessary for real change.

Priority Conversations – Which generate clear distinctions between the things that will move the organisation towards its goal and everything else that needs to be done. They also ensure that resources of time and money are properly focused on these few things that really matter.

Accountability Conversations – In which teams understand and work with collective, as well as individual, accountability. This requires team members to become truly aligned, rather than just 'buying in' to decisions – or, worse, leaving the room not supporting the decision that has been made.

Delivery Conversations – In which the Leadership Team owns and drives the three underpinning imperatives of consistent and sustained delivery for all projects – engaging and mobilising stakeholders, developing and involving a wider group of leaders, and creating a culture that embraces and supports change.

Learning Conversations – In which Leadership Team members get beyond the usual win-lose debates and use the full range of experience and expertise in the room to expand their understanding of each issue, create new and better options for how to proceed and so make better decisions.

What's stopping teams from acting to realise their potential?

Leaders described three key reasons why it's difficult to develop a Leadership Team. The book includes guidance on how to overcome all three.

▲ *Understanding the problem.* It provides a framework to help you understand what is working and what isn't in a team, and what the benefits would be of shifting different aspects of its functioning.
▲ *Deciding how to begin.* It provides guidance on how to judge whether you are ready to commence a team development programme – and gives you the confidence to take the initiative.
▲ *Finding a route map to success.* It identifies the steps to follow to get started, including the creation of a business case. It also contains a comprehensive toolkit to develop those aspects of the team that most need attention.

The first steps to changing your team

A CEO must start by deciding whether he has the right team around the table. How big should the team be? Who is part of the CEO's desired future and who will be able to make the journey? Who should be given a chance and who should be dealt with before a programme starts? Guidance on all these questions can be found in Chapter 14.

In Section 3, I have set out in detail the steps to get started. These include:

Step One – *Commit, and begin.* Change will only start when you start to act. Be honest with yourself and address the reasons why you haven't started before.

Step Two – *Clearly articulate the rationale.* To win the support of others, consolidate your own commitment and sustain action, even when the going gets tough, you will need a clear and powerful rationale.

Step Three – *Decide who will manage the change.* While the CEO or MD will have to lead the initiative, they will need expert help to manage it. The nature of the skills needed is described in detail.

Step Four – *Win support.* To succeed, the MD/CEO will need at least the support of the members of the Leadership Team – and probably other stakeholders too. We have a proven and engaging method for doing this.

Step Five – *Collate views and assemble the case for change.* Once the team and other stakeholders have been involved, their views can be used to collate a business case and provide the impetus for getting started.

Step Six – *Run a launch workshop.* This needs to take the initial energy and harness it to provide support for and commitment to a sustained programme of team development. We have a tried and tested approach for doing this and a model agenda is included.

You've read the summary, so why read the book?

You need the detail. If you're serious about team development, you'll want to get beyond the summary of the key ideas set out here to understand, and test for yourself, the concepts and their underpinnings in more detail.

It's designed to be an accessible and interesting read. Business books can be dry. I have included numerous case studies, models and illustrations – and stories from the Maasai – to illuminate and animate the ideas.

It tells you how you can improve your team. Theory and ideas are interesting, but what really matters to you is whether you can apply them in your own team. Section 4 contains a comprehensive toolkit for getting started, developing your ability to hold the Six Conversations and sustaining the changes over time. ▲

INTRODUCTION

Most of us have glimpsed, however briefly or partially, the potential of working in a great team. We know, in our guts as well as our heads, that great teams can deliver results so far beyond our initial expectations that they genuinely astonish us.

Two of the leading academics in this field, Katzenbach and Smith, have identified a number of things that these extraordinary teams have in common, including:

- ▲ Exceptional performance – they outperform all reasonable expectations of the group, including those of the members themselves
- ▲ High levels of enthusiasm and energy
- ▲ Personal commitment and willingness to go the extra mile
- ▲ Great stories of 'galvanising events' – turning points in their history, where they succeeded against the odds
- ▲ More fun and humour than other teams

This certainly echoes my own experience of working in and with great Leadership Teams. But it doesn't begin to capture the sheer excitement of being part of a team that is truly working wonders.

What's missing is the joy of feeling rapid progress, the respect you feel from both above and below, and the thrill of tackling the really big challenges – because you know you can.

Being able to give your best is incredibly rewarding. But it's also hugely challenging, as you try to raise your own game, knowing that everyone around you is doing the same. Leadership Team meetings become a pleasure to look forward to – a unique opportunity to get support to deal with your own problems and work together on getting to grips with what really matters for the whole organisation.

Once you've been part of a team like this, you'll never forget it. Or the colleagues you shared it with.

Katzenbach and Smith end their book on the subject with a great definition of a high performing team:

> 'A small group of people so committed to something larger than themselves that they will not be denied.'

I have experienced this kind of team and it changed my life – to the point where I decided to dedicate my career to creating such teams and experiences. I hope the excitement of your memories of great teams remains strong enough for you to want to come with me on the journey through this book.

If you do, I'll help you understand what makes these teams so special, then take you through the practical steps needed to take your team from wherever it is now to becoming a truly high performing Leadership Team.

Leadership is in trouble

We all know about the massive problems confronting leaders and organisations. Markets are globalising. Competition comes from all over the world. Customers are ever more demanding, staff are less loyal, and running organisations is increasingly a matter of knitting together people, cultures and processes across continents.

All this is happening against the backdrop of global economic fundamentals which promise lower growth for years, if not decades, to come.

None of this, of course, is news to anyone in a leadership position. When I talk to leaders in organisations, they consistently tell me three things:

'I'm incredibly busy. My days start early and end late. I get hundreds of emails a week. I have back-to-back meetings every day and I'm having to work evenings and weekends just to keep up.'

'I'm frustrated. I can see the potential of this organisation, but progress is incredibly slow. We're finding it hard to make the few percentage points of growth in our annual plans – let alone the transformational changes we need to break through to the next level.'

'It should be more fulfilling. I worked hard to be in a leadership position, because I wanted to make a difference. I wanted to change our market. I wanted to help this organisation, and the people in it, reach their potential. I thought leadership would allow me to leave something really worthwhile behind. Most of the time, though, it feels like a treadmill. Dragging this organisation along, barely managing to do enough to keep paying the bills, is not what I signed up for.'

Does any of this sound familiar?

If you're in a leadership position, it's probably because you've got a proven track record of excellence in your field.

You've worked hard to get to the top, driven on by seeing the mistakes others make and by the certainty that you could do better.

But now you're up there, is the view what you hoped it would be?

Leadership has always been tough. Today's economic and business contexts give leaders plenty to think about. As ever, though, the key leadership issues are to do with change – social, cultural, commercial and organisational shifts. These massive challenges are too much for even the most talented individual leader to tackle alone.

The good news is that we can create Leadership Teams that will work in this new environment.

We don't need a new sort of person. But we do need a new sort of team.

You're not alone

Leading an organisation or a department should be exciting. But the grand challenges of overseeing change and transformation, of creating a powerful long-term plan and seeing it through, are only too rare. More often our time is hijacked and dominated by a mass of smaller everyday problems. If this sounds like you, you are in good company.

The leaders we meet are usually bright, articulate, ambitious people, full of potential and ideas. Most work in teams with other bright, articulate, ambitious colleagues. Yet many of the leaders I meet are dissatisfied with their work and their lives – and how the two connect.

Many leaders would love to change all this. They want to lift their own performance and that of their organisations to another level. But the system does little to support the transformational initiatives that are necessary for real change.

I saw the effect of all these frustrations when I was working with Tim, the CEO of an advertising agency. He was keeping the agency's head above water through difficult times, but doing it had drained the energy and optimism out of him:

'I'm 41, and it feels like my best years are behind me,' he told me. 'I'm exactly where I wanted to be – and now I'm here, I hate it.

'I spend every day fighting fires and micromanaging people and battling to keep the investors calm. I used to have a vision and ambitions for the company. Now it's just about survival.'

Leading an organisation should be exciting. But the grand challenges of overseeing change and transformation, of creating a powerful long-term plan and seeing it through, are only too rare.

Tim knew he wasn't working as well as he could. He told me that at our first meeting. He knew he wasn't seeing enough of his wife and children, too.

'They're getting used to me not being around. I sometimes wonder if they even notice when I'm not there.'

Like so many leaders in his situation, Tim felt powerless to change what was happening around him. Like so many, he felt stressed, isolated and pressured. The financial rewards were good, but they were nowhere near enough to compensate for the personal price he was paying, both at work and at home.

When we first met, Tim could see no happy ending ahead, other than a merger or a buyout. He was casting around for an exit strategy, because he saw no chance of getting what he needed or achieving the goals he thought worthwhile.

He was the boss, yet he felt trapped.

There is hope

I was delighted to meet Tim, because I quickly recognised that the solution wasn't complicated and that there were some simple

tools and approaches that could help him find a way forward.
I felt the buzz of excitement that comes when you know you are going to be able to make a difference, help someone and create a mutually beneficial business relationship at the same time. If Tim's enthusiasm had been almost extinguished, I saw my job as making it burn bright again.

I'll tell you later about the results of some research we organised into CEOs' opinions of their own leadership groups. The comments weren't pretty. Very few saw their own teams as delivering anything remotely like the performance they could – and should – be capable of.

So the key challenge for the individual leader – and the organisation's best hope of making profound and lasting changes – is to change an ordinary leadership group into a genuine Leadership Team that can really deliver results by driving transformational change throughout the organisation.

But how can that be done? How do we start to weld a group of individuals, all of them drawn from different business disciplines and backgrounds, into a single Leadership Team with shared objectives, trusting relationships and productive, creative ways of thinking and working together?

How do we take these people, all of whom have succeeded so far by being strong and individualistic leaders, and help them work as one towards an ambitious set of common goals?

How do we take these people, all of whom have succeeded so far by being strong and individualistic leaders, and help them work as one towards an ambitious set of common goals?

It's not easy, but it isn't complicated either. The good news is that there is a range of techniques and approaches, developed, honed and thoroughly tried and tested over many years, which allow us to tackle these big challenges purposefully and methodically, with the near certainty of producing dramatically better teams.

We have become obsessed by the myth of the heroic individual leader. We have either lost sight of the importance of Leadership Teams, or lost hope of changing them for the better.

This book aims to address both of these things, focusing on Leadership Teams and providing a clear way of understanding and developing them.

First, though, we need to understand a little more about the leadership landscape and how we arrived here.

Leading clever people

In Rob Goffee and Gareth Jones's book, *Clever: Leading Your Smartest, Most Creative People*, the authors say that today's thinking about leadership has completely missed the point. They point out that, in today's knowledge economy, organisations are highly dependent on people with high value expertise – they call them 'clevers' – who are often:

▲ Unimpressed by hierarchy (they value cleverness more than position)
▲ Organisationally savvy (and don't want to be led)
▲ Resistant to feedback (and won't thank you for doing the right things, either)
▲ Hard to replace (and they know it)
▲ Bored easily (and given to asking difficult questions)
▲ Inclined to expect instant access (to leaders and to other clever people)

In this brave new world, the work of leadership changes. In the old world, leadership was focused on making individuals more valuable to their organisations through concepts like productivity, motivation and engagement.

In the new world, leaders are faced with the task of making their organisations more valuable to the best people.

It's easy to find these talented, hard-to-lead 'clevers' in most organisations. The first place to look is around the boardroom table.

Leadership research has got lost

If the people sitting around the boardroom table are some of your most important, most valuable and most potentially hard-to-lead individuals, the job of selecting and developing them becomes ever more important.

The challenges facing these leaders are tougher than ever, and the people they are leading are demanding new things from them. This should be a time when scholarly thinking and research has a huge contribution to make. Most leaders I talk to, however, find little value in most of today's books and theories on leadership.

The vast majority of leadership research has been conducted by examining the people who have achieved positions at the very top of organisational hierarchies. Worse still, most of it has only been engaged in studying the characteristics of individuals.

Researchers have studied everything they can think of about individuals to see what differentiates good leaders. Nothing so far shows a significant correlation with leadership success or organisational performance. To use the terminology of social science, the correlations (between performance and individual leadership characteristics) are weak and the causal connection (with organisational performance) is indeterminate.

In plain English, that means these studies tell you little that's going to be of any value.

One mark of the stage reached by these lines of inquiry was an article published in the *Harvard Business Review* in November 2011, examining the correlation between ear lobes and leadership potential. Yes, really! (Senior, 2011)

Is it just me, or does that smack of desperation? Surely projects like this are signs that leadership thinking and research is taking us down the wrong path.

Leadership is relational, and contextual

You can't have leadership without followership. Interestingly, there is excellent research (with strong correlations) on what followers need to produce high performance. The key elements are:

- ▲ A sense of community and belonging
- ▲ Authenticity in leaders (people they can trust and believe in)
- ▲ Significance (they feel important)
- ▲ Excitement (they get stimulation and arousal from their leader, as well as from the job)

Meeting these demanding needs across a large organisation of diverse people is clearly more than any one individual can do alone. The kinds of relationships required with employees call for the whole Leadership Team to be involved and working in concert.

Leadership is also contextual. One of the reasons why the research on individual leadership characteristics is failing is that it does not take account of the different situations in which leaders are operating. Differences ranging from macro-economic background, sector and organisational history to the needs and composition of the team all have an impact on the type of leadership required. A leader who succeeds in one context may fail dismally in another – and vice versa.

> *'It is the pattern of relationships within organisations, not the fact that great men sit on top of them, which makes it possible to exert influence and enhance organisational performance'*
> (Weick, 1979)

Since leadership depends on the context, no leader can be well equipped for every situation. Leaders may, of course, fit better in some places than in others. But even if they are in situations they are well suited to, they are unlikely to be brilliant at everything that's required of them. Even where there's a good fit at one point in time, the pace at which the challenges facing today's leaders change means this is unlikely to last.

A new perspective on leadership

Not all research and thinking on individual leadership is flawed. There are some important ideas and work out there – both in academia and in organisations.

There is, however, a huge imbalance between the thinking, research and practice on individual leadership and the equivalent study of Leadership Teams. This book is an attempt to begin to redress that balance.

Leading today's organisations, and the 'clevers' on whom they depend, demands the skill, experience, talent and expertise of more than one person. The most important group to help the overall leader of the organisation is the team immediately around him. Often called the Executive Team, it may also sail under many other flags. For the sake of simplicity, I will refer to this team from now on as a Leadership Team.

The underpinning idea of this book is a simple one. If no leader can do the work alone, then we need to look at leadership in a different way. My contention is that the most important unit of leadership is the Leadership Team, rather than the individual within it.

We all know that a team that functions well can perform at a level greater than the sum of its parts and that a poorly functioning team makes it impossible for everyone to give their best. This isn't just folk wisdom. It's backed up by decades of research into group functioning and effectiveness, going back to the work of giants like Kurt Lewin and Ron Lippitt in the late 1930s.

The implications for Leadership Teams

While the idea of a high performing Leadership Team is a simple one, its implications are profound. Leading together is much more complex than leading as an individual. Leading together at the top of an organisation is more challenging still.

How do Leadership Teams access the huge resources of expertise and experience available within the team? How do they make decisions they will all support? How do they create an environment for one another in which all the members can give their very best?

The discussion also opens up new questions.

> *'Not finance, not strategy, not technology. It is teamwork that remains the ultimate competitive advantage, because it is both so powerful and so rare'.*
> (Lencioni, 2002)

- ▲ What is the work of the Leadership Team – the work that only it can do?
- ▲ What kind of example are the Leadership Team members setting today – and what kind of example would they like to set?
- ▲ How can they learn and improve together?

Underpinning all these questions, and many other key issues, is one vital and oft-forgotten truth:

Leadership Teams are made up of human beings.

Like all members of the species, each brings great strengths and glaring weaknesses, passions and hang-ups, potential contributions and personal needs. They are also all 'clevers' – and require the same things to deliver high performance.

Very few Leadership Teams function anything like as well as they could. This book aims to set out why that is, what collective leadership can be, why it matters, and how you can do it in your team.

A different kind of business book

A dialogue, not just an exposition

One of the great mistakes made in much business literature is the presentation of ideas as if they were universal truths. Apart from the fact that the arrogance of such a positioning jars with me, it's patently untrue. If there was one single way to solve any problem, we would have found it long ago and everyone would be doing it.

I don't know you or your organisation. The approaches in this book represent only one way of succeeding. Some organisations do well with an emphasis only on individual leadership. Others somehow manage to make progress with little effort or investment in leadership at all.

While it is possible to succeed without focusing explicit attention on creating a really effective Leadership Team, our research suggests that this success is much harder to win, and to sustain over time. It is my contention that neglecting or accepting the current poor level of performance of your Leadership Team leads directly to the busy, unproductive and frustrating experience of leadership I have been describing.

> *While it is possible to succeed without focusing explicit attention on creating a really effective Leadership Team, our research suggests that this success is much harder to win, and to sustain over time.*

Much of the work of leadership takes place in conversations. To help you and your situation, we need to bring together your knowledge of your context, organisation, goals and people with my ideas about Leadership Teams.

I see this book as a dialogue in which we can explore both areas. I have included questions for you to reflect on that will illuminate your situation and bring you new perspectives and ideas for moving forward.

This book is also designed to help you understand how you can improve your Leadership Team – including the practical tools you can use. Some of these require more expert knowledge than others and I have made this clear in each case where it applies.

If you have any questions about the book, or about how to develop your own team, I'd be happy to help in any way I can. My contact details can be found on our website: www.OneThirdMore.co.uk.

Informed by my experiences, and by those of leaders and members of Leadership Teams

If we are to have a conversation, it's important for you to know a little about me and where my ideas come from.

I had a 15-year career with Boots and Barclays in which I held director-level roles in functions as diverse as strategy and operations, property and HR. In each of these, I was a member of a senior Leadership Team. Like most leaders, I found that some of these teams produced incredible results and were amazing to work with. Others underperformed and were an ordeal to be part of.

I became fascinated by the potential power of these teams, and by the fact that so many seem to be dysfunctional. In 2003 I set up a consultancy, OneThirdMore, to focus on understanding them better and helping to create truly high performing Leadership Teams.

As we shall see, the potential gains from creating a productive, creative team environment can be transformational, cascading down through the organisation from top to bottom.

The name of my business, OneThirdMore, is a very conservative nod to the huge figures that members and leaders of these teams put on the value, in bottom line financial terms, that could be realised if Leadership Teams could be made to work to their full potential.

These numbers may or may not be referring to exact changes in turnover or profit figures. What they do represent is the aching feeling these CEOs have that there is vast untapped potential in their Leadership Teams – and that unleashing it is what is required to make the transformational changes they yearn for in their organisations.

What have the Maasai got to do with Leadership Teams?

You must by now be wondering about the references to the Maasai in the Executive Summary or, at least, about the image on the front cover of this book.

I have learned a huge amount from my own business experiences – good and bad – in senior Leadership Teams at big companies like Barclaycard and Boots and from working with Leadership Teams in industries ranging from publishing to aviation.

But I have learned even more from the time I have spent with the Maasai. Before I met them, my knowledge was limited to images in coffee table books of photogenic clothes, colourful beads and radiant smiles. Over my many trips to Kenya, I have learned that there is far more to this ancient people, whose culture has survived and thrived intact for hundreds, probably thousands, of years.

Far from being the group of primitive tribespeople I expected to find, the Maasai, I discovered, have some remarkable and special ways of living and working together. These have made possible an incredible odyssey that has taken them from prehistoric times in the cradle of man to the modern era, in which they are wrestling with the problems of overpopulation, climate change, HIV/AIDS, globalisation and many other 21st-century challenges.

At the heart of the Maasai way of life is a distinctive, and very different, approach to one another and to getting things done together, which I explain more below and throughout the book.

The Maasai think in terms of the community first and the individual second. They place enormous importance on working together and supporting each other, rather than relying on competition to fuel performance, as we do, almost unconsciously, in Western business.

Looking at Leadership Teams from a Maasai-influenced perspective can shed new light on the dynamics of teams and communities and the way ideas are examined and decisions are made.

Looking at Leadership Teams from a Maasai-influenced perspective can shed new light on the dynamics of teams and communities and the way ideas are examined and decisions are made. Staying alive and thriving in the harsh, pitiless environment of the savannah, where resources are scarce and danger is always present, calls for levels of co-operation and collective working that are truly eye-opening and inspirational.

To my surprise, the things I have seen and the lessons I have learned in that extraordinary, hostile environment have turned out to be directly relevant to the way people interact in the boardrooms and high-rise office blocks of London and Paris, Frankfurt and New York. After all, group endeavour is as old as humankind, and not limited to the last few decades of Western management research.

This book, though, is about Leadership Teams in Western businesses. The role of the Maasai references is simply to cast a new and unusual light on the way we approach Leadership Teams and how we might work together more productively to find success when demands are sky high and resources are scarce. No more, no less.

Practically useful

If you're leading an organisation, you're busy and you need practical and accessible help. The ideas and tools in this book are simple, but powerful.

Leadership isn't, in my view, something individuals grapple with as part of their 'Personal Development Plan'. Neither is it the preserve of the HR department. Leadership and strategy are inseparable. Leadership is every bit as much about concrete things like numbers, plans and delivery as it is about more human concepts like relationships, accountability and learning.

Above all, leadership is about the work you're doing today with your colleagues, and about how you can do it better to be more effective, more successful and happier.

Leadership and strategy are inseparable. Leadership is every bit as much about concrete things like numbers, plans and delivery as it is about more human concepts like relationships, accountability and learning.

Finding what's useful to you

You may not want to read this book from cover to cover. To help you find the things that are most relevant to you and your situation, every section is divided into clearly labelled subsections.

If you want to jump quickly to a synopsis of my key ideas, there's an Executive Summary of the entire book on pages 11-17.

Case studies and anonymity

To illustrate the ideas and tools I am recommending, I have included a number of case studies. Some of these are based on teams I was part of, some are stories of clients I have worked with and others have come from leaders we talked to as part of our research.

To protect both individual and commercial confidentiality, all of these stories have been made anonymous, which has required the modification of some of the details. As the Maasai say, 'It may not have happened exactly this way, but the story is true.'

References and further reading

I have drawn on the work of many other theorists and thinkers. I have attributed these ideas wherever possible and a full list of references and recommendations for further reading can be found on page 348-352.

Are you thinking sceptical thoughts?

No two organisations are ever at exactly the same stage of development. No two leaders will ever have exactly the same view of the challenges facing them.

When I talk to business leaders about how we can improve Leadership Team performance, I get reactions ranging from enthusiasm, via curiosity, to thinly veiled hostility.

Most leaders believe there is potentially scope to build more effective Leadership Teams. Many others know it's a desirable goal, but wonder whether it can really be done. Some sceptics believe that leaders – and teams – are born and not made, and that no process or technique on earth can make them perform better.

So which of these reactions sums up your position? What's actually on your mind today?

▲ 'I have a team that isn't working well.'
▲ 'I have a team that is working just fine, but I'm interested in building teams and I'd like to see your take on it.'
▲ 'I'm already engaged in building a team and would like to know more about the tools and techniques I might use.'
▲ 'I instinctively feel that having a powerful, more effective team would be good. But I struggle to make the business case for the time and investment involved.'
▲ 'I am convinced I should do some work on building my Leadership Team, but I just don't know where to start.'
▲ 'I think all this team stuff is guff and I'm looking forward to tearing your arguments apart.'

Wherever you are as you start on this book, if you've read this far, you must at least be curious. ▲

SECTION 1

Why Leadership Teams matter, and why you should develop yours

MAKE OR BREAK
How your Leadership Team shapes the company's future

Leadership Teams are a special case. They are not like other teams.

The Leadership team that lost its way

A few years ago, a huge industrial processing company suffered a logistical meltdown.

It was at a particularly busy time, and orders had picked up on top of an anticipated seasonal peak in demand. These stresses combined with some staffing problems and the usual range of operational glitches to create a perfect storm.

The problems fed on one another and created new issues. What started in one factory was soon affecting the other plants and even the company's suppliers. Soon raw materials and part-finished inventory completely clogged their plants and warehouses. The flow of finished product shipped out slowed to a trickle, leaving customers fuming on several continents. Even when the chaos was sorted out and things started moving again, the huge backlog of orders caused knock-on problems that lasted many weeks.

At the centre of the storm were the operations director and his team. He was a serious, capable logistics specialist, with half a lifetime of management and problem-solving knowhow behind him. Yet this experience had traumatised him. Several months later, when I talked to him about ➤

the day the earth stood still, he was shaking as he spoke of it.

'I honestly don't know how I got through it,' he said. 'It was brutal. I never, ever, want to feel that kind of pressure again.'

The disaster was too big to gloss over and the operations director and his team were the natural targets for everyone's anger and frustration. People who had no idea what had caused the problem and whether it could have been avoided, decided they knew enough to pin the blame on the operations director. When it was suggested that he should perhaps have lost his job, insiders pointed out that no sane person with the necessary expertise would have been at all eager to take his place.

In the first 45 minutes of my initial meeting with the company's Leadership Team, I saw three people close to tears as they recalled that nightmare. I had asked a simple starter question – 'What's it like to work in this team?' – and then sat back and listened. As the members of the group told their tales, it became obvious that they had felt let down, even punished, just when they had most needed the team's help.

The Leadership Team had not given them support and resilience, ideas and wisdom, or even just a place of safety in which they could candidly discuss the problems raining in on them.

Yet it was no one person's fault. The cause was a constellation of human and technical issues. In the pressurised environment, and amid all the recriminations, the team had taken too long to solve the problem and this had come at a profound human cost.

The team was made up of very strong individuals, but at the point when the organisation had most needed the Leadership Team to function at its best, its members had simply not been able to work well enough together to deal with what faced them.

You couldn't blame the operations director, or his CEO, for not knowing how to build a high performing Leadership Team. Hardly anyone does. ▲

Your single biggest opportunity

In fact, when you think about it, the very idea of a business team is a metaphor, an analogy drawn from the world of sport. You would never pick a sports team with eleven goalkeepers or fifteen prop forwards or one composed entirely of opening batsmen. You'd pick a team to play together, carefully assembling complementary strengths. But Leadership Teams in business generally come together by default, as the people who have risen to the top in various functional specialities suddenly find themselves in the same room, trying to play the same game. Even getting everyone kicking in the same direction is often an achievement.

The team I've just been describing had actually performed no worse than most Leadership Teams would have done if they'd been exposed to the same problems and the same pitiless scrutiny. You may not have seen such painful examples, but you will recognise the truth that Leadership Teams, left to themselves, seldom deliver everything that might be hoped for.

The good news is that this can be changed, relatively quickly and relatively cheaply, by the right intervention and investment in the Leadership Team. In this case, an effective team might or might not have been able to avoid the problems in the first place. These team members would, however, go on to learn that problems could be resolved more quickly and at far less personal cost once they improved the way they worked together.

It is quite possible that the value offered by a tried and tested programme to improve Leadership Team performance is the single biggest opportunity available to most businesses, not least because it is not dependent on external circumstances or competitive factors.

Imagine the costs, the effort and the risk involved in developing and launching a new product or breaking into a new geographical market, the kind of business initiative that might make a difference of several percentage points to the bottom line.

Now imagine how much a business might gain if the Leadership Team could be truly effective and could fully exploit the talents and potential within it. The boost could be comparable, but there would be nothing like the downside risk that comes with every new product development or geographical expansion.

It is quite possible that the value offered by a tried and tested programme to improve Leadership Team performance is the single biggest opportunity available to most businesses, not least because it is not dependent on external circumstances or competitive factors.

Whether the organisation – which could be a company, or a division or business unit within a large corporation – is doing well or not, raising the effectiveness of the Leadership Team will always pay off, almost by definition.

The industrial processing team in the case study eventually came to understand, through the work we did together, how the team dynamic could add value, so the Leadership Team genuinely became more than the sum of its parts. The individuals learned how to trust and help each other and how to handle difficult and explosive issues – often in ways that generated unexpectedly positive outcomes. This initiative was certainly beneficial to the company, producing clearly identifiable gains, yet it had taken a disastrous failure to highlight the potential for improvement.

Breaking out of the silos of misery

Every industry faces unprecedented and unpredictable changes that guarantee the past will be no guide to the future. When old solutions will not work, there is an absolute necessity to make the most of the collective wisdom and creativity of the Leadership Team to chart a way forward.

What Leadership Teams need to do that individual leaders can't

They must choose the right trade-offs

Robert Kaplan and David Norton's famous and influential work on the Balanced Scorecard (Kaplan and Norton, 1996) identifies four separate areas that an organisation must manage to generate sustainable success:

▲ Financial
▲ Customer
▲ Processes/internal
▲ People/learning and growth

I worked recently with one of the oldest and most respected companies in newspaper publishing, an industry that has found itself, for the second time in thirty years, caught in a maelstrom of disruptive change. No-one could blame the Leadership Team for the problems raised by the advent of electronic publishing, but the changes were happening so fast that the business needed to create the capacity to reinvent itself just to survive.

'Nobody's faced these problems before,' Greg, the chief executive, told me on Day One.

'Customers want everything for nothing online, and advertisers don't believe we can deliver the value they want. We need a new infrastructure and there are no experts to tell us what to do, because nobody in this industry has a clue what will happen next.'

If anyone could potentially devise a strategy to ride this unstoppable wave of change, it should have been the group of people in Greg's Leadership Team. But every departmental head was fixated on the problems in his or her own area. They were each stuck, as one of them told me, in 'a silo of misery'.

Attitudes were critical and defensive, when what was needed was a source of support and help and a place of safety where colleagues could compare notes and work collaboratively to tackle the problems. All the key issues had interdepartmental implications and this kind of collegiate approach was going to be essential to get to grips with them. But there was little sign of it – or even of basic trust between the team members – when I first met them.

The work we did to improve the confidence and performance of this Leadership Team did not resolve the future of the newspaper industry. But it did help the CEO re-energise and reshape his Leadership Team and put the company's performance back on track. As frequently happens, he had to make some politically sensitive decisions, including rationalising the membership of his top team. But once the right people were used to being and working together, within a framework that promoted trust as well as rigour, the group ethos changed completely and positive changes came thick and fast. ▲

Leadership Teams have to make trade-offs between these elements, but they are simply not susceptible to direct comparison. How do you decide whether to invest in a new product launch or make an investment of a similar size in new plant, or in leadership development? Trade-offs and decisions like this are at the very core of organisational leadership.

Launching a new product means investing heavily up front, in development, production and marketing costs, followed by a new income stream later in the year, if all goes well. By contrast, investing in Leadership Team development will create added value that will usually be difficult to quantify and will inevitably be realised over a longer time scale.

Only the Leadership Team can make these sensitive, judgement-based trade-offs and assess the best course of action within the chosen strategy. And it must do this despite the fact that team members will often be evaluating alternatives using quite different criteria and applying their own subjective assessments.

Only they can manage the big issues – which are all cross-functional

The real issues in today's organisations are always cross-functional. Developing brands, launching complex products, improving processes and building loyalty (to name just a few) are all beyond the scope of any one discipline or department.

Most organisations pay far more attention to managing the Financial and Customer perspectives of their business than they do to the other Balanced Scorecard perspectives, largely because these are directly concerned with the quantifiable results that are the principal interest of external stakeholders.

> *The real issues in today's organisations are always cross-functional. Developing brands, launching complex products, improving processes and building loyalty (to name just a few) are all beyond the scope of any one discipline or department.*

Leadership Teams often place much less focus on the areas of Processes and People. As well as being influenced by the external stakeholders' emphasis on Financial and Customer metrics, teams also neglect them because Financial and Customer issues can often be managed within the scope and resources of individual departments, whereas Process and People issues can only ever be managed cross-functionally.

The weak role and influence of the HR department in many Leadership Teams shows how people issues like morale, communication, leadership, training and performance management are often neglected.

'I'm lucky if I get 15 minutes in meetings,' Laura, an HR director, told me.

'Nobody's really listening and they're all waiting for me to shut up so they can get on with the "real" business.'

Unlike, say, Finance, Processes do not usually have a single owner in the organisation. Problems often arise where Processes cross organisational boundaries. Branding, for example, will necessarily involve production, sales and customer service. When the cross-disciplinary processes go wrong, customers pay the price in the form of delays, added costs or shortfalls in quality.

The demarcation issues that occur can take several forms. They can develop into turf wars, where departments jealously guard every activity they see as their own. Alternatively, they can lead to situations where each department does what it is formally charged with doing and then stops there, rather than trying to make life easier for those in the next part of the production or distribution chain.

Team meetings give participants the time and space to understand the difficulties and get to grips with these boundary issues before they can cause friction and affect performance.

Effective Leadership Teams collectively manage these big issues, which transcend organisational boundaries. Indeed, one of the main reasons for their existence is to deal with such challenges, for if the top team doesn't do it, then who can?

They have to reconcile conflicting needs

To make the right decisions for the organisation, Leadership Teams need access to the best possible information. This is typically dispersed across a number of individuals, each with expertise and access to data in a particular area.

How openly they contribute their information – or how grudgingly they share it – can be a key factor in determining the Leadership Team's ultimate performance. Assembling a complete 360° picture of a complex situation, based on all the available information, is vital when it comes to making major decisions.

Leadership Teams have to reconcile different perspectives arising from departmental needs and from differences in expertise and viewpoint between individuals. They must be able to integrate these disparate views and manage the political and interpersonal dynamics that hamper communication. Being able to piece together information from different sources and understand its significance is one of the keys to understanding situations, creating options and making decisions.

They need to pull together when the world wants to pull them apart

To make sense out of great complexity, large organisations are divided up into pieces. Whether the division is based on functional, geographical, market or other factors, the result is to separate elements which are part of the whole. Issues over silos, boundaries, handovers and interdepartmental tensions are familiar to all leaders and are an inevitable consequence of the need to organise large numbers of people (Oshry, 2007). David Nadler (Nadler and Spencer, 1998) memorably called these the 'centrifugal forces' acting on any Leadership Team.

The separating forces between these elements are powerful, ranging from reward systems to the tendency to identify more closely with those who share interests, expertise or physical space with us. These forces are potentially destructive. The Leadership Team is by far the most important factor in balancing them by integrating elements of the organisation and making work happen effectively across boundaries – both through its handling of specific tasks and through the leadership and example its members provide by the way they co-operate with their colleagues.

Being able to piece together information from different sources and understand its significance is one of the keys to understanding situations, creating options and making decisions.

The Leadership Team, too, is affected by these forces of separation, and a key ingredient for overcoming them is the glue formed by the relationships that exist between Leadership Team members.

It's human nature to like those whose thought processes resemble our own. We all do it, though, and learning how to build positive relationships with people who have different backgrounds, attitudes, styles and assumptions is a major challenge. Again, it's not easy. But it can be done.

Where this glue is weak, Leadership Team members are only too familiar with the kind of meetings that descend into unproductive buck-passing, dominated by parochial views and defensive reactions.

Finger-pointing and blame-shifting, with each member focusing narrowly on his or her departmental 'patch', are not uncommon. More often, however, problems arise from individuals arguing passionately for the perspective they truly hold to be the best assessment, option or decision, and being reluctant to move on to get behind shared, collective decisions. This is understandable, but it is not consistent with the constructive, reasoned conversations Leadership Teams require if they are going to explore complex and sensitive issues, balance competing needs and find creative ways forward.

They balance short-term and long-term imperatives

Short-termism is always going to be a problem in a world where external stakeholders are hungry for immediate success.

Money and attention are unavoidably drawn to the areas that will produce short-term growth and profit, boosting performance today or in the very near future, but issues with less immediate impact on results are much harder to prioritise.

Investments in the Processes area may take a year or more to feed through into measurable performance gains, while investments in People typically take longer still. That's a long time in business, and the external stakeholders won't hold their breath. They just want to see results, and they will leave it to the chief executive and the Leadership Team to handle the tricky decisions involved in balancing out long-term priorities with short-term delivery imperatives.

In practice, this means having the strength and determination to stand up and resist the clamour to focus only on instant solutions and instant results – and that's something only a solid and unified Leadership Team can do. In a sense, it is like fighting against gravity. There is always the constant pull towards quick fixes and dramatic action, not least because many of the structures and processes in organisations predispose them towards short-termism.

Sustained and genuine transformation can only be achieved by delivering in the short term and simultaneously addressing the root causes of today's symptoms. This is a nettle that only the Leadership Team can grasp, and it is one of its most challenging responsibilities.

They have to deal with three, very different, kinds of work

The range of tasks facing Leadership Teams is broader than any other kind of team. They have to be able to think broadly and creatively to develop strategy. Operational delivery requires speed and detail, whilst governance has characteristics that demand rigour and process skills.

These varied challenges require modes of thinking, agendas and ways of working together which are equally distinct. A tool for helping to address these by separating Leadership Team meetings can be found at page 330. ▲

WHAT MAKES
Leadership Teams different?

There is a broad assumption that everything we know about teams also applies to Leadership Teams. Just applying what we know about teamwork in general is never going to take us far enough.

Leadership Teams are a neglected subject. There are thousands of books on leadership and almost as many on teambuilding. Some are useful, but many of the books and approaches that claim to help with teambuilding are grossly simplistic. Leaders at all management levels have become wary of quick fix solutions and ineffective teambuilding days that revolve around crossing rivers on makeshift rafts.

But even amid all this hype about teams, very little attention has been paid to the specifics of Leadership Teams and the challenges they face.

There is a broad assumption that everything we know about teams also applies to Leadership Teams. Some of it does. But the literature on teams often overlooks the many differences that make Leadership Teams unique. Just applying what we know about teamwork in general is never going to take us far enough.

Functional teams, project teams and Leadership Teams

Let's get back to basics.

What types of teams do we find in large organisations? How do they differ? What exactly is a Leadership Team, and what makes it distinctive?

We can think in terms of three main types of team – functional, project and leadership.

Functional teams

Functional teams work within a single discipline, often running a department. In marketing, for example, there will be people with their own groups to manage in areas like branding, campaign planning, creative execution and pricing. In finance, there may be specialists in cost control, investment planning, payroll and decision support.

Because each functional team has its own area of expertise, its members will often have similar backgrounds and viewpoints. This can lead to a narrow frame of reference and a lack of understanding of the needs and challenges of other parts of the organisation.

And while every department – from production and R&D to HR and sales – makes its own contribution, it is only at the top that the strands are brought together to contribute to an overall responsibility for the organisation's survival and profitability. No functional team will ever be in control of all the elements of profit or other ultimate financial outcomes.

Project teams

Project teams are usually multi-disciplinary, with members drawn from different departments. Individuals in the project team generally find themselves reporting to their bosses in the 'home' department as well as the project team leader.

The goals, deliverables, scope and authority of project teams are usually clarified at the beginning so they can operate with a clear mandate and within agreed parameters.

When the project comes to an end, the project team is usually dissolved. Project teams are therefore focused on fixed and finite goals, to be delivered within specific time frames, and are not usually expected to look out at broader perspectives.

Leadership Teams

Leadership Teams are qualitatively different. Leadership Teams are composed of the people who run the organisation, or who head a profit centre within a larger organisation.

Unlike functional and project teams, they are responsible for the organisation's overall performance. They are accountable for profits and losses to stakeholders such as investors, holding companies, boards of trustees or, in the public sector, political leaders. If organisational results are good, the Leadership Team will get the credit. If things go wrong, it's the Leadership Team that will carry the can.

Leadership Teams bring together leaders from different functional areas, each contributing to a broad multi-disciplinary picture that's backed up by different technical skills and organisational perspectives.

At its best, the Leadership Team is in a position to piece together a complete and near-perfect view of the organisation and its world. In practice, though, this seldom happens.

Types of teams

Functional teams	Project teams	Leadership Teams
Single discipline	Usually multi-disciplinary	Multi-disciplinary
Clear area of expertise	Fixed goals	Diverse areas of expertise
No direct responsibility for the organisation's success or failure	Finite time frame	Direct responsibility for the organisation's success or failure

What distinguishes Leadership Teams?

If we look more closely at Leadership Teams, we see that these differences of role and context produce an environment where both the task and the human dynamics are qualitatively different from those of other types of teams.

They can't delegate responsibility for strategy

Every organisation wants its senior leaders and other teams to be strategic in the way they operate. Some are, some aren't. Developing more of a strategic approach outside the boardroom is almost always desirable.

If the Leadership Team isn't creating strategy and making strategic decisions, there's no-one else who can fill that gap. While most members of Leadership Teams will recognise this imperative, very few would claim their own teams are fully achieving it.

There's a reason for this. There is an 'organisational gravity' that constantly forces them away from a strategic approach (see table below). Fighting this gravity, so that it can be genuinely and consistently strategic, is a – perhaps the – real challenge for every Leadership Team.

How organisational gravity frustrates strategy

A strategic approach requires...	But 'organisational gravity' works against this...
Long-term thinking	Short-term performance demands
Focus on the external market	Internal complexities and pressures
Cross-functional solutions	Organisational boundaries and politics
Value-based decisions	Many issues are only uncertainly and distantly related to financial outcomes

They work with complexity and ambiguity

The Leadership Team has to understand and manage the wider environment, from investors to economic pressures and from customers to markets. It has to integrate all these elements with a range of internal factors, from organisational structure to morale and from processes to culture. The pace of change in the context managed by a Leadership Team is greater than in other teams, and everything from markets to organisational goals is usually in a state of constant and rapid flux.

Decisions are, therefore, inevitably far more ambiguous and complex than at any other organisational level (Nadler and Spencer, 1998), with the team juggling many interests and responsibilities.

What it decides will have far-reaching effects on results, departments, careers and even markets. The stakes are high, and coming up with the right answers is often a matter of judgement, rather than calculation.

In this environment, there are frequently several 'right' answers to any question (as well as a multitude of wrong ones). Decision-making is often as much about gaining influence in the group and winning support for an idea as it is about understanding and assessing facts.

There's a different structure of authority

The team leader is usually the managing director or CEO, the person ultimately accountable to the organisation's funders, usually shareholders or a parent organisation, who are often relatively remote, with little direct contact with the team.

Because they are much further removed, their focus will always be on outputs, rather than methods. Ultimately, these stakeholders are interested in measurable results. What happens within the organisation to create those outputs is seldom their concern.

...when strategy fails, accountability is clear – and often ruthless.

As a result, the Leadership Team is usually able to operate with a high degree of autonomy to match its high degree of accountability. It can take make-or-break decisions or embark on major strategic changes in a way no other team in the organisation can.

The corollary of this is that, when strategy fails, accountability is clear – and often ruthless. This accountability for results places high demands on the leader of the team, often putting him or her under great pressure, which in turn bears down on the other members of the Leadership Team.

The fact that the leader can hire or fire team members (and may do so quite often) inevitably has a significant impact on relationships within the team. Insecurity, misplaced competitiveness and anxiety about personal performance often have a destructive influence on how individuals interact with the leader and with each other, leading to defensive and risk-averse behaviour.

One interesting side effect of the CEO's power to hire and fire team members is that the HR director, who should usually be best placed to deal with human and interpersonal issues in the team, can find this difficult. If Leadership Team members think of the HR expert as the CEO's confidant in discussions about capability, promotion and exit, it will inevitably inhibit this person's ability to play a part in improving team function, as they will not be seen as an honest broker.

The line-up changes frequently

Leadership Teams are always in a state of flux. People do well and get promoted or are lured away to new challenges. Others do less well and leave, of their own volition or otherwise. Turnover is usually much faster than in functional or project teams. Often the team will welcome a new person every few months, with each line-up change introducing new dynamics, demands and questions.

CEOs face the same challenge as the manager of a football club, where creating and maintaining a strong team involves a never-ending cycle of building and rebuilding. As individual talents come and go, the dynamics of the team alter and members have to learn – and often relearn – how to work together.

Turnover is usually much faster than in functional or project teams. Often the team will welcome a new person every few months, with each line-up change introducing new dynamics, demands and questions.

The team may never be the finished article. Like the greats of football management – the Shanklys, Fergusons, Wengers, Mourinhos and Guardiolas – the CEO must excel in spotting and developing new talent while facing the same challenge of constantly integrating new acquisitions into an existing team dynamic.

They are made up of high performers

Another key difference between Leadership Teams and other types of team is the kind of person you find round the table. By the time he or she is invited to join, each Leadership Team member will already have a high level of expertise within a particular discipline and a proven track record as a group or departmental leader. As individuals, these people will usually be highly driven, competitive, ambitious and confident of their own views and opinions.

Critically, their success to that point will often have been based on individual, rather than collective, leadership skills. Very few Leadership Teams are made up of a set of people who intuitively operate as 'team players'.

Each member of the Leadership Team is therefore likely to bring a big personality, a lot of determination and considerable self-belief. The challenge is to harness this individualistic energy and flair in a context that demands close, co-operative collaboration with other forceful talents.

They are necessarily political

The job of Leadership Teams is to get results, usually by making things work across boundaries – both within the organisation and also with other organisations like partners, customers and suppliers.

Each individual controls some of the resources and levers needed to deliver the changes sought by each of the others. Team members must negotiate to promote the changes they believe are most important.

There are also the more unhelpful, but natural, aspects of politics, with personal ambition and desire for influence continuously at play – whether in the foreground or beneath the surface.

Conflict is inevitable – and desirable

The nature of the challenges facing Leadership Teams means that conflict is part of the work. Bringing together the different views of the enormously complex situation facing any organisation needs to create conflict. Unlike all other work groups, the Leadership Team has no-one beyond or above it to arbitrate when these views can't easily be reconciled. The team must both create conflict and resolve it. As one article so clearly puts it: 'The absence of conflict is not harmony. It's apathy.' (Eisenhardt, Kahwajy and Bourgeois, 1997).

Each member of the Leadership Team is therefore likely to bring a big personality, a lot of determination and considerable self-belief.

Not all conflict is good conflict, however. The conflict teams need is generative, constructive and involves bringing together ideas and perspectives to find new solutions that are better than individuals could have found alone. Too often, though, teams are stifled by conflicts based on personal

Thomas-Kilmann modes of conflict

Assertiveness
Focus on my needs, desired outcomes and agendas

Competing
Zero-sum orientation
Win/lose power struggle

COLLABORATING
Expand range of possible options
Achieve win/win outcomes

Compromising
Minimally acceptable to all
Relationships undamaged

Avoiding
Withdraw from the situation
Maintain neutrality

Accommodating
Accede to the other party
Maintain harmony

Cooperativeness
Focus on others' needs and mutual relationships

antagonism or which involve attempts to force win-lose conclusions.

The most widely used model for understanding the different modes of conflict was developed by Thomas and Kilmann (Thomas, 2002) and is shown above.

The sources of destructive conflict are many. The absence of fully shared collective goals and priorities, personal mistrust or lack of understanding, failures to take accountability or deliver on it, and an inability to learn and reflect together are all potential underlying causes for this kind of dysfunction.

The way to consistently reach the heights of genuinely collaborative conflict shown in the top right box of the model is to develop each of these aspects of the team. In Section 2, I will describe the Six Conversations through which teams can address all of these issues. In Section 4, I have included a range of tools that can be used in this context.

One of these tools, Resolving Conflict, on page 336, also offers a practical method for understanding and addressing destructive conflict for teams that have an immediate and pressing need to do this and cannot afford to wait for the team development programme to address all the underlying causes. ▲

3
WHAT LEADERS SAY
about Leadership Teams

Even chief executives who classed their current teams as performing well said the organisation could perform 45 per cent better if the Leadership Team could realise its full potential.

Keeping your head down, to avoid it being shot off

The most visible place to see the effectiveness of the Leadership Teams is in their meetings. And these are the subject of the most frustration in the leaders we talk to in the course of our work. As one former client put it:

> *'Members of my team behave as though I'm the only one with responsibility for the organisation as a whole. No matter how hard I try, team meetings feel like a series of reports from department heads.*

> *'Each person contributes their update with the main goal being to avoid criticism or blame for whatever is going wrong. As they speak, others are reluctant to contribute as they fear it will be seen as interfering in another area – and may well be repaid with critical commentary when their turn comes to speak.*

> *'Even on the big issues, that involve more than one function, some dominate unhelpfully and others are reticent. Decisions are hard to reach and we often leave the room with a different understanding of the conclusion. As a result we end up revisiting the same issues over and over again. Delivery of anything significant is painfully slow.*

'We all know that it's not working, and that it's hurting our ability to change the business and deliver our numbers, but it's seen as my job to put it right and I can't do it alone.'

This description resonates with my own experience, as well as with that of almost every leader I have spoken to. The similarities in these stories led us to wonder just how much else would be common across all Leadership Teams.

Our research

The scarcity of research focused on the very distinctive group endeavour of Leadership Teams prompted us to plug some of the gaps. We gathered data from leaders in a wide range of private sector companies, public sector organisations and not-for-profits.

We collected first-hand perspectives from detailed face-to-face interviews and assembled quantitative data from business leaders to develop an understanding of the impact of Leadership Teams and the factors that differentiate the best teams from their weaker brethren.

Could do better: every Leadership Team underdelivers

The first surprise was the discovery that all Leadership Teams, almost without exception, thought they could and should do far better.

Even those chief executives who classed their current teams as performing well said they felt the organisation could perform 45 per cent better if the Leadership Team could realise its full potential.

These are startling figures.

Leaders who said their current Leadership Teams were underperforming told us that if they were working to maximum capacity and effectiveness, they would deliver 90 per cent more.

These are startling figures. I was initially sceptical. But as the picture became clearer, it emerged that the figures these CEOs quoted were remarkably consistent across many different industries and sectors. I wouldn't claim huge statistical validity for these exact figures, but their scale and consistency demands that they be taken seriously.

While other research is limited, there are a few authoritative studies on the relationship between team cohesion and results (Katzenbach and Smith, 1993), (Smith and al, 1994), (Hambrick, 1995), (Cohen and Bailey, 1997), (Ernst and Young, 1998). All point to a very significant impact.

Even if you discounted the figures from our research by half, developing the team would still be the biggest value opportunity available to most CEOs and Leadership Teams. And it is certainly the one with the greatest potential to transform their working experience into something much more exciting, motivating and rewarding.

The rest of the figures, and the research generally, highlight several important points:

- ▲ There is a broad consensus among both leaders and members that their teams are underperforming badly.
- ▲ Even the best Leadership Teams offer a huge amount of untapped potential for improving profits and operational results.
- ▲ The leaders we spoke to were desperate for a solution and were unsure where they could find one.
- ▲ Those who had experience of efforts to develop their teams often found that the approaches used were not focused or rigorous enough to deliver much in the way of sustained change.

In other words, both CEOs and other team members already know there is latent performance buried and neglected in Leadership Teams that fall short of realising their full potential.

RESEARCH SUMMARY

Our research on Leadership Teams consisted of two main parts.

Harvesting the wisdom and experience of members of Leadership Teams

We carried out interviews with a wide range of leaders, from organisations of all types, to ask them about their experience of Leadership Teams – good ones, bad ones, their present ones and what they had learned about them.

What separated the better teams from the poor ones? How were they created? Had people been involved in deliberate attempts to improve the effectiveness of Leadership Teams? If so, how well had these interventions worked?

We built on the findings of these interviews and the existing literature to create the Six Conversations which are the foundation of this book – and of all our work with Leadership Teams.

These are effectively a set of 'competencies' for teams that are leading organisations. While no two teams are the same (any more than individual leaders are), these competencies represent the ways the best Leadership Teams interact – and what they need to work on if they are going to improve their effectiveness.

The Six Conversations are described in detail in Section 2 of this book.

Quantifying the impact of the differences between teams

Following on from the identification of the Six Conversations, we engaged a much larger group of leaders to give us their views on how great the differences were between high performing and underperforming Leadership Teams – and the impact of those differences.

Our survey has generated a huge volume of data. There's too much to include here, but it's worth looking at a summary of the most interesting findings.

We asked members of Leadership Teams to rate the effectiveness of their teams on a six-point scale. Teams were categorised as underperforming if they were rated in the lower two categories, and high performing if they were rated in the top two categories.

The scores indicated overleaf represent the average scores for each area or question, from respondents who rated their team as underperforming (grey bars) and those who assessed it as high performing (orange bars).

➤

1. The biggest differences between high performing Leadership Teams and those that are underperforming are in the areas of Relationships and Accountability, followed by Ambition.

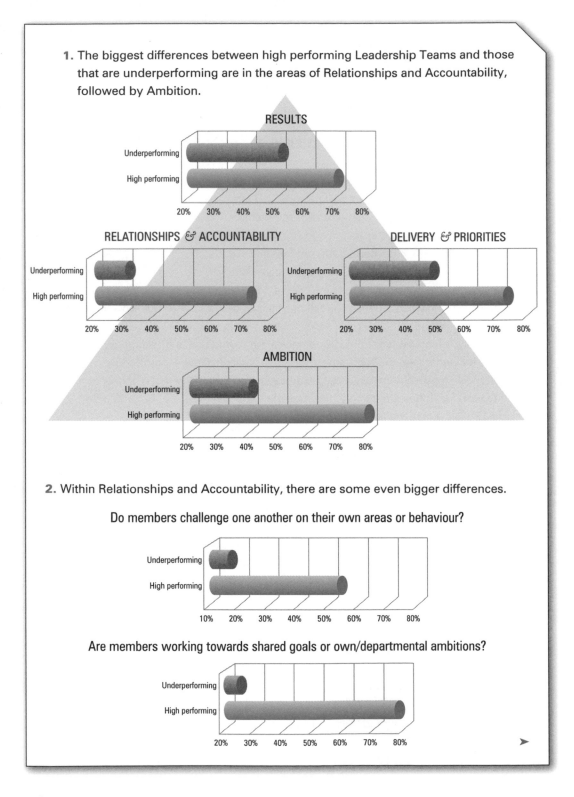

2. Within Relationships and Accountability, there are some even bigger differences.

Do members challenge one another on their own areas or behaviour?

Are members working towards shared goals or own/departmental ambitions?

How much open debate is there about the issues facing the organisation?

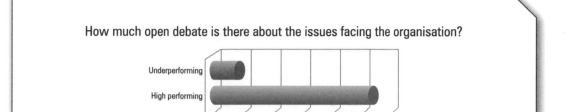

3. Within Ambition, the gap between high performing and underperforming teams is less extreme. Members of both types of team feel challenged by what they have to achieve but, perhaps paradoxically, the individuals who feel more stretched are those in high-performing teams.

How stretching is the goal the team are working towards?

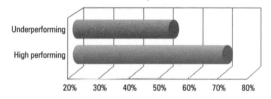

4. What differentiates them appears to be how motivating they find the ambition and how aligned they are about it.

How motivating is the team goal you are working towards?

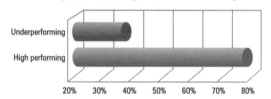

How aligned is the team about the goal you are working towards?

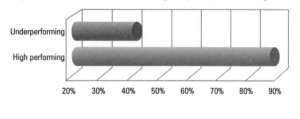

➤

5. The most dramatic figures are for the potential uplift in results that team members envisage if the team were ever to be as effective as it could be.

If the team worked to its potential how much extra performance could it get?

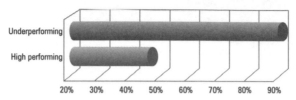

6. In addition to hard business outcomes, there are big differences in the effect on team members and their performance.

How much does being part of this team help you achieve your own goals?

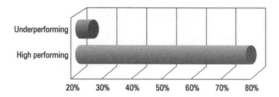

How much of your own potential is being realised by this team?

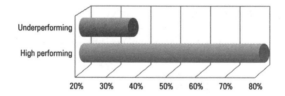

Despite the belief among respondents that there are huge potential benefits, few Leadership Teams have addressed the development of the team in a sustained and systematic way.

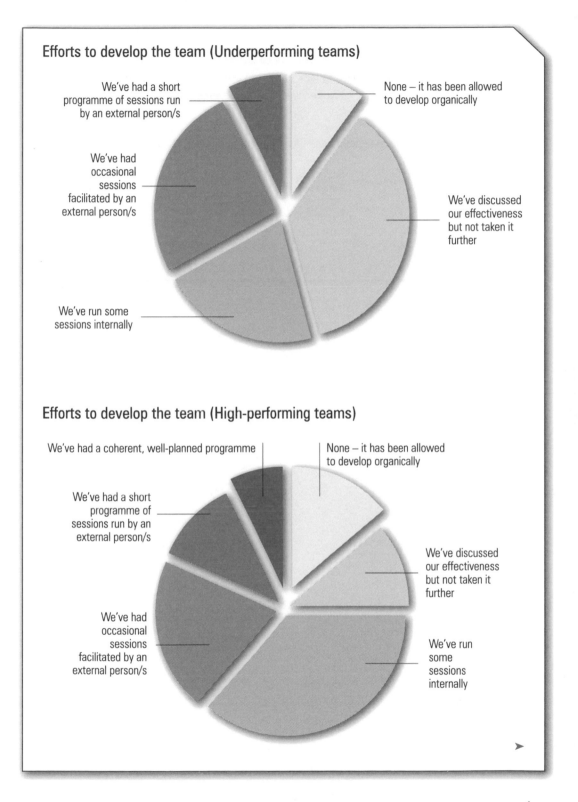

Efforts to develop the team (Underperforming teams)

- We've had a short programme of sessions run by an external person/s
- We've had occasional sessions facilitated by an external person/s
- We've run some sessions internally
- None – it has been allowed to develop organically
- We've discussed our effectiveness but not taken it further

Efforts to develop the team (High-performing teams)

- We've had a coherent, well-planned programme
- We've had a short programme of sessions run by an external person/s
- We've had occasional sessions facilitated by an external person/s
- None – it has been allowed to develop organically
- We've discussed our effectiveness but not taken it further
- We've run some sessions internally

7. Part of the reason for failing to work more consistently on team functioning seems to be the disappointing lack of effectiveness of some of the interventions. High-performing teams, however, seem to value these interventions more. ▲

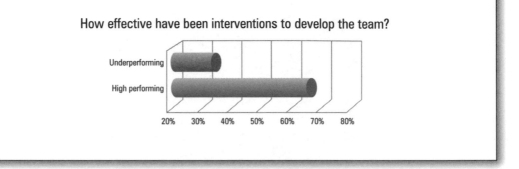

How effective have been interventions to develop the team?

WHY LEADERSHIP TEAMS MATTER, AND WHY YOU SHOULD DEVELOP YOURS

IF DEVELOPING LEADERSHIP TEAMS IS SO IMPORTANT,
why isn't everyone doing it?

As we have already seen, individual leadership attracts far more attention than the role of Leadership Teams. And our strange attitudes to leadership get us into all sorts of trouble.

Too many heroes, not enough teams

As we have already seen, individual leadership attracts far more attention than the role of Leadership Teams. And our strange attitudes to leadership get us into all sorts of trouble – politically and socially, as well as in business. We admire the wrong people, for the wrong reasons. We are obsessed with the idea of heroic individual leadership – the Great Man Theory of history.

This is the theory that says that Elizabeth I fought off the Spanish Armada, Winston Churchill won World War II, Gandhi gained independence for India, and Bill Gates created desktop computing. They didn't do these things singlehanded, of course. But it's easier to simplify and attach one name to great achievements than to learn the details about the complex path these changes took and the various people who contributed to each of these successes.

We expect our leaders to be strong, decisive visionaries, and we consistently undervalue the contributions made by the Leadership Teams they assemble around them.

We're wedded to our stereotypes of Great Leaders. We expect our leaders to be strong, decisive visionaries, and we consistently undervalue the contributions made by the Leadership Teams they assemble around them. This is causing serious problems for leaders today who are trying to get things done, because, by oversimplifying what leadership is about, we fall into the trap of drastically underestimating the importance of Leadership Teams and the impact they have on performance and outcomes.

It's not just outsiders who make this mistake, though. Leaders themselves also fall, far too easily, into the stereotype of the lone, heroic figure, singlehandedly willing the team on to greatness.

Leaders of teams know that they are dependent on the performance of those around them to succeed, but they can't see a way past the dysfunction to realise that potential.

The leaders I talk to want to act as charioteers, harnessing the energy and power of their teams and using all their strength to keep the energy heading in the right direction. Many will have had experience of this, and they know it can be an exhilarating ride. All too often, though, they end up working as mediators, spending most of their time managing individual egos and bridging fractured and fractious relationships.

Polishing fish

I have been coaching both individuals and Leadership Teams for many years, and I've had great results with both. But my own experience of working with individual leaders has often been dispiriting. However much the individual changes and develops, the fundamental challenges a leader faces almost always relate to other people and other areas of the organisation. Kurt Lewin (Sansone, Morf and Panter, 2004) articulated this as long ago as 1937 as a mathematical equation:

$$B = f(P \times E)$$

or Behaviour is a function of Personality x Environment.

Lewin's intention was to get beyond the 'nature versus nurture' debate by showing that individuals are always a product of both their own inherent preferences and style and the environment that surrounds them. In changing behaviour, therefore, the best results come if you can shift both the individuals and what lies around them.

I know that I can help almost any leader perform better, and find practical ways to bring out the best in other people. But I have found myself wishing, time and again, that we had those others right there in the room, so that they could all work things out together and find ways to resolve the bigger, deeper issues that hold organisations back from delivering value and realising their full potential.

Coaching individuals who are working in an unhelpful team environment, without these others, is like polishing fish. You take your fish out of the muddy, murky water, polish it till it shines and then pop it straight back into the same unhealthy environment, where everything quickly reverts to normal.

You need to fix the pool, as well as the poissons. Otherwise, nothing changes.

The leaders I speak to know this. Yet few of them, as we have seen, take the action necessary to address the team, rather than just the individuals.

There's an apparent paradox here. If all these highly intelligent and experienced leaders believe that the scale of bottom line benefit from creating a high performing Leadership Team is so large, why aren't they doing something to realise it?

In our research, leaders and members of Leadership Teams quote several reasons why their teams fail to address the underlying problems and fulfil their potential.

Six things that get in the way of developing Leadership Teams

'It's never the right time to start'

Leadership Teams can always find good reasons to put off looking at team development. Because of the fluidity of their membership, they may be waiting for a new member to come on board. Or perhaps a reorganisation is imminent, or team members want to wait for the start of the new financial cycle.

There are also always other tasks and challenges that seem more urgent and that must be attended to straight away. Leadership Team development is one of the many victims of the 'tyranny of the urgent'. Dealing with the problems facing the Leadership Team is important, yes, but it is often set aside in the face of the huge pressures of grappling with day-to-day challenges.

Yet, by failing to deal with weaknesses in the way they go about their business, Leadership Teams stack up problems for themselves. Delays contribute to a situation in which there will always be ever more urgent matters to address, and the team ends up spending all its time firefighting.

Once this vicious circle is established, addressing the development of the Leadership Team never seems quite urgent enough to prioritise. It never quite gets to the top of the list, and the list just keeps getting longer.

'We don't have the support we'd need'

The work that's needed to develop the effectiveness of a Leadership Team takes time. It becomes a lot easier when external stakeholders are supportive and understand the implications of this work.

But it can sometimes be hard to help them see the link between something as intangible as team effectiveness and financial impact. CEOs and Leadership Teams need to convince their stakeholders that investing time and resources in a sustained effort to develop a powerful team will boost performance in ways that will make a large and measurable difference, even if this may not be immediately reflected in quarterly outputs and results. Often, they need to convince themselves first.

> *...addressing the development of the Leadership Team never seems quite urgent enough to prioritise. It never quite gets to the top of the list, and the list just keeps getting longer.*

'We don't really have a plan'

When it comes to developing a Leadership Team, good planning disciplines and a proper business case are often neglected. Most team development work is based on only a vague understanding of what needs to be done and the bottom line value expected from it. Leadership Team development is seen as being about 'soft' skills and unmeasurable results, and it is denied the rigorous planning and scrutiny given to other business initiatives.

Developing a Leadership Team should be treated like any other business task. Planning is vital, but it is hard to know before you begin what the sequence of steps will be. This kind of project needs to be planned out clearly and to take an emergent approach to design.

Because the project is competing for resources with other initiatives that do have defined targets, deliverables and timescales, the Leadership Team will need to give as much thought to deliverables, investment and ROI as it would in embarking on any other investment.

'We don't have the skills we need'

Members of Leadership Teams all have their own specialist skills and expertise. But they usually have little training and less knowledge when it comes to the skills needed in their roles as members of the unique environment that is a Leadership Team.

They may even not know what skills they lack. Understandably, they assume that everything they already know about teamwork will apply to Leadership Teams. Some of it does. But team members usually have much to learn – and it often touches on factors they may have been completely unaware of.

'Past awaydays haven't translated into real change'

When a company becomes aware that its Leadership Team is not functioning as well as it could, the reaction is often to organise an awayday.

While these may help – and may even deliver new insights – they are not the answer. More time needs to be invested to create lasting and effective transformations. Sustained effort and focus is needed. Without this, the benefits will quickly decay as soon as team members are thrown back into the melee of their everyday work.

Developing a Leadership Team should be treated like any other business task. Planning is vital, but it is hard to know before you begin what the sequence of steps will be.

As a result, many team members have become sceptical about renewed attempts to develop the team, as they have seen so many previous efforts that were halfhearted or poorly followed through and have made so little difference.

We need help – but where can we find it?

While there are widely understood methods and approaches for most other forms of investment, this is often not the case with team development. Expert help is usually needed.

The obvious place to look for expertise and support is HR. But many HR professionals have little experience of the very specific methods and skills required to develop teamwork in the unique environment of the boardroom.

The few HR specialists who do are usually so weighed down with the challenges of keeping systems running smoothly and addressing the plethora of other people issues in the organisation that it's hard for them to give the necessary focus and attention to the functioning of the top team. They are also, of course, greatly disadvantaged by being members of the team themselves, and by the effect this has on their relationships with others in the team.

Most organisations of any size have relationships with some external coaches. Often those coaches are tainted by a close association with one or more board members. However skilled these executive coaches are, they, too, are unlikely to have the specialist knowledge and experience required to develop a Leadership Team.

If these are the symptoms, what's the antidote?

Each of these reasons for not developing Leadership Teams is understandable. All are also capable of being overcome, and in Section 3 I'll show you a set of steps to take that will get you started with your team by successfully addressing all of them.

If you're impatient to get to the detail of how to make changes you can go straight to that point. However, so far we've talked a lot about symptoms. One of the reasons for some of the medicine not working is a failure to properly understand both the patient and what's wrong before we reach for a cure. Let's first spend some time getting a deeper understanding of both. ▲

CHANGING YOUR TEAM
is easier than you might think

The assumption may be that great teams somehow just happen – that they depend on luck, or, at least, a mystical and elusive personal chemistry. But the truth is, great Leadership Teams can be created. It doesn't take magic.

Working in a high performing Leadership Team is exhilarating. Getting things done is easier. Simple things become routine, harder things become easy and you find you can wrestle effectively with even the thorniest challenges facing you. You and your colleagues surprise yourselves, both individually and collectively, with what you're able to achieve.

Team meetings are something you to look forward to. They become a refuge from the day-to-day pressures and tasks – a place where you get support, insight and ideas that mean you can dive back into the fray with new energy and new solutions. The Leadership Team, rather than members' own departmental teams, becomes each person's first loyalty.

The results such teams produce win you all respect – from both above and below. Criticism and scrutiny are replaced with curiosity about how you're delivering so much.

It's not easy. Far from it. Your appetite grows to do even better. The challenges you set yourselves are greater and the demands you make of yourselves are higher.

Most of all, though, there's a real satisfaction in doing all this together, with people you trust, respect and care about. You want to raise your game for the others in the team, as well as yourself. And the others all want to do the same.

None of this will come as a surprise to anyone who has felt the joy and energy of being part of a great team. What does initially surprise many of the leaders we work with – and may surprise you – is that such teams can be created. All this is possible. You, too, can create an unforgettable experience like this with your current team.

It's not magic

Creating a team that functions well, exploits the amazing strengths each member brings and complements the inevitable weaknesses that every member also has can lead to dramatic improvements. It can transform an organisation's results, culture and prospects, quickly and permanently.

Many people seem to think successful Leadership Teams are a magical phenomenon – occurring, like the origins of life, only through a rare and unlikely constellation of circumstances. The assumption may be that great teams somehow just happen – that they depend on luck, or, at least, a mystical and elusive personal chemistry.

But the truth is, great Leadership Teams can be created. It doesn't take magic.

Leadership Teams have a finite number of simple characteristics – and they can be acquired relatively easily. Instead of concentrating only on the individuals who spearhead organisations, CEOs can learn how to form and develop outstanding Leadership Teams. Leaders from across the organisation can be brought together to analyse problems, gain a shared understanding of them and work together to create better solutions.

Real changes can be generated surprisingly quickly

Creating an effective Leadership Team requires changes – in the way each individual behaves, in the ways you interact, in the processes you employ for getting work done and in the way that work is organised – as the team develops and practises new patterns of behaving, talking and relating.

It is perfectly possible to take a normal, uninspired, disparate collection of people and talents and set in motion a process that will help it evolve into a powerful, unified and productive Leadership Team.

You can do it, and it can happen quickly. A complete and sustainable transformation will take time, but the first positive signs of change will be visible, and making a real difference, within weeks. You just need to know how to go about it.

When that new understanding starts to show through in real, practical changes, dramatic results can follow surprisingly fast. These early results add their own energy and momentum, and the pace of change will accelerate as you go through the gears.

We have all been part of at least one great team – and we'll never forget it

Here's a simple thought experiment. Think back to a time when you were part of an extraordinary and positive achievement. It can be almost anything, from winning a school painting contest to running a marathon or turning a business loss into a profit.

- ▲ What do you remember most about the people behind that success?
- ▲ What did it achieve?
- ▲ How did it feel to be part of it?

When I talk to people about their memories of positive events like these, I see them light up. There is excitement and energy, even when what's being remembered happened many years ago.

When you recall your own chosen experience, I'm sure you'll find that it involved teamwork. You may be remembering crossing that finishing line, but you didn't get there only because of your own hard work. You were there because of the encouragement you had from your spouse or parents, the support of the people you trained with, or the tips and advice you received from a friend who had been there before. Probably a bit of each.

Now look at the team you have today. Imagine what you could all achieve together if this team worked as well as the team involved in your best memory of success. How far could you go if this team worked as well as that one?

So how can my team reach that level?

Section 3 of this book sets out the details of how you can develop your own team, whatever its current level of effectiveness, using a set of simple and extensively proven methods.

But before we start to look at tools and techniques, we need to understand what high performing teams do differently, how they do it and the effect that these differences make.

How does your own Leadership Team score today?

Rather than thinking about these important issues in the abstract, it may be useful to carry out a self-assessment test to establish where your own Leadership Team stands in relation to the issues that directly affect its performance.

Before reading the next chapter, take a moment to score your own team on the scales opposite. ▲

Imagine what you could all achieve together if this team worked as well as the team involved in your best memory of success. How far could you go if this team worked as well as that one?

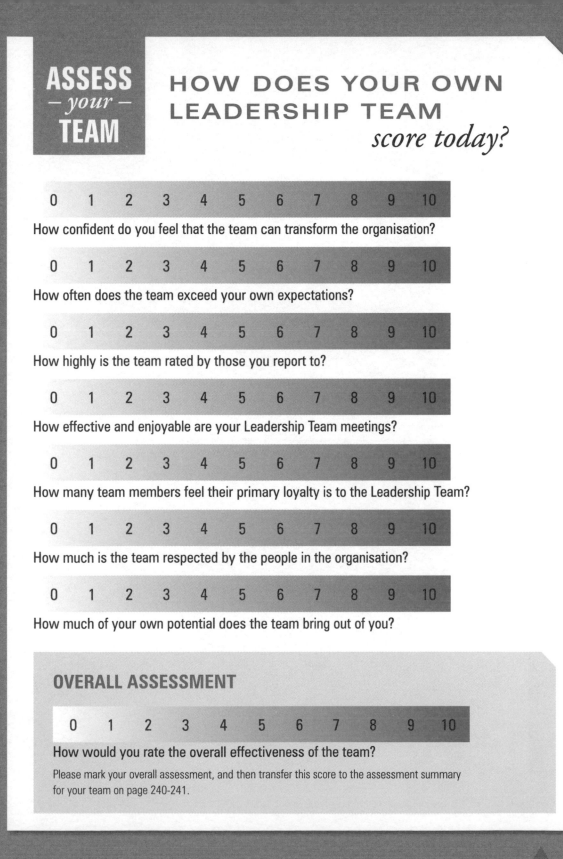

ASSESS
— your —
TEAM

HOW DOES YOUR OWN LEADERSHIP TEAM *score today?*

| 0 | 1 | 2 | 3 | 4 | 5 | 6 | 7 | 8 | 9 | 10 |

How confident do you feel that the team can transform the organisation?

| 0 | 1 | 2 | 3 | 4 | 5 | 6 | 7 | 8 | 9 | 10 |

How often does the team exceed your own expectations?

| 0 | 1 | 2 | 3 | 4 | 5 | 6 | 7 | 8 | 9 | 10 |

How highly is the team rated by those you report to?

| 0 | 1 | 2 | 3 | 4 | 5 | 6 | 7 | 8 | 9 | 10 |

How effective and enjoyable are your Leadership Team meetings?

| 0 | 1 | 2 | 3 | 4 | 5 | 6 | 7 | 8 | 9 | 10 |

How many team members feel their primary loyalty is to the Leadership Team?

| 0 | 1 | 2 | 3 | 4 | 5 | 6 | 7 | 8 | 9 | 10 |

How much is the team respected by the people in the organisation?

| 0 | 1 | 2 | 3 | 4 | 5 | 6 | 7 | 8 | 9 | 10 |

How much of your own potential does the team bring out of you?

OVERALL ASSESSMENT

| 0 | 1 | 2 | 3 | 4 | 5 | 6 | 7 | 8 | 9 | 10 |

How would you rate the overall effectiveness of the team?

Please mark your overall assessment, and then transfer this score to the assessment summary for your team on page 240-241.

SECTION 2

*What makes a
high performing
Leadership Team?*

*The Six Game-Changing
Conversations*

THE SIX GAME-CHANGING
conversations

What is the biggest single difference between a great Leadership Team and a less successful one? It's simple. Great Leadership Teams know how to talk.

This is not a question of articulacy – top managers are often quite capable of articulating the hind leg off a donkey, without necessarily achieving much. It is about knowing specifically, as a team and individually, how to talk and what to talk about.

It's about having the right conversations, at the right times, with the right approaches – and getting the right results. Our research condensed this down into six areas of discussion. We call them the Six Game-Changing Conversations.

These are:

1. Ambition Conversations

2. Relationship Conversations

3. Priority Conversations

4. Accountability Conversations

5. Delivery Conversations

6. Learning Conversations

Most Leadership Teams touch on all these issues from time to time. But even when they do, they don't always do it effectively – and often miss out or don't fully address some of the critical elements.

Each of the Six Conversations is different and requires different approaches, skills and processes. Distinguishing them allows us to define, understand and approach each of them more rigorously and effectively.

The Six Game-Changing Conversations are ongoing, dynamic and interdependent. High performing teams constantly cycle through all of them, adjust the sequence, relate them to each other and consciously balance the time they invest in each.

The best Leadership Teams hold all six conversations regularly, systematically and rigorously. They use them to address the key problems that hold their organisations back, including the thorniest, most challenging and irreconcilable issues – the ones lesser Leadership Teams rarely get to, let alone solve.

Teams that do this create better results for the organisation – and a more rewarding experience for every member of the Leadership Team.

The Conversations Pyramid

The Six Conversations build from the bottom of what we call the Conversations Pyramid.

LEARNING
conversations

ACCOUNTABILITY
conversations

DELIVERY
conversations

RELATIONSHIP
conversations

PRIORITY
conversations

AMBITION
conversations

AMBITION
conversations

The pyramid is read from the bottom upwards. Ambition Conversations are the foundation of everything. They define the purpose and direction of the team.

Relationship Conversations create the human connections necessary to deliver the Ambition. Only when these are strong enough do team members hold one another robustly and constructively to account in Accountability Conversations.

Priority Conversations define and decide the most important things required to deliver the Ambition, and Delivery Conversations ensure that the Leadership Team takes responsibility for seeing that those priorities are successfully achieved.

In conjunction with the other five conversations, Learning Conversations ensure that the team makes full use of the contributions of all team members – and that the team as a whole continually improves.

The pyramid integrates leadership and strategy

In this model, the subjects that are traditionally seen as being concerned with leadership are on the left face, while those that are normally seen as strategy are on the right face.

These two sides are yin and yang to each other, mutually interdependent.

Working on leadership and strategy is not enough for success, if you treat them independently. You must work on them both together, so that you can deal with the way each drives and supports the other.

This is one of the central tenets of this book. Working on leadership and strategy is not enough for success, if you treat them independently. You must work on them both together, so that you can deal with the way each drives and supports the other.

That, of course, is not how it plays out in most organisations. Leadership development and strategy work are often tucked away in separate departments. HR looks after the 'soft' leadership issues, and finance or business development departments look after the 'hard' strategy aspects.

This is not a recipe for success. Leadership issues are seen as less critical, and they get swamped in the torrent of everyday tasks and challenges. Strategy always looks great in a deck of smart PowerPoint documents, but it often fails in execution because its implementation is poorly led, communicated and managed.

Two conversations bridge both strategy and leadership

Ambition Conversations and Learning Conversations straddle both sides of the pyramid, which goes a long way towards explaining why these aspects are so rarely handled well in Leadership Teams. 'Learning' becomes an intangible, soft issue, often neglected because of its unquantifiable relationship to performance. 'Ambition' becomes a set of purely rational numbers and dry statements which fail to engage and excite the leadership, let alone the rest of the organisation.

What makes Ambition Conversations different from strategic discussions about goals, for example, is the emotional element. They are not just about what could be done, but what must be done, what would be worth doing, what would fire and inspire and animate the whole organisation.

Similarly, what makes Learning Conversations more than just HR's business is the fact that they are grounded, realistic, content-based and strategic in nature, as well as being about essential human interactions. Learning conversations are how Leadership Teams integrate the human and strategic elements of their organisation, and the other five conversations, to create genuine transformation.

Tapping into the collective knowhow

We know, from CEOs' comments and our own experiences, that today's Leadership Teams generally underperform – in most cases by a wide margin.

> *We know, from CEOs' comments and our own experiences, that today's Leadership Teams generally underperform – in most cases by a wide margin.*

To realise their full potential, Leadership Teams must pay attention to what they talk about and how they do it. This means learning how to excel at each of the Six Conversations and how to strike the balance between them.

Most Leadership Teams already have all the knowledge, data and expertise they need to succeed. What they don't always have is a way to combine their collective knowhow to understand challenges, generate fresh insights, identify new options for action and make better decisions.

The Six Conversations are the key to doing this successfully. Changing the way the Leadership Team interacts can and will transform the performance of both the team and the organisation.

Understanding the conversations

In the chapters that follow I will introduce each of the Six Conversations. For each one I will set out:

What exactly it is

What is the nature and purpose of the conversation – and how does it differ from some of the related conversations you might read about in the business literature or recognise in your own team?

Why teams struggle

We know from our research and experience of working with teams that there are factors which get in the way of having each conversation effectively – and, therefore, of harvesting the full benefit from it.

To overcome these factors, it is important to understand them. This understanding will also provide you with the reassuring recognition that they are common to all Leadership Teams, not just your own.

What a good one looks like

Good conversations do take place in most Leadership Teams. They just don't happen often enough. You will, therefore, have experienced effective conversations of all six types.

This section describes what good looks like for each conversation, so that you can recognise good ones when they are happening, recall good examples from the past and move your team towards more frequent and consistent conversations of each type.

Good conversations do take place in most Leadership Teams. They just don't happen often enough.

The benefits

Improving any of the conversations will require some investment of effort. This section describes the payoffs you can expect for achieving success.

A relevant case study

In relation to each conversation, I have included a story from our research or work with Leadership Teams. These case studies both bring the conversation to life and show how it has generated a transformational impact in a team and the organisation around it.

I have also opened each conversation chapter with a story from my experience of the Maasai which I hope will offer an illuminating and even provocative view from a completely different perspective. ▲

7 AMBITION

conversations

Great Leadership Teams aim high. They create goals that mean something to each person and that are worth fighting for, even when the going gets tough.

Under the acacia tree

Mobilising an entire community for transformation

The people of Merrueshi, a Maasai community, met as they always did when there was something important to discuss, under the big acacia tree in the centre of the community.

Merrueshi is in a poor rural area. There is little water for farming or domestic use, and the region has been largely ignored by the government far away in Nairobi. But there were huge changes on the way, including the double-edged benefits of a new road that would bring Merrueshi into closer touch with the outside world but also open it up to many new challenges. Some were obvious to many – like the risk of introducing crime and disease, including HIV/AIDS. Others were only visible to a few – such as the potential arrival of land speculators.

Critically, though, this greater integration with the outside world threatened a terminal erosion of the ancient Maasai culture and traditions.

It was time to start thinking hard about how people wanted the community to develop, how they could protect their culture in the face of the coming changes and how they could make their home a better place to live.

At Maasai meetings, everyone, old and young, is given a chance to speak. One by one, people rose to their feet, said their piece and sat back down. Some were eloquent and impassioned, others brief and succinct. There were conflicting views and varying interpretations of what the coming changes meant for Merrueshi, but everybody listened with courtesy and patience.

➤

The sun rose and sank in the sky. Night fell, and the meeting was paused. The process continued early the following morning, with many of the children still wiping the sleep from their eyes.

Although the meeting started with many different points of view, the people of this isolated community gradually began to share their thoughts and build a vision of a meaningful goal. At the beginning of the conversation, ideas about how the community could be changed were diverse, unfocused and imprecise. As everyone had their say, the picture became clearer. Bit by bit, vague hopes began to turn into a concrete intention, and by the close of this initial conversation, the first of many, everyone was united around the vision of a community worth working and striving for.

No-one could fully forecast the changes ahead, but it was clear that a single, powerful solution was needed which would help them respond to whatever was coming their way.

After all the speakers' views and opinions had been heard, a vision emerged around which the community's energy coalesced. Education emerged as the dominant theme. There was a passionate desire for the Maasai children to be better equipped for whatever future might lie ahead.

From a huge sprawling discussion, a single conclusion emerged. The community needed a school. Not only would it provide an education, it would also play a vital role in teaching children the Maasai culture. It would be a Maasai school, built, staffed and populated by the Maasai.

Over the months that followed, the hard work began. A charity, the Maasai Association, was created. Supporters were recruited and rallied across the world. Funds were raised. Links were formed with the National Education Department in Nairobi. Over a period of two years, people from every part of the community contributed to the construction of a small primary school.

That school was just the beginning. Today, Merrueshi is a transformed place, with the primary school and a successful secondary school that has drawn in more than 800 pupils from surrounding areas – and from far away, across the Tanzanian border.

The energy of that original meeting has generated many more amazing changes. Merrueshi now has a maternity unit, a health centre and a mobile clinic that criss-crosses the region. There's a Maasai cultural centre and a thriving women's co-operative, a visitor centre to encourage outsiders to get involved and even a computer station to facilitate access to the resources available on the internet. The momentum for change is unstoppable, but each innovation is carefully managed to ensure that the identity, values and culture of the local people are honoured and preserved.

It all started when the members of a community came together to wrestle with finding a shared way forward and a future they could all believe in, in the face of great uncertainty. It all started with an Ambition Conversation beneath an acacia tree. ▲

Starting Leadership Team transformation

Although there are many definitions of the word 'team', they all involve some kind of common or shared goal. In practice, we have found that this is often missing, indistinct or simply not shared across the Leadership Team. The transformation to a great Leadership Team, therefore, starts with Ambition Conversations.

These begin by exploring what team members truly, deeply want for the organisation and trying to discover what would motivate each of them to take real risks and confront the big issues that hold the organisation back.

Establishing the Leadership Team's ambition is fundamental. The team will need to have many conversations about priorities, delivery, relationships, accountability and learning, and these will all be seriously compromised, and far less effective, if they are not brought into focus by a clear, shared and motivating ambition.

> *Although there are many definitions of the word 'team', they all involve some kind of common or shared goal. In practice, we have found that this is often missing, indistinct or simply not shared across the Leadership Team.*

What are Ambition Conversations?

The Maasai people of Merrueshi got together and talked to determine their goals for the community – to decide what, for them, would constitute success and what they wanted to reach and work for together. But the talking was also about understanding and articulating why they wanted what they did.

In business, too, even potentially great teams often set out without a clear realisation of what they might be able to accomplish and why this would be a worthwhile and engaging ambition.

Great Leadership Teams aim high. They create goals that mean something to each person and that are worth fighting for, even when the going gets tough. By having genuine and profound Ambition Conversations, just like the one under the acacia tree in Merrueshi, they can start to form and shape a vision of the future. And once the right goals are in place, the Leadership Team can start thinking and working as a single force as it decides how to reach these distant destinations.

Goals are also about emotion, not just numbers

A big part of leadership is about inspiration – making team members feel that they are part of something bigger than themselves, and helping them achieve more than they think they can.

Organisations can work on an inspiring goal (often labelled 'the vision') – but this is often so vague that it's not clear what anyone needs to do differently to achieve it. Alternatively, they may work on rational, practical – often eminently logical – targets, which usually have the fatal flaw of being too dry to engage or excite anyone. Even the few businesses that do both usually end up with a disconnect between the two. Ambition Conversations are about forming goals that fully incorporate both dimensions.

Using ambition to excite, motivate and engage is something that calls for harnessing emotion. In business, there is a tendency to focus on numbers – on boosting sales by so much year on year, or on spending so much less. But most great journeys of achievement start with emotion, rather than percentages. They emerge from a big idea, like 'How would it be if our customers never had to worry about X?' or 'Wouldn't it be wonderful if we could launch our product so that every household could afford it?'

'The winning strategy combines analytically sound, ambitious but logical goals with methods that help people experience new, often very ambitious goals, as exciting, meaningful and uplifting – creating a deeply felt determination to move, make it happen, and win, now'.
(Kotter, 2008)

Ambition Conversations are emotional and personal, as well as commercial and organisational. They involve people talking about what matters to them – and about what they truly and deeply want for themselves and the business. This makes them quite different from the usual conversations about goals and targets that happen in Leadership Teams when they look at planning, budgeting and all the other familiar business processes.

Starting to have Ambition Conversations is exciting, but it can also be difficult. Leadership Teams can't see at the outset where they are going to end up, and the journey can have many twists and turns. It can take personal courage, especially in the early stages, for members of the team to stand up and talk about the things that matter most to them. There will be many different perspectives, ideas and needs to be discussed before an Ambition Conversation arrives at the kind of goals that will light up and inspire the team's efforts.

What's needed, though, is goals that will do more than engage and inspire. Ambition Conversations begin with this and then let the thinking flow on through to the practical, the rational and the quantifiable. Both dimensions are important and they need to flow together seamlessly.

By making the commitment to be courageous, open and bold, teams can break through to a level of understanding rarely found in day-to-day business. The picture of the future that emerges is always greater and more powerful than existed before the team began talking about it. Not all differences can be resolved and reconciled, but engaging in a genuine Ambition Conversation is an important step towards forging a Leadership Team that is truly more than the sum of its parts.

Ambition Conversations are the key to unlocking the kind of ideas and energy that will be needed to turn an organisation in a new direction and put it on a new path to a different future.

A good Ambition Conversation lifts the organisation's sights beyond the familiar annual battle to improve performance by a few percentage points here or there. Big leaps don't happen bit by bit.

No-one is excited or inspired by piecemeal, incremental goals. Ambition Conversations are the key to unlocking the kind of ideas and energy that will be needed to turn an organisation in a new direction and put it on a new path to a different future.

Forming goals with the power to motivate

Goals are a tool that can be consciously used to channel the drive and energy of individuals and teams and to bring ambitions into sharp focus. But it is only recently that psychologists have paid serious attention to the importance of goal-setting and the techniques that can be employed to make a goal act as a powerful force in driving performance and change.

We all know, from interviews with successful athletes and sporting champions, that goal-setting and visualisation techniques are now used almost universally by people who are dedicated to wringing the last ounce of performance out of themselves. They use them because they work. But most leaders I meet have only a vague idea of how this is done and why it is successful in helping individuals achieve performance and results that were previously beyond them.

Leaders do not generally understand the scientific basis for this kind of goal-setting. They don't realise, for example, that how a goal is conceived and expressed is vitally important or that the necessary skills can be learnt, like any other set of techniques. As a result, many business goals are so abstract and ill-defined that they cannot possibly offer the inspirational beacons and touchstones that would change behaviour and improve performance. The process of setting goals is every bit as important as the final product, and this is often overlooked in organisations.

But anyone can learn the art of creating a rich, engaging picture of the future and a clear, motivating and exciting vision.

At the personal level, it begins with clarifying and refining your goal to make it as real and sharply defined as possible. It needs to be a rich picture, rather than an abstract idea. Since the visual sense is strongest in most of us – 50 per cent of the brain's pathways involve vision – this is the obvious starting point. But psychologists have found that it pays to consciously involve the other senses as well.

The theory of goal-setting has been extensively studied by psychologists in many fields. Neuro-Linguistic Programming (NLP) has synthesised much of this research and a summary of the key elements is shown in the box on page 86.

The process of setting goals is every bit as important as the final product, and this is often overlooked in organisations.

Imagine it's already happened

One of the most important discoveries of the last fifty years was the development of the Paradoxical Theory of Change, first described in 1970 by Gestalt therapist Arnold Beisser (Beisser, 1970).

Beisser's breakthrough research showed that the best way to make change happen was often to behave as if it had already occurred.

This sounds like a very strange way to change your world, but it is not nearly as illogical as it might seem. In fact, everyday life throws up plenty of examples to prove the point.

For instance, many of us have had to deal with the problem of needing to work with someone who rubs us up the wrong way. One approach is to grit one's teeth and put up with the situation. But the best way to improve this relationship is to start acting as if it is already strong. The resulting change in your approach stimulates new responses from them and this changes the dynamics of the relationship, making it possible for both people to open up and

NLP THEORY ON ACHIEVING OUTCOMES

Knowing your outcome is vitally important. Many people do not have conscious outcomes. Others know what they don't want. NLP highlights the importance of individuals moving towards those things they want. Without outcomes, individuals are simply wandering purposelessly. Outcomes enable people to focus on achieving their goals.

NLP suggests there are several criteria for a well-formed outcome.

1. **It needs to be positively stated.** It must be what the person wants, rather than what the person doesn't want. Outcomes must be capable of being achieved – and it's impossible to work towards a negative.

2. **It needs to be able to be tested.** There must be a way to use the person's senses to know that it has been achieved. Without this, there is no way to measure progress towards its achievement.

3. **It must be sensory.** The person needs to know what they would see, hear and feel when it is achieved.

4. **It must be within the person's control.** The individual needs to be able to begin and sustain progress towards it. Control and responsibility for achieving it must be with the person, rather than with someone else.

5. **It must make sense in context.** The outcome has to be available and relevant in the appropriate circumstances.

6. **It must maintain the best of what already is.** The outcome must preserve the positive aspects of the current situation. ▲

see each other's point of view. Even if this change has happened as result of a deliberate, conscious, almost mechanical initiative, it immediately makes the relationship less tense and antagonistic and greatly improves the chances of getting good work done.

In the same way, individuals and teams can work towards goals by starting their thinking from imagining that the goals have already been achieved. So that, for example, whatever the perceived barriers to success were, they have been overcome. Instead of accepting the limitations imposed by current thinking, people can scale up their ambitions and fix their imagination on bigger, bolder, braver and more compelling goals.

'I don't want them thinking I'm a flake'

While some of today's business leaders understand the psychology of goals better than their predecessors, most don't apply this understanding as widely as they could. Others still see these techniques as being a bit 'out there' and suspect.

The quantity and quality of research on the subject, however, means that the efficacy of such techniques, whether with individuals or in teams, is beyond doubt. The only question is to what degree leaders choose to use them.

Today's leadership culture still continues to place a disproportionate emphasis on analytical thinking, and those who want to try different approaches often find themselves having to introduce them by stealth.

One successful leader told me recently that he believes creative visualisation is definitely helping him achieve his goals.

'But I don't tell people I'm doing it,' he said. 'I don't want them thinking I'm a flake.'

This is a man who is known for his rigorous logic and shrewd financial assessments. His use of visualisation is a learned technique he deploys and values alongside his analytical skills. But while he is happy to talk to anyone about columns of numbers, he is oddly reticent about his goal-setting habits.

Goal-setting in Leadership Teams

Goal-setting in teams is just as important as it is for individuals. It uses the same well proven principles, but doing it in teams requires more time and more careful thought.

When a Leadership Team's members' goals coincide, they can create a powerful motivating force. When everyone in the team is pulling in the same direction and working towards a unified purpose, it immediately becomes easier to achieve the goal.

On the other hand, in the absence of a unifying team purpose, conflicts inevitably arise – and resolving them is often impossible.

Why teams struggle

Without a clear, compelling ambition around which the Leadership Team are aligned, mobilising the organisation towards transformational change can feel like running through treacle. Even modest changes seem to take a huge amount of effort to get moving, and yet more to sustain.

The Leadership Team, too, suffers if it doesn't have an ambition as a shared touchstone. A vacuum of common purpose gets filled with competing agendas and priorities and the team feels disparate.

Whilst the need for ambition is clear, the environment in which Leadership Teams operate makes it hard for Ambition Conversations to happen.

The Leadership Team, too, suffers if it doesn't have an ambition as a shared touchstone. A vacuum of common purpose gets filled with competing agendas and priorities and the team feels disparate.

Many goals and no single ambition

Many factors, including individual priorities and the simple power of habit, tend to make people focus on and talk about what they know, which is usually their own part of the organisation. It is hard for them to see the bigger picture of where the Leadership Team and the organisation are heading. Even when they do, their version of the bigger picture tends to be skewed and partial. It will come with their own biases and is almost certain to miss out important aspects of other parts of the organisation.

Leadership Team members often have goals for their own departments that have developed independently of others' targets and the organisation's broader goals. Indeed, in some cases the organisation may have nothing that could rightly be called a single goal. More often, though, the shared purpose that should be unifying the organisation to work towards a common goal is unfocused or layered.

They jump too soon from ambition to action

Even when shared purpose is discussed in Leadership Teams, the ingrained habit of focusing on action means that they almost always move too fast from fully exploring and clearly articulating their ambitions to discussing the details of how to reach the destination.

The Leadership Team of a recycling company decided that its ambition was to double its sales and dominate the market. Logically enough, on the face of it, suggestions flowed thick and fast on how to achieve the goal. People piled in to contribute other ideas and mention other challenges, and the debate quickly became about the methods and feasibility of reaching the goal.

But there were several other things that needed to be talked about before the team moved on to discuss implementation.

Why, for example, had they chosen market domination as their goal?

Why was doubling the size of the business the right target, rather than going for a 50 per cent increase, or a 200 per cent improvement?

More importantly, did that goal motivate and excite them? And why would anyone else in the organisation, outside the Leadership Team, care and be inspired by this goal?

This Leadership Team needed to understand what would be motivating and compelling about dominating the market. Perhaps they would be able to ensure that more waste would be recycled properly and play their part in cleaning up the environment. Would this ambition be meaningful and motivating enough to sustain the team in the face of the challenges of transforming the organisation? Or could they align around the goal of dominating the market so as to create a bigger, more sustainable business that would give its employees more job security?

By moving on too quickly, they virtually guaranteed the usual weary reaction from people in the organisation: 'Oh, yeah. Just another meaningless set of numbers sent down from the top. Next year's will be different again. We'll just keep our heads down and keep going...'

Companies underestimate the importance of emotions

When Leadership Teams move too quickly from goals to action, they end up with dry, anodyne statements of intent that aren't compelling or even memorable. If an organisation ends up with a statement of intent, rather than a vision, employees will not be motivated and the emotional power of a well-chosen and well-articulated ambition will be squandered. People, including the Leadership Team, will feel nagged, rather than excited, and the organisation will not be inspired to move towards its goals.

It's unfamiliar and difficult

Talking about what's important to each team member isn't something Leadership Teams normally do. Using personal passions to set the direction of the organisation is counterintuitive. The financial goals and strategy are set and agreed, so surely it would make more sense to spend time discussing how to deliver those? What if the direction that emerges is in conflict with them?

Even when you are able to get started on an Ambition Conversation, it's challenging. Initially the ideas that emerge do have many similarities, but bringing them together into a single memorable and compelling articulation is hard. I've seen teams abandon the effort, just when victory was in sight.

If the team can find the courage to start an Ambition Conversation and see it through, the rewards are high. Every ambition I have been involved in creating has pushed out far beyond the organisation's existing goals and strategy, and every one has mobilised new ideas, energy and action.

What does a good Ambition Conversation look like?

The characteristics of a great Ambition Conversation are simple to describe, but less easy to achieve.

Motivations are explicit

They begin with a deep understanding of what each member of the team really, deeply wants to achieve or leave as a legacy in the organisation. Each of these people joined the team, and sustains the extraordinary degree of commitment required to deliver their roles, for a reason. Most teams don't understand very much about these reasons. They are buried under the demands of the everyday.

Both themes and differences are explored

The motivations of the Leadership Team will have some overlap. They will also be diverse. The themes that emerge will become the raw ingredients of the Ambition. The differences represent a sample of the massive diversity across the people in the organisation, all of who need to be engaged if the Ambition is to have genuine transformational power.

It's challenging to process such a wide range of closely held desires. The tension produced, however, is potentially creative. The temptation is to try to find consensus quickly by rationalising differences and retreating into abstractions. This may reduce the tensions, but it also moves people further away from the power of the raw motivations and ideas.

When Leadership Teams move too quickly from goals to action, they end up with dry, anodyne statements of intent that aren't compelling or even memorable.

A good Ambition Conversation will hold this tension while the similarities are respectfully, deeply and fully explored.

They wait for alchemy

Every great Ambition Conversation I have seen starts energetically and gradually becomes increasingly uncomfortable. Resolving all the elements into something clear and finding a succinct way to articulate it that retains the energy and excitement of the conversation is hard. It takes time.

Most leaders are impatient for a solution, a resolution to the tension, and become agitated when this doesn't appear quickly. Struggling for a really clear and inspirational articulation starts to feel like a self-indulgent use of people's time, given the many other urgent topics they could be discussing.

Staying with the conversation is vital at this stage. Many an organisation has begun this process with good intentions and bailed out when it became frustrating. Most of the dry, uninspiring mission and vision statements that are adopted in organisations were originally produced as a way to reach a result when any conclusion seemed better than prolonging a frustrating and unclear discussion.

The few teams who stick with it, though, eventually light on an idea that is worth the effort. This idea is like the seed in a child's crystal growing kit, and the Ambition forms around it. It's often a single word, but it can also be a more nuanced concept. In one team, it was the desire to regain the important place the organisation had previously held in the community around it.

Most leaders are impatient for a solution, a resolution to the tension, and become agitated when this doesn't appear quickly. A good Ambition Conversation will hold this tension while the similarities are respectfully, deeply and fully explored.

At one publishing company I worked with, it was a pun. 'Inspiring people' was a description both of what the Leadership Team members saw as the best of themselves and also of what they wanted to deliver to their readers. It became the touchstone that galvanised everything else.

It doesn't stop there

There's usually a lot of energy and excitement in the room when the idea emerges and is shaped into words that form the basis of how it will be communicated. This isn't the end of an Ambition Conversation, though. There's more work to do.

The statement or idea needs to be translated into a vivid description of the organisation when it is achieved. What will you hear and see around you? What will your people experience? What will look different to your customers and stakeholders?

As well as these critical descriptions of the end state, how will it translate into your strategy and figures? What will you be doing that you aren't doing now? What will you stop doing? What sort of revenue, profit and cost figures will you need when you get there? How will your processes need to be different?

These are all demanding questions to answer, but they are what give substance and credibility to your aspirational Ambition. Clarity about all this is needed if you are going to take an Ambition and turn it from a noble intention into a compelling quest.

Its only 1% about the words - and 99% about the communication

The final piece of the jigsaw is finding a way to tell the story that gives it life. Screensavers and posters on the wall have their place but, alone, will turn even the most exciting ambition into wallpaper.

Each of your Leadership Team members needs to be able to tell, and sell, the story in a way that includes not just what the Ambition is but also why it was chosen. You also all need to be able to paint a rich and credible picture of the destination. Words on paper can never do this. It's all about how each team member, in his or her own style, brings it to life for your people. It takes thought, and practice.

Finally, you need to agree how you will take the tier of leaders below the Leadership Team on the same journey you have travelled. Telling them is no substitute for taking them through a similar process. How and where will you do that?

> *When they are facing major challenges, people need powerful, compelling, emotional reasons to take on the hard work and levels of risk that may be involved.*

The benefits of Ambition Conversations

It is easy to find out if your Leadership Team already has a shared ambition that can drive performance and form the foundation for great achievements. Simply ask each member of the team, 'What are we trying to achieve in our organisation and why?'

If the team is aligned around a common ambition, you will find that:

Everyone talks about the same ambition

All the members of the team give substantially the same answer. While people will articulate it in their own words, some key terms and phrases – the ones which hark back to some shared meaning – will be repeated. There is an art to summing up a high-flying ambition in ringing and memorable terms that will become part of the organisation's vocabulary.

The goal is compelling

People understand the goal and feel it is worth stretching for. It changes their view of what the organisation can be and resets their ideas of what is possible. This change of perspective alters attitudes and behaviour, encouraging everyone to look at problems and opportunities in fresh and constructive ways.

The excitement is genuine

You can see people start to sparkle with enthusiasm and excitement when they talk about goals that have some emotional meaning and significance for them as individuals. They become animated and you'll see their eyes shine and hear their voices rise as they explain what the Ambition means to them.

The goal changes the game

Goals need to be worth the effort. They need to promise real change. When it's inspired by a dramatic, ambitious goal, the team's conversation becomes more speculative, more inquiring and more aspirational, going further than the old, narrow focus on how to be a percentage point or two bigger or marginally more cost-efficient than the previous year.

Clear ambitions make tackling challenges easier

Ambitions provide strong foundations. If they are vividly imagined, clearly defined and articulated in a way that is exciting and motivating, they provide a new impetus to deal with obstacles, problems and difficult decisions.

When they are facing major challenges, people need powerful, compelling, emotional reasons to take on the hard work and levels of risk that may be involved. They must understand what their destination is and why, and they must have a personal investment in the ambition.

Compelling ambitions create energy and momentum

We worked with one substantial business-to-business organisation, with a turnover of £200 million. A few years earlier, it had gone through a period of rapid growth as a result of changing its business model. It had moved from just selling products to installing and operating them as well, and it had got the timing just right.

Now, though, progress had slowed. There was less recruitment and investment. We found a Leadership Team under huge pressure to ramp up growth. Everyone was working flat out and there were no extra resources to help them deliver. With no clear way forward, the company's executives were drained and despairing.

We began by starting a conversation about how big the business could be and what the Leadership Team could be aiming for.

'I know you've got your own vision and ambitions for the company,' I told the CEO, 'but please keep all that to yourself for now.'

The conversation began – as often happens in practice – with someone saying they felt the company could be 20 per cent bigger. This is so often the kind of opening bid in an Ambition Conversation that we have come to see it as part of the process.

In this case, as people loosened up, everyone started insisting that there was a lot more potential in the business. They were talking about far more than 20 per cent – and the more they talked, the more convinced they all became. They talked about why they wanted the company to grow and agreed that many customers in their market were making do with inferior solutions and could certainly benefit from their product. They also started to talk about a number of untapped applications for their product, which offered a huge potential for new markets and revenue.

> *Ambitions provide strong foundations. If they are vividly imagined, clearly defined and articulated in a way that is exciting and motivating, they provide a new impetus to deal with obstacles, problems and difficult decisions.*

By the end of the conversation, the Leadership Team had moved on a long way from the original suggestion of 20 per cent growth potential. Team members were unanimous in thinking that they could, and should, double the size of the business within four years. This goal was proposed by the team member who had seemed most sceptical at first – and it went a lot further than the ambitions the CEO had been keeping under wraps at the start of the conversation.

What had happened? The Ambition Conversation had enabled the Leadership Team members to become excited again, to see bold possibilities, to generate the energy needed to make some real changes and to think again about how to realise their ambitions for the organisation. A year later, growth had surged again and the team was on track to deliver its new Ambition.

Are Ambition Conversations needed in your team?

Ambition Conversations are needed for teams who want to:

- ▲ Uncover, and address, differences in the team about direction and destination.
- ▲ Shift the organisation's ambitions to a higher level of aspiration.
- ▲ Re-energise itself and others to move beyond today's challenges and limitations.
- ▲ Break out of its current trajectory and aim for something that's genuinely better.
- ▲ Free itself from today's problems and obstacles and look at what is truly possible.

If this is what's needed in your team, you can see tools for developing Ambition Conversations, Reimagining the Future and the Ambition Line, on pages 242-255. ▲

When ambition provoked transformation

One of my clients, Diane, was brought in some years ago to head a telecoms operator at a time when the business seemed to be going nowhere.

The company was a joint venture of the divisions of two larger parents. But it had never really got off the ground. Diane inherited what had already become a backwater, an unloved, uninspiring division of the parent companies' empire, with no great ambitions and no obvious USP. It had a modest number of low-value subscribers and was mainly staffed with employees shifted across from one of the parent companies, not all of them entirely willingly. One manager had described his secondment as 'being sent to the salt mines'. Customers were not impressed with the offering or the service, and the parent company saw no reason to invest in making things better.

Diane viewed the situation differently. She saw exciting potential in the parent companies' large customer base, all of them prospective telecoms customers. But her first task was to encourage the Leadership Team to take charge of the company's destiny. She began by sitting down with her team and challenging them with one simple, provocative question.

'What are we up for here?' she asked. 'Are we just going along for the ride, or do we really want to do something with this business?'

As Diane had hoped, this led directly to a frank and wide-ranging Ambition Conversation. People talked about their frustrations with the products they could offer, the service customers experienced and the lack of investment. They talked about what they could do if some of these barriers were removed, and how little it would actually take to change the company's ethos and performance. As the conversation went on, a vision started to emerge of what a successful company would look like. Suddenly, it was clear ➤

that the organisation still had the opportunity to become something unique and attractive in the marketplace. And once the team members focused on that vision, they saw exactly what needed to change.

The common rallying point was that the market desperately needed a provider that would make life easier for customers. They needed straightforward tariffs and decent customer service. Instead of sweeping up at the bottom of the market, providing cheap products and services, the company could start offering attractive monthly contracts on the latest smartphones. If they could get the investments they needed, none of this was as impossible as everyone had assumed.

Together, the members of the Leadership Team were able to paint a picture of a very different organisation. It would be better for customers, better for employees and better still for the parent companies, as the new-look organisation stood every chance of grabbing profitable market share.

Fired up with their new sense of purpose, the members of the Leadership Team channelled their excitement into convincing the two parents to support the new approach. Both parents bought into it, the investment money was made available and their transformation began.

Less than two years after the first Ambition Conversation, the company was unrecognisable. It had gained a big slice of market share and won a fistful of awards for its simple tariffs and good customer service. It had become an exciting place to work and a source of significant growth for the parent companies.

By challenging themselves and changing their aim, the Leadership Team members had saved the business and given themselves new excitement and motivation for their work. ▲

AMBITION *conversations*

| 0 | 1 | 2 | 3 | 4 | 5 | 6 | 7 | 8 | 9 | 10 |

How clear and vivid is your ambition?

| 0 | 1 | 2 | 3 | 4 | 5 | 6 | 7 | 8 | 9 | 10 |

How transformational is your ambition?

| 0 | 1 | 2 | 3 | 4 | 5 | 6 | 7 | 8 | 9 | 10 |

How motivated and excited are members of your team about your ambition?

| 0 | 1 | 2 | 3 | 4 | 5 | 6 | 7 | 8 | 9 | 10 |

How aligned are you around the ambition?

| 0 | 1 | 2 | 3 | 4 | 5 | 6 | 7 | 8 | 9 | 10 |

How clearly linked are your strategy, plans and budgets with your ambition?

OVERALL ASSESSMENT FOR AMBITION CONVERSATIONS

| 0 | 1 | 2 | 3 | 4 | 5 | 6 | 7 | 8 | 9 | 10 |

What is your overall assessment of the Ambition Conversations in your team?

Please mark your overall assessment, and then transfer this score to the assessment summary for your team on pages 240-241.

RELATIONSHIP
conversations

If ambition is the foundation, it is the web of relationships between the various members that provides the mortar to bind the Leadership Team together and allows it to function

---

A TALE FROM THE MAASAI

A Maasai welcome

...and treating colleagues as people

I'll never forget the first time I went to visit the Maasai. We all got into a van – about ten of us, Brits, Americans and some other Europeans – and set off on our nine-hour journey from the airport. This meant nine hours' bumping along roads that got progressively worse, until we were just dodging between trees. They called it a road, but it was pretty much a matter of just driving across the rugged savannah.

That kind of travelling tends to take the edge off your boyish enthusiasm. By the time we got to our destination, we were hot, dusty, tired and fed up. The Americans were ratty because they were jet-lagged too. I suppose we'd expected to find a village of some sort, but the place we arrived at seemed to be in the middle of nowhere.

There are no villages in Maasailand. Each family lives in its own boma, a cluster of two or three low, windowless, sticks-and-cow dung huts, ringed by two thick fences made of spiky thorn-tree branches. The inner fence keeps your cows and goats out of your home, while the outer circle keeps the lions and hyenas from eating your cows and goats. Beyond the outer fence, there will be no other homes for maybe a mile or two. Nobody has a next-door neighbour.

Eventually, we stopped near a single, isolated boma. 'Right, we're here,' said our guide. We clambered stiffly out of the dusty van – and were confronted with an extraordinary sight.

➤

Standing among the trees was a welcoming party of about fifty people – tall, mostly red-clad warriors, women in beautiful bright clothes, beads and earrings, and children with dazzling smiles. Some of them had walked ten miles to be there. No-one had arranged it. People had heard we were coming and just decided they should come together to make us welcome. Some of them had been sitting chatting and waiting patiently for us for hours.

The Maasai believe in welcomes. They set a lot of store by them. Every single one of the people who had gathered near that boma made a point of coming over and individually welcoming each of us, warmly, cheerfully and unhurriedly. When that was done, they danced and sang to entertain us, and then walked off into the bush, back to their homes.

I have since found out that the Maasai take welcomes very seriously in more normal day-to-day contexts as well. It made me think about the cursory greetings we exchange with colleagues when we get together for meetings – or even when people visit our homes. Our attitude is perfunctory and superficial, as if this is something we'd rather not spend time doing – and it's certainly not usual to schedule even a few minutes for welcomes and greetings at the beginning of the ten o'clock board meeting.

Perhaps it's no wonder, then, that the interactions in these meetings of ours are at best stiff and formal and at worst even hostile. Our Maasai welcome got me thinking about how much difference it would make to the discussions that follow if we chose to invest just a little more time in properly connecting with each of our colleagues as people before getting down to business. ▲

What are Relationship Conversations?

In our work with Leadership Teams, we often find that the existing relationships between the leaders simply aren't strong enough to sustain the work they have to do.

As we have seen, Leadership Team performance is built on foundations of ambition. A good Ambition Conversation makes the organisation's destination clear and explores why the team feels so strongly about reaching it.

But if ambition is the foundation, it is the web of relationships between the various members that provides the mortar to bind the Leadership Team together and allow it to function. Relationship Conversations enable the team to work productively and well.

As a colleague of mine puts it, 'The work of any group of people can never be better than the strength of the relationships that underpin it'.

Put simply, Relationship Conversations are interactions in the team which build and sustain the connections between individual team members.

Relationships are founded on understanding

The quality of your relationship with any individual is built on growing the intersections between the two of you – particularly in three fundamental areas (Levin, 2011):

▲ Understanding and respecting the important purpose of the other person – what they are for.
▲ Understanding the concerns they have about not achieving their purpose.
▲ Understanding the circumstances or obstacles that affect their purpose.

If thinking in terms of personal purpose sounds too 'deep', it doesn't have to be. Many perfectly functional relationships operate without great insight on either side into these issues. But if you think about your own life, you'll find that the best relationships – those with the power to make big changes and in which you have been able to contribute your talents most effectively – do involve this kind of understanding.

'The work of any group of people can never be better than the strength of the relationships that underpin it'.

It's rarely helpful to ask questions about purpose directly of someone. People may well be unclear themselves about it, and unless you already have a very strong relationship with them, direct questions are likely to be experienced as intrusive.

The way we develop this understanding of others, in a Leadership Team context, is to start by talking with them about the shared goals and priorities of the team and their own work. Through this, both trust and insight will grow and the understanding of the person behind the role will deepen.

Learning how to listen and make time to communicate about people's needs and wants enables team members to understand their colleagues' perspectives and motivations. It all begins with the recognition that each person has his or her own unique framework of reference and needs.

You can see the strength of relationships in what people talk about

Perhaps the most visible way of assessing the strength of the relationships in a team is to examine what they do and don't talk about. This is illustrated in the Interaction Staircase:

The Interaction Staircase

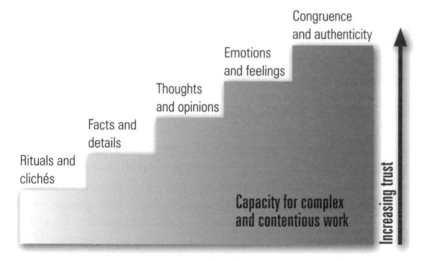

The degree of trust, and thus the strength of relationships in the team, is shown by how much they interact on the level indicated by each of the steps. High performing teams have the trust and relationships that allow them to operate at all levels. The best teams regularly and fluidly move between the levels and this further builds trust as well as creating an environment in which even difficult, sensitive or controversial issues can be effectively wrestled with.

Weaker teams interact only on the lower steps, trust is harder to build and this limits their capacity to work on the more complex or contentious issues.

The Leadership Team's task of understanding today's complex organisations and continually transforming them is work of the greatest importance, presenting huge challenges. To not only succeed, but to excel, requires strong and resilient relationships. Put simply, the greater the team's level of trust, the better it will perform – and the more the team members will enjoy the journey.

Strong relationships are a necessity not an option

No one comes to work to fail or to make things harder for their colleagues. No one in the Leadership Team is there to sabotage it. People may have been holding back from a full commitment to the team and their colleagues, for all kinds of historic or personal reasons. But these reservations can almost always be overcome if they are recognised, acknowledged and, in some cases, resolved, within honest Relationship Conversations.

Leadership Teams that have created strong relationships can operate more effectively because everything can be discussed openly and candidly. Diverse views are welcomed and valued and the Leadership Team can work through the many challenging conversations and decisions it will inevitably face (Raes A. M., 2011).

These conversations can be difficult. Leadership Teams often have to talk about complex, ambiguous topics and about questions which may have many right answers, or none at all. They need to be able to improve things that are already going well, and to talk about things that are going wrong. They must be able to keep going, without being distracted or deflected, until they arrive at a common understanding of the situation and options and agree on the best way forward.

Leadership Teams often have to talk about complex, ambiguous topics and about questions which may have many right answers, or none at all.

To do this, they need to be able to talk freely and openly, with the confidence that all contributions, even on sensitive issues, will be received as constructive and useful.

Strong relationships make leading easier

The tasks facing each member of a Leadership Team are complex, and no-one can tackle them alone. Each team member needs practical support, especially in addressing the inevitable cross-functional issues.

Even initiatives that look as if they are wholly within a single function will require significant support from other areas, and the many big cross-functional projects will require even more co-operation between Leadership Team members.

But leaders need emotional support, too. Leading is exciting and challenging, but it can also be tough. People in leadership positions are under constant pressure. When close, supportive relationships have been developed within the team, the members know they are working in an environment of trust. No-one seeks to blame others, and when the inevitable mistakes are made, team members will get the help they need to fix them.

Blending complementary strengths

Within any Leadership Team, the members will each have their own profiles of strengths and weaknesses. In a balanced team, with good working relationships, team members can use their strengths to make their own distinctive contributions and also help compensate for other members' weaknesses. Strong relationships within the team make it second nature for members to turn to each other for support and insight.

Why teams struggle

Most leaders will recognise only too readily the lack of cohesion and other symptoms described below. The result is a team in which it's hard to get the most important work done. Some of the most important issues are hard to raise, and even harder to work through productively. Others can't even be tabled. Leading a team like this can feel like having one hand tied behind your back.

Yet conversations in Leadership Teams that are focused on how to build better, more trusting and productive relationships are quite unusual. There are many reasons for this but two, in our experience, play the biggest part.

The first is the challenge of making them a priority. It can be hard to focus on relationships and behaviour when there are immediate and pressing items on the agenda – particularly when it's not easy to see, or quantify, the positive impact that spending time on relationships might produce.

Perhaps more significantly, senior people in most organisations are used to being managed intellectually and to focusing on the task. Talking about the human dimensions, motivations and relationships can feel uncomfortable and even threatening at first. It often requires some confidence to be built both in one another and also in the value of understanding one another better, before they can flow naturally.

Even when Leadership Teams can see the importance of Relationship Conversations and are prepared to invest in them, it's not clear how they should go about it. They don't have simple, accessible and time-efficient methods.

Talking about the human dimensions, motivations and relationships can feel uncomfortable and even threatening at first.

The result is that these conversations don't happen, at least not often enough, and this leads to a number of painful and damaging symptoms in the team.

Important but contentious issues are neglected

Our research has shown that, even in teams that work well, only 60 per cent of team members feel they can constructively challenge one another without the fear of provoking destructive reactions. In underperforming teams, this figure falls to just 33 per cent. Yet, difficult though they are, these conversations are often the most important ones, offering the greatest scope for resolving damaging problems or discovering untapped opportunities.

When team members don't feel secure enough about their relationships with one another, it can become difficult or even impossible for them to talk about and resolve the issue – and the team then has to find new, less effective, ways to discuss it. Often this involves the CEO brokering a solution – or even mandating a decision to avoid wasting time on the anticipated conflict.

People duck out of conflict

When a Leadership Team lacks relationships strong enough to discuss difficult issues, members often pull back from the conversation when they sense that conflict is likely.

While it is unusual for Leadership Teams to have explicit rules of conduct, unspoken norms evolve and are generally observed. But incidents that have caused problems in the past can affect the

team's cultural norms for years to come, sometimes even after all the original protagonists have left the organisation.

There may, for example, be a tacit agreement that one team member must never be challenged about product implementation times, because he once became so defensive that the atmosphere was poisoned for weeks.

Newcomers to the team will be warned off as part of their informal initiation: 'Oh, no. Don't even go there. Michaela tried it and he got so irate we were all side-tracked for an hour and never reached the main item on the agenda.'

Conflict is a necessary and potentially creative part of the functioning of every Leadership Team and relationships need to be strong enough both to allow it and to manage it productively.

The CEO becomes a mediator

The larger the Leadership Team, the more relationships there are, and the more potential conflict.

Some CEOs I've met spend a huge amount of time managing relationships and resolving conflict. Often, the various people involved in talks with the leader don't even know the CEO is having similar conversations with others in the group. It is all too easy for the team leader to get bogged down in micro-managing unproductive relationships, rather than steering the team towards its goal.

> *'The moment there is suspicion about a person's motives, everything he does is tainted.'*
> Mahatma Gandhi

One very well-respected leader heads a large industrial plant. When we asked him how he used his time, he admitted spending a huge amount of it managing relationships between the members of his team to ensure that issues didn't get tangled in interpersonal tensions. He also had to invest time in coaching team members individually on how to orientate themselves towards other team members.

The style he described is what is known as 'hub-and-spoke' leadership, as illustrated in the diagram on page 108.

While this leader was successful in many ways, this came at a great personal cost. He was working flat out for nearly ninety hours a week and this approach was responsible for a significant proportion of that. Worse still, by managing the issue himself, he was actively getting in the way of finding a better team solution.

Hub-and-Spoke Leadership

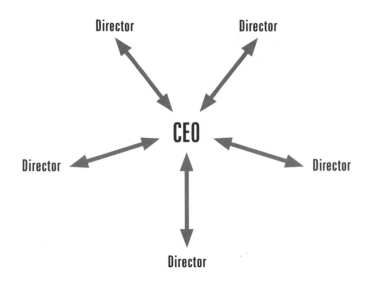

Destructive conversations take place on the sidelines

One organisation we worked with clearly needed help developing relationships within the Leadership Team. We spoke to each leader individually, and they all told us the same story.

'We have awful, unproductive meetings that leave everyone frustrated,' the finance director explained. 'And then, for the next two hours, people are in and out of each other's offices, moaning about how bad it was, the decisions they don't agree with and how unhelpful so-and-so was.'

This often happens when relationships in the Leadership Team are not strong enough to support people in raising difficult issues. Saving these up to chew over in the safe environment of an ally's private office may ease the emotional pressure, but it does nothing to address the underlying problems. It can even help lock the organisation into the status quo.

...employees soon pick up on the fact that the Leadership Team is having problems. When this happens, the team not only fails to address important issues but is also guilty of modelling unhelpful behaviour to others in the organisation.

Unhelpful side conversations seldom stay within the confines of the Leadership Team. At least some team members are likely to be talking to other people in the organisation. And even if they aren't, employees soon pick up on the fact that the Leadership Team is having problems.

When this happens, the team not only fails to address important issues but is also guilty of modelling unhelpful behaviour to others in the organisation.

What does a good Relationship Conversation look like?

They are focused on 'us'

The subject of a Relationship Conversation is always 'us'. This might mean two individuals talking about their relationship or the Leadership Team as a whole talking about the relationships within the group.

Whether they are about personal or team relationships, Relationship Conversations focus on exploring the areas of the relationship that will advance the team's work. The question will always be the same: 'What aspect of the relationship needs to be discussed to make it easier to achieve what we need?'

They address problems directly

Whatever approach is taken, Relationship Conversations are characterised by clear, honest discussion of the interpersonal aspects of team functioning. As well as dealing with obstacles, at their best they include an exploration of where and when the team works together at its best as a source of both confidence and ideas for how to improve effectiveness.

They will also always explicitly acknowledge, and directly address, the areas of interaction that inhibit the team from dealing with the issues it faces. These areas of dysfunction, whether between pairs of team members, subsets of the group or the whole team are discussed and examined in order that agreements can be made on how they can be reduced or eliminated.

They conclude with action

Productive Relationship Conversations will result in clear commitments by some or all of the team to make the changes required to improve team functioning and effectiveness.

In the example on page 108, when we discussed the hub-and-spoke diagram, all the members of that company's Leadership Team recognised it immediately.

In the Relationship Conversation that followed, we explored with them the reasons why the hub-and-spoke approach had come to be their norm and the problems that gave them all, as well as the CEO.

It didn't take long for them to decide that they wanted a different, more collective model and the CEO ended up drawing the diagram below to summarise the way they wanted to operate, with the CEO facilitating the team and its interactions, as well as participating fully as a member of it.

The remainder of the conversation was spent agreeing a set of rules for how they would work together – both inside and outside board meetings.

Leadership that enables the team

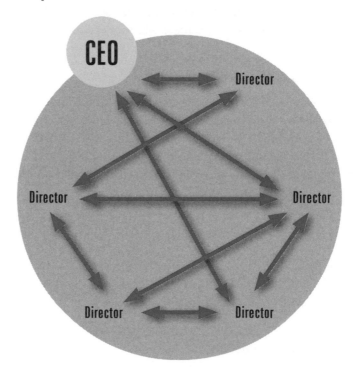

Trust is evident

The paradox of teams who have Relationship Conversations is that an outside observer would be surprised that they are needed. Team members interact with each other surprisingly robustly, but also skilfully. Mutual confidence is easy to see and conversations can, therefore, be focused on really getting to grips with the issues with no-one worrying about how even potentially controversial or sensitive contributions might be received.

Working so productively on the task, however, is only possible because the team has invested the time to understand their colleagues, respect one another's strengths and trust that everyone is working to the same end.

The benefits of Relationship Conversations

The gains from improving relationships in the team are profound, but often indirect.

Behaviours change as trust develops

Relationship Conversations usually result in small, practical changes to the behaviours that have become disproportionately obstructive and are impeding effective collaboration. As relationships build, team members understand one another better. Negative assumptions about motives are replaced with real information about why colleagues behave as they do and what they are seeking to achieve.

By dissolving these damaging suspicions, the team can create an atmosphere within which trust can grow. Increasing trust encourages all the team members to feel their views are respected and valued. It becomes easier to be motivated and excited and there is much more emotional investment in the work.

Through its investment in relationships, the team creates a safe environment in which even the most challenging issues can be addressed without blame or recrimination.

When all the members of a Leadership Team have good relationships, there are no limits to what can be discussed. Through its investment in relationships, the team creates a safe environment in which challenging issues can be addressed without blame or recrimination.

It becomes easier to focus on the real issues

Conversations quickly become more directed and much more purposeful. Team members look beyond personal dynamics and get to grips quickly and directly with the big issues, without worrying about the possibility of running into defensive or hostile reactions.

When people hear team colleagues question or comment on their work, they don't feel threatened or defensive. They don't suspect their colleagues' motives or worry that they are being undermined. When there is criticism, everybody understands that it is directed at the issue, not the individual.

Conversations become more challenging – and more productive

Paradoxically, while many things get easier, conversations often become more challenging – because the real work, which has the power to transform the organisation is, by definition, tough.

'People are unreasonable, illogical and self-centred. Love them anyway.'
Mother Teresa

These more robust debates make it easier to test alternative courses of action and take the kind of bold but calculated risks that can move the whole organisation forward.

Each member of the team thrives

When positive relationships have been established, all the team members know that they can count on the support of their colleagues. This creates a stimulating, trusting environment that can transform the performance of the individuals involved, the team and the organisation.

As team members get closer to an environment that helps them give their very best, the trust within the team makes it easier for members to refine their own skills and abilities, to give and receive feedback, to learn from one another and to give of their best.

Side conversations are productive and useful

Side conversations are common, but rather than being used to discuss how unhappy everyone is, they are now about how subgroups can work together to take action on the issues under discussion. They are productive, helpful and never secretive.

Are Relationship Conversations needed in your team?

Relationship Conversations are needed for teams who teams want to:

▲ Understand the different traits brought to the group by each member and how these strengths can be used better.

▲ Defuse tensions and build stronger relationships by deepening team members' appreciation of one another.

▲ Identify 'blind spots' in the team and gaps in the team's collective make-up that need to be addressed.

▲ Be able to talk about even the most difficult subjects without worrying about defensiveness, antagonism or politics.

▲ Dissolve personal tensions and replace them with robust and trusting relationships.

▲ Create a framework that is a support to all of its members as they tackle the many challenges facing each of them.

If this is what is needed in your team, you can see tools for developing Relationship Conversations, Speed Feedback and Seeing Styles, on pages 256-267. ▲

Enemies become allies

Simon was the operations director of a textile company. Alex was the marketing director. Simon needed at least six months' notice whenever Alex was planning to launch a new product and the two of them had fallen out in the past over deadlines, standards and poor communication.

Like many others, this Leadership Team had a history of dissent and tension, and it had tended to dodge the difficult conversations. But a breakthrough happened when we formulated a series of one-to-one Relationship Conversations in the team.

Each member of the team sat down with each of the others, in turn, and talked about how they made life difficult for each other and what they could do to help one another more. There was palpable tension when the time came for Alex and Simon to sit together.

Simon took the initiative by going straight to the heart of what had become a sensitive and undiscussable tension between them.

'I think we're missing a trick by not communicating well about what we need from each other. For instance, when you're brainstorming new products, why not give me a heads-up? I'd love to be involved. I may be able to contribute something and the extra notice of what's coming will really help me.' He could see Alex was a little wary, but he pressed on.

'I know I get very stressed when I'm struggling to hit your deadlines, and it's really not about you personally. It's just that it's frustrating when I can't get things done as well as I'd like to. I'd love to find a way to make it work better.'

Simon's honesty encouraged Alex. 'Yeah, I find it really hard when all our planning and good ideas get snarled up and delayed. I know I clam up when I feel I'm being criticised and that doesn't help. I'm worried about involving you that early in the process, though, when we're really just starting to explore possibilities.

➤

'I'm also nervous about the interaction with my team. With all the friction over recent times, I'm afraid that Operations aren't exactly flavour of the month.'

Alex agreed. 'I know what you mean. My team probably wouldn't respond well if you showed up in a production scheduling meeting. I suspect we may both have been complicit in some of the finger-pointing and negativity that has been going on.'

Now it was Simon's turn to be surprised at his colleague's candour. 'Actually, it would be great for me to get a better understanding of how you guys do the production planning. I think we should tackle this head-on. Let's sit down with the key members of each of our teams and map out our approach to product launches – from soup to nuts.'

The conversation continued. When time ran out in the team meeting, they agreed to meet again to work through the details. While others in the team didn't know much about the work they were doing, the new spirit of co-operation between them was clear for all to see.

Over the following months, they still had their disagreements. The nature of their roles made that inevitable. But these were now dealt with faster, more constructively and with better solutions. The team no longer had to tiptoe around issues affecting both of them. And they each knew that they had a supportive colleague to work with, rather than a destructive and antagonistic adversary.

The arrangement to communicate more about product launches was important in itself. But what was far more significant was the unspoken agreement to turn over a new leaf and work more collaboratively together. Simon and Alex never became best friends outside the office – and they didn't need to. But they soon found they were able to work much better together, and a lot of the tension disappeared from their working relationship. Life got easier, not just for both of them but for the whole team. ▲

RELATIONSHIP *conversations*

0 1 2 3 4 5 6 7 8 9 10

How strong is the trust between members of your team?

0 1 2 3 4 5 6 7 8 9 10

How much open, constructive debate do you have about the difficult issues and choices facing the organisation?

0 1 2 3 4 5 6 7 8 9 10

How freely are members of your team able to challenge one another on their own areas of responsibility, on decisions they have made and on their behaviour?

0 1 2 3 4 5 6 7 8 9 10

To what degree are your team members working together towards a shared goal, rather than pursuing personal or departmental ambitions?

0 1 2 3 4 5 6 7 8 9 10

How much does your Leadership Team lead by example?

OVERALL ASSESSMENT FOR RELATIONSHIP CONVERSATIONS

0 1 2 3 4 5 6 7 8 9 10

What is your overall assessment of the Relationships Conversation in your team?

Please mark your overall assessment, and then transfer this score to the assessment summary for your team on pages 240-241.

9 PRIORITY *conversations*

Creating priorities is tough. There is always an element of risk. The best Priority Conversations recognise and address these risks directly so that, as well as a list of priorities, what emerges is a confidence in the team to back its judgement and gamble its precious resources, time and money on the chosen set of key issues.

A TALE FROM THE MAASAI

What matters for the Maasai

...and the meaning of poverty

On one visit to Kenya, my friend John and I took a walk through Kibera, Nairobi's slum area, with four of the Maasai warriors. A million people live here – in the world's third-biggest slum – in improvised shanties of cardboard, plastic and rusting corrugated iron, crammed in tight along chaotic, ramshackle streets. The vista, complete with uncountable hordes of people rushing about their business, seemed to stretch all the way to the horizon.

Kwenia, one of the warriors, sighed heavily and shook his head.

'Man,' he said. 'Those people are so poor!'

'What do you mean?' John asked. 'You're wearing everything you own, Kwenia. Aren't you just as poor as them?'

Kwenia smiled at our lack of understanding.

'I don't mean they don't have things,' he said, patiently. 'I meant they don't seem to have community. We don't have things, but we have a very strong community.'

His words made me think about what being poor really means. In the West, we have a lot of possessions – houses, cars, furniture, iPads, the list goes on and on – but we, too, often have little in the way of meaningful community. The wealthier members of our society have the most possessions, of course, but most of us ➤

seem to lack a true sense of community, with the really close ties that encourage people to truly look after one another.

The Maasai are materially poor, but immeasurably wealthy in terms of the relationships they enjoy – relationships that offer support and a trusting, supportive environment. Taking care of and being there for one another is a core value in their culture. This is a type of wealth we often lack, and we'd probably gain a lot if we invested more, as they do, in building and sustaining our relationships with others.

I love going to Kenya and spending time in a Maasai community because, for me, watching the way the Maasai people focus on what is important is a profound and stimulating experience. The background noise and clutter of life disappears, and I find it becomes easier to concentrate on matters that are important right now. Imagine, though, what a Maasai would make of our world, if he were to visit us…

Some time ago, three Maasai warriors, Kobole, Sipoi and Kwenia, were invited to spend some time working as guides at Seattle Zoo. Kakuta, the founder of the Maasai Association, had given his services to help the zoo to design its savannah enclosure. Now the wonderful new enclosure was completed and the Maasai warriors were going to help show the animals they know so well to the public. They would also be there to answer visitors' questions about their lives at home in Kenya.

Although they had been keen to visit Seattle, after about a week there, the three Maasai guides became intensely homesick. They were surprised and horrified by some of the things they saw in America. Above all, they were baffled to find that even such a wealthy country had people with no homes – and apparently no-one to care for them.

The issues around homelessness are complicated for us, but their concern cut to the core of the issue. With so much wealth around, why did no-one seem to be caring for these people in need? It was a simple, telling observation, and it illustrates the chasm between our societies when it comes to priorities.

While that might sound like a line from a socialist manifesto, it has real relevance to how individuals work together in 21st-century organisations, where the work is so complex and interdependent that genuinely collaborative approaches and mutually supportive attitudes are vital for success.

Whenever I visit the Maasai, I find that my thoughts gravitate to profound personal questions. I can see with startling clarity that certain things are crucial to me, whereas others, which may have been occupying a lot of my time, aren't – and I'm prompted to make decisions that put those priorities back in the centre of my focus.

Whatever technique we use, when we can concentrate on priorities – something that seems to come easily to the Maasai people – the world becomes a simpler place, and the things that really matter start to move forward. ▲

What are Priority Conversations?

There's a well-worn allegory about time management, popularised by Stephen Covey (Covey, 1990), that's based on the story of a young student who approaches his master for advice. The master tells him to bring a bucket and gestures to a pile of big rocks.

'Put these big rocks in the bucket,' he commands.
The student does as he is told.
'Is the bucket full?' the master asks.
The rocks come right up to the top of the bucket. You couldn't fit a single extra rock in.
The student is puzzled. Of course it's full.
The master passes him a box of small pebbles and tells him to add them to the bucket. The pebbles slip into place around the rocks quite easily.
'Is the bucket full?' the master asks again.
'Well, yes,' says the student. 'It is now. Look at it.'
The master smiles his guru smile, points to a small heap of sand and tells the student to add it to the bucket. The fine sand pours in to fill the spaces between the rocks and the pebbles.
'Is the bucket full?' the master inquires.
'Yes,' the student says. 'Yes. I think so. It must be. With the sand there, nothing else can possibly fit in.'
The master smiles his enigmatic smile again, and the student knows there is more to come.
'Pour in the water from that other bucket,' the master says. 'You'll find there's plenty of room.'
As always, of course, the master is right. The bucket absorbs plenty of water, despite already seeming so full.
As always, the student hates the master's mannered, self-conscious teaching style. But he has to admit he's learned an important lesson.

Managing time in the hectic environment of a Leadership Team is a perennial challenge. As that student discovered, though, you have to put the big rocks in first. When they are in place, it's surprising how many of the smaller issues will still fit in around them. On the other hand, if the sand and pebbles go in first, there's no chance of getting the big rocks in at all.

Put simply, Priority Conversation isolates the big rocks and makes sure they get put into the bucket first.

Why teams struggle

No-one needs to be reminded about the importance of prioritisation. We all know how hard it can be to prioritise in practice. And if it's hard for us individually, it's even harder in a team.

Every team that we have worked with struggles to decide priorities, to resource them properly and to strip away other activity as well as they would like. This leaves team members often feeling individually overwhelmed and the entire team frustrated. They know that the things that need to happen to really make a difference just aren't getting the focus and resources that they need. Vital work misses deadlines and fails, with wearying predictability, to fully deliver its intended results. It saps the energy of not only members of the team but also of the whole organisation.

Every team that we have worked with struggles to decide priorities, to resource them properly and to strip away other activity as well as they would like.

So why do Leadership Teams find it so hard?

Prioritising requires courage

Priority decisions have to be taken in the real world, in the context of ever-shifting markets and a lack of full knowledge about what the competition is doing. The Leadership Team can never know in advance that it has made the right choices. But while making incremental changes may seem like the safer bet, with less risk of the company falling flat on its face, playing safe makes it difficult to make the big leap forward.

All of the candidates for organisational or team priorities will have merit. And all teams are under pressure to deliver better results, faster. Compromising anything on the long list of the candidates, therefore, means removing something else that has clear value – whether that means stopping work on it completely or just reducing investment in it in some way.

As well as compromising initiatives by the sheer volume of change that is being attempted at one time, valuable learning is sacrificed. Spectacular successes are made more unlikely and painful learning is often masked. It's often unclear whether failure has revealed something important about what works or whether it was simply a case of not investing enough to make it work.

Subsequent prioritisation then becomes harder still and, in the absence of clear feedback about what works, teams are forced to spread their investments of time and money to hedge their bets. One leader I worked had a memorable way to describe his antidote to this; 'We try to hit a few initiatives very hard. That way it becomes much easier to hear the echoes.'

Members of Leadership Teams know, intellectually, that focusing more time and effort on a few things will advance them faster and produce better results than trying to push forward on too many things at once. Knowing this and acting on that knowledge when the pressure is on are very different things. The temptation to add 'just one more thing' is hard to resist and even the best teams can succumb to it.

'We try to hit a few initiatives very hard. That way it becomes much easier to hear the echoes.'

There are just too many priorities on the list

While it's beguiling to feel that the Leadership Team has a comprehensive, all-encompassing list of priorities, a long list does not help get things done. I had a client once who told me, a little shamefacedly, that his team had a list of seventeen strategic priorities.

One of the main reasons Leadership Teams find themselves juggling with unmanageable numbers of priorities is the difficulty of convincing some team members that their departmental or personal priority is not a priority for the team. Too often, issues which are important to just one member of the team make it on to the collective list. This may be politic, but it's not prioritisation.

Research shows that seven is the largest number of items that people can easily remember and concentrate on (Shiffrin and Nosofsky, 1994). A Leadership Team that is working on more than seven priorities needs to rethink its approach. The aim should be to reduce the number of items to seven or fewer. People cannot focus fully on a list of priorities that they cannot remember or easily communicate to others.

They start at the wrong end

It's tempting, when talking about priorities, to start by (implicitly or explicitly) sorting through everything that's already going on to find the things that need to rise to the top.

There are a number of problems with this approach. The most important is that it makes it impossible for the team to step back from the tactical, day-to-day tumult of everything that's going on. Many of these smaller issues will be symptoms of bigger, underlying causes – and it's these things that offer many of the most important candidates for the Leadership Team's priority treatment.

The sheer volume of current issues and activities also makes it difficult, and much more time-consuming, to work through them.

Even when a team can find the time to process a full current list of activities and needs, it's an almost impossible task. Promoting any one item involves relegating others, and that's really tough for any team or individual to do. Everything that's currently going on is happening for a reason. Discussions that try to lift some things up and demote others rapidly get stuck in arguments over which should be defended. It's like trying to get the big rocks into the bucket by going through its contents, pebble by pebble, and arguing each one in or out.

Vague phrasing leaves too much wiggle room

Faced with drawing up a list of priorities, Leadership Teams have good intentions. But their efforts to get agreement often lead them into using vague language that leaves so much scope for interpretation that it doesn't provide a means for the team, or others, to know what should be elevated and what should be stopped.

Without clarity, there can be no shared understanding of what the priorities really are. Team members will want to stand up for issues or projects that they have an investment in and words are often carefully chosen to avoid provoking sensitivities. Teams think they have made progress when they have created a document describing a set of priorities nobody can disagree with. Too often though, they have created a list without real discrimination.

For instance, I have seen teams cite 'customer focus' as a key priority. It's a powerful concept and it can be a compelling way to harness effort. The problem is that unless the team members are all absolutely clear about what 'customer focus' means for the organisation, for their departments, and for them, it can mean all things to all men.

What does customer focus really mean? It's easy to envisage a situation in which the heads of all the departments argue cogently that everything they do is about customer focus. For one person, it might mean new product development. For another, it might mean achieving keen pricing through the lower costs that come from improving financial controls. For someone else, it might mean on-time delivery. These are all important. But unless the Leadership Team articulates exactly what it means about customer focus, it won't help the team or the organisation make decisions to advance some things and stop others.

Priorities become pyramids

When Leadership Teams start to work on priorities, they often fail to fully consider how an issue or project will look as it is interpreted down through the organisation. At each level, an item creates another set of things to do, until what should be a simple list has broadened out into a pyramid.

Suddenly, instead of focusing on the six immediate tasks to hand, the Leadership Team is looking at a long and complicated range of activities across the organisation – not all of which it would want to see pushed forward.

New rocks are forced into full buckets

Writing a list of key priorities is difficult. But it isn't the hardest part of a Priority Conversation. The list has to be turned into real change in the focus and activities of the people in the organisation – and that must start with the Leadership Team.

Members of Leadership Teams tend to be driven, determined and blessed or cursed with an extraordinary work ethic. Part of the reason they are overloaded is that they constantly try to take on too much. They accept too easily new things arising simply being added to their lists, without corresponding deletions.

What does a good Priority Conversation look like?

The discussion is about causes, rather than symptoms

Creating a short list of priorities requires the courage to strip everything back to reach the essentials.

In many cases, the issues that are raised as candidates for the priority list are actually symptoms of fundamental problems. If the top priorities are shrewdly defined, addressing them will cure these symptomatic issues and carry the organisation along the road towards achieving its ambitions. Priority conversations, therefore, require the team to examine, at a deeper level, the underlying issues that hold the organisation back and the work that will be required to address them.

Priorities emerge that can be communicated to everyone

When the Leadership Team has distilled its key priorities, it needs to be able to explain them in terms everybody can grasp. Even the most junior member of the organisation should be able to understand, and apply, its priorities. Certainly, those making decisions about the deployment of human and financial resources should be able to do so.

America's best-known budget carrier, Southwest Airlines, managed to boil its priorities down to seven basics, including fast turnaround at airports, punctuality and great customer service.

In many cases, the issues that are raised as candidates for the priority list are actually symptoms of fundamental problems.

Safety – the most obvious requirement for any airline – did not have a place on the list, as it was regarded as a given. Southwest's Leadership Team recognised that you could not 'out-safety' your competitors and make that a source of competitive advantage.

Southwest pays lower salaries than other airlines and works its staff and equipment hard, fitting in more flights per crew per day. But its strategy places an explicit priority on valuing its employees and sustaining a distinctive working culture. Staff are encouraged to show initiative (Southwest's singing and rapping flight attendants have become YouTube stars) and treat customers as individuals, and they are given a stake in the company's success through generous share ownership schemes.

Every employee knows the airline's priorities and is encouraged to bend the rules or improvise, when necessary, to get the flights away on time or to serve customers better. As a result, staff work with a sense of purpose and engagement and Southwest is always able to recruit good people who are looking for something more than just a wage packet.

People talk and listen as Leadership Team members, not departmental heads

It's natural that team members arrive at most discussions with their heads full of the potential and problems of the issues for which they are responsible.

But the best Priority Conversations take place when each member is able to set those interests aside and individual departments' narrower concerns are subordinated to a truly organisational perspective.

Risk is accepted as the price of progress

Creating priorities is tough. There is always an element of risk. The best Priority Conversations recognise and address these risks directly so that, as well as a list of priorities, what emerges is a confidence in the team to back its judgement and gamble its precious resources, time and money on the chosen set of key issues.

Priority decisions make real changes to what key people do

There's always a big danger that the new list of priorities simply adds to the workload of the organisation's key people, rather than being the prompt for corresponding reductions in effort elsewhere.

There's always a big danger that the new list of priorities simply adds to the workload of the organisation's key people, rather than being the prompt for corresponding reductions in effort elsewhere.

Team members find themselves adding new work to their to-do lists, or they find ways to rationalise the new priorities so they are seen as supporting the existing agenda.

The best Priority Conversations, therefore, follow through the list of collective priorities to allow team members to revisit, together, the agenda facing each individual. Team members will each describe their own revised priorities – and also all the other work they need to do. The team can then play a part in challenging that list and redeploying resources as needed, until everyone is sure that what's needed for each member to give the new priorities the required focus is realistic and achievable.

The benefits of Priority Conversations

Everyone knows about the few things that really matter

When an organisation's middle managers have a conversation about what needs to be done, they need to be able to refer immediately to the priorities determined by the Leadership Team and use them to inform their decisions. Delivering this clarity deep into the organisation, and cutting through all the other communication they receive, requires a small number of clear and powerful messages.

Nordstrom is one of the top retailers in the United States, a high-end department store with a reputation for excellent customer service. When I met Nordstrom's CEO, a few years ago, I was struck by the inspiring, charismatic way he talked about what his company did and what it stood for. Afterwards, I was invited to attend Nordstrom's monthly sales meeting, at which awards were being given to high-achieving employees.

Throughout the meeting, the company's twin priorities, to 'sell more product' and 'give great customer service', were emphasised again and again. It was evident that Nordstrom's whole workforce was perfectly aligned around two very clear and straightforward imperatives.

Even the most junior member of the organisation should be able to understand, and apply, its priorities.

Later that day, I had my own experience of Nordstrom's commitment to its customer service priority. I needed some formal trousers and found a pair I liked, but they were too long. The store's tailoring service assured me the trousers could be shortened in just twenty-four hours. But I was flying out the next morning. I explained the problem and the assistant disappeared to make a call. He quickly returned, having persuaded one of the tailoring team to make the adjustment immediately. Thirty minutes later, the new trousers were ready to wear.

Because everyone, from the Leadership Team to the sales assistant to the tailor, had understood and bought into Nordstrom's clearly defined priorities, the individuals involved took it upon themselves to deal with the problem straight away. They didn't have to get authorisation or go through any procedures. I was a customer who needed service that went beyond the normal routine, and it was clear to them that their job was to help me out.

The Leadership Team is focused on ambition

Good conversations about priorities create Leadership Teams with a focus on what really matters. Clear priorities are articulated in ways that are simple, memorable and easy to apply. They provide answers to two key questions:

1. 'What are the most important things needed to reach our ambition?'

2. 'What do these change about what I need to do?'

Through being able to answer these questions themselves, Leadership Team members are able to help their own teams find solutions which reinforce rather than dilute the overarching organisational priorities.

Bold changes win more support

Every organisation has many tasks to address and issues to solve at any one time. But they can't all be tackled at once. Clear prioritisation allows the Leadership Team to make bigger, bolder changes – and to benefit from the fact that big, dynamic changes are easier to communicate and more likely to inspire the whole workforce to move in the same direction. One CEO I know likes to talk about 'creating messages that break through the background noise'.

Clear prioritisation allows the Leadership Team to make bigger, bolder changes – and to benefit from the fact that big, dynamic changes are easier to communicate and more likely to inspire the whole workforce to move in the same direction.

Priorities make decision-making easier. In any large organisation, thousands of decisions of varying importance are made each day. A short, clearly articulated and fully understood list of priorities will guide decision-making at every level.

If everyone knows the overriding priorities, it becomes easier for people to support them and to check that everything they do is in line with the changes that need to be made. Employees, from the Leadership Team right down to front-line staff, can use a known and explicit priority as a touchstone for their day-to-day actions and decisions.

Whether people are handling customers' problems on the fly, or discussing future policies and procedures in an internal meeting, they can take operational decisions on their own initiative, because they know what the organisation needs of them.

Are Priority Conversations needed in your Team?

Priority Conversations are needed in teams who want to:

- ▲ Fully understand the range of issues that must be balanced and traded off.
- ▲ Find ways to compare the very different types of issues and work.
- ▲ Work through the total picture of existing and potential work and reduce it to a deliverable set of priorities for the organisation.
- ▲ Give the necessary leadership time and focus to key initiatives to ensure that they are implemented as effectively and quickly as needed.
- ▲ Deal with any over-dependency the organisation may have on a few critical and overloaded individuals for its success

If this is what is needed in your team, you can see tools for developing Priority Conversations, the Priority Matrix, the Rapid Sort and Challenging Big Rocks, on pages 268-283. ▲

One decision that changed almost everything

It started as an almost throwaway comment in an early team meeting of a financial organisation I worked with. We were talking about priorities and energy was low as the team went down a long list of familiar candidates.

'If we were serious about setting ourselves apart from the competition, we'd sort out the call centres,' muttered Steve, the operations director. There was a discernible rolling of eyes around the room from others who'd heard him climb on this soap box many times before.

The MD, Adam, who was new and looking for something different to galvanise the team, picked up on the aside. 'What's on your mind, Steve?'

He had lit the touch paper, and Steve set out in detail just how much the customers hated dealing with them. The company's customers were businesses who generally only needed to contact the call centre when there was a problem. When they did, they found the service slow at best and often didn't get their problem resolved in one call. They were frustrated and felt exploited by a company they saw as happy to take their money when all was well, but frustrating and slow to resolve things when the customer needed help.

Steve went on to complain that no-one ever took the issue seriously, as the situation was just as bad among all the major competitors in the sector. He pointed out that operations, in general, and the call centres, in particular, had long been a neglected area of the business – in terms of both management attention and investment.

Adam immediately saw that there was an opportunity. If the competition was equally poor, then a company that could do better could gain a genuine advantage. He pressed the conversation on but was shocked at what he heard.

When ringing the call centres for assistance, customers had to deal with several layers of automated voice messages. ➤

But they still often found, when they finally got through, that they were talking to someone who could not help them.

The call centre staff were demotivated and deeply cynical, after years of neglect and broken promises. The IT systems they had to use were also dreadful. There were a number of different applications, some of which were so ancient that they still used an old green-text-on-black-screen interface. Some were unreliable and it wasn't uncommon for the data in one system to clash with that from another.

As Adam asked more questions, Steve became clearer and more positive than he had been before about both the issues and his ideas for the way forward. It became clear that solutions to all of the problems were possible, if difficult. Gradually, the energy level rose, as the team began to see the opportunity and realise that it was achievable. By the end of the meeting, a number of areas of work were identified and every member of the team was deputed to look at scoping the work required.

At the next meeting, these plans were discussed and it was clear that the scale of change was bigger than everyone had thought. Even so, the team decided to make being the best in their industry for customer service their Number One priority.

As radical as this revolution had seemed at first, the further the team got into it, the bigger it became. Initially, changes were needed in training, recruitment and IT. Soon, processes were being modified, reporting was overhauled and marketing and sales were involved, as the time came to take the new message to the market. Every part of the organisation was affected. Both people and finances were redirected to accelerate the changes.

Three years on, the process is still continuing. The difference is that the company is now consolidating and stretching its lead over the competition, rather than establishing it. And customers have noticed. Market share has increased, with significant gains at the competition's expense, and the company has even managed to raise prices and margins on the back of the stronger service proposition. ➤

It was a tough call to make, but prioritising a new way to their destination is now described by the team members as the best decision they ever made.

Having to face up to a problem like this changed the way they operated. From that point on, they have been braver and more confident. They look carefully at every single decision and work as a team to create a vision for it. They now feel like a Leadership Team that has come of age and decisions like this have played a big part in the long period of unprecedented success that they are now enjoying. ▲

PRIORITY *conversations*

0	1	2	3	4	5	6	7	8	9	10

How aligned are your priorities with your ambition?

0	1	2	3	4	5	6	7	8	9	10

How good is your team at stopping or deferring activity to allow you to focus on your priorities?

0	1	2	3	4	5	6	7	8	9	10

To what degree have you dedicated enough resources to deliver all of what's needed from your priorities?

0	1	2	3	4	5	6	7	8	9	10

How well do people throughout the organisation understand and follow your priorities?

0	1	2	3	4	5	6	7	8	9	10

How much of the focus needed to deliver your key priorities are members of the Leadership Team able to give them?

OVERALL ASSESSMENT FOR PRIORITY CONVERSATIONS

0	1	2	3	4	5	6	7	8	9	10

What is your overall assessment of the Priority Conversations in your team?

Please mark your overall assessment, and then transfer this score to the assessment summary for your team on pages 240-241.

10

ACCOUNTABILITY
conversations

'When cross-functional teams have problems making decisions, leaders blame mistrust or poor communication. But the problem isn't trust or people – it's the decision-making process'

(Harvard Business Review, 2011)

A TALE FROM THE MAASAI

Loolpapit's changing world

Loolpapit was a young warrior when the fateful meeting took place under the acacia tree. His manhood ceremony was well behind him, but he had not yet married.

He'd been brought up like generations of Maasai men before him. From the age of just five or six, he was taught how to herd goats and cows. Every day, he would get up before sunrise with his father, eat and head out in the first rays of savannah light to take the goats and cattle out to pasture.

These trips could cover many miles, as the two of them searched to find enough food for the livestock. During these long days, Loolpapit was schooled by his father. Rather than the Three Rs, he learned all there was to know about livestock farming – from disease control to breeding, and from helping with calving to getting the best price at market. Like all his peers, his highest ambition was to own and manage as large a herd of goats and cows as he could.

The schooling went beyond the art of animal husbandry, though. His father taught him the culture and ways of the Maasai people. He eagerly drank in his father's stories and grew to understand the traditions, rituals and values of his people.

Loolpapit's sisters' lives also had a fixed pattern. They would play their part in the daily routine of survival by rising early and helping their mother prepare food, collect water, find firewood and, at the end of the day, milk the goats and cows. While their role was different, their schooling was similar. They, too, would learn how to succeed ➤

in the Maasai way in this hostile environment.

This was the background within which Loolpapit sat and listened to the big discussion about community development. When the conversation moved to a consensus about the building of a school, he, like many others, could see only some of the implications for himself and his people.

Everyone present, whether they had children or not, wanted the Maasai children to have the choices and opportunities that education would surely bring. It was clear, though, that these benefits would come with significant challenges.

First, people would have to work together to overcome the significant barriers of costs, logistics and Kenyan politics to build a school for the community. This, in itself, was intimidating, and there were many who doubted it was possible.

Beyond that were some huge challenges for every family. The most obvious of these was that their hand-to-mouth existence would somehow have to generate the extra funds required to pay for schooling for the children. An equally big worry for many was losing the help of the children in herding the animals and sharing the domestic duties. If the kids were at school, how could the parents alone possibly do all that was necessary?

A decade on, it's clear that the impact of that decision has been far greater than anyone had foreseen. Loolpapit's children's lives are very different from his own childhood. His own family life is far from what he would have expected when he was tending the animals in the savannah with his father.

He is married to Kisinyinye, and they now have four children: Sarah (10), Lema (9), Saruni (6) and Kiranto, who is just 5. Sarah and Lema attend the primary school. Saruni and Kiranto will also go to school as soon as they are old enough.

Where Loolpapit used to help his father herd the animals, he and Kisinyinye now manage the herding and domestic duties without help from the children. But of course, as they are Maasai, one solution to the challenges this presents is to work with other families and support each other's efforts to an even greater degree than before. Even so, life is much tougher today without the support their parents had from the children.

The financial challenge is greater still. Primary school costs $50 a year for each child, and secondary school is $400 per year. That's a lot for a family with four children.

Loolpapit and Kisinyinye's main source of income is their herd. A cow is worth $200, but they need to increase their herds, for both calves and milk, rather than deplete them by selling off their animals. So they have both had to find ways of creating additional sources of income.

Maasai ingenuity and creativity have been very much in evidence as they have risen to these challenges. Loolpapit works as a guide and security guard at the tourist camp ➤

in the community. He has also invested in an old motorbike and runs a taxi service, 'Bada Bada', for the locals for 150 shillings a ride (about $1.50). Kisinyinye sells milk from the cows directly to the staff of a cement factory which has opened nearby, and she is part of a women's co-operative that makes and sells beadwork to tourists.

The changes in Loolpapait's family and way of life are replicated in every boma. For many, they are deeply unsettling and cut to the heart of their identity as Maasai.

And yet, amazingly, almost every child in the community now goes to school. Every family continues to take on these challenges and changes and works hard to find ways to adapt. Like many other families, Loolpapait and Kisinyinye know the real challenge – finding the cost of secondary schooling for all four of their children – is yet to come.'

Despite all this, they and every family in the community remain steadfast in their collective commitment to the decision made all those years ago, under the acacia tree, to build the school and educate the coming generations.

Because every family has stood unswervingly behind the original commitment – like Loolpapait and Kisinyinye – the education project has succeeded beyond all expectations, and transformed the community's future. ▲

What are Accountability Conversations?

All the most important issues that Leadership Teams tackle are cross-functional and multi-disciplinary. From branding and service to customer retention, quality and personnel issues, every single one of these major issues requires co-operation and collaboration across departmental boundaries.

Product launches are an example that's familiar to everyone. The organisation needs to design the product, work out how and where it is to be manufactured, arrange packaging and distribution, decide on pricing and develop a marketing plan. That is going to involve at least four departments, several members of the Leadership Team, and, potentially, huge numbers of other employees.

So who among all these contributors is to be held accountable for the success of these efforts?

How do you go about making sure accountability is clear and understood, when all the work that matters most is fundamentally collective?

The traditional approach is to break the work down into objectives and contributions for all involved. That is clearly important. But it's not enough.

Every part of the work relies for its success on every other. The elements are interdependent, and this cannot be addressed if the work is only broken down into fragments and assigned to individuals in a piecemeal way. Interdependency calls for the project to be managed as a whole, in a way that pays attention to both the individual elements and the way they link together.

When success depends on cross-functional collaboration, it is not enough to pin the responsibility for getting the right results on any one member of the Leadership Team. It makes practical sense to give one person the job of taking the lead, but that person can't be left alone to take on complete accountability for tasks that span several different departments. But that is exactly what happens in most organisations. It even happens in situations where some other members of the team, whose support will be needed for successful implementation, are clearly not in full agreement.

When success depends on cross-functional collaboration, it is not enough to pin the responsibility for getting the right results on any one member of the Leadership Team.

In addition to the familiar notion of individual accountability we need something more. I call this extra dimension 'collective accountability' – and it is one of the key elements that distinguishes successful Leadership Teams from their less effective peers.

The good news is that achieving collective accountability, and making great decisions, is a process that can be learned.

Collective Accountability

Conventional business thinking has focused on individual accountability, but that has never been enough in the context of Leadership Teams. Individual accountability is concerned with the acknowledgement and assumption of actions and decisions by one person. Less familiar is the notion of collective accountability which is concerned with the same things but in cases where a group of people need to act or decide together.

Drawing on Miles Kierson's ideas (Kierson, 2009), we have developed a new approach to Accountability Conversations. This approach is vitally concerned with exploring the quality of the decisions that are made – and the relationship between team members and the decisions they take.

The process starts with a very specific definition of collective accountability. The term may not be new, but in this context, collective accountability is concerned with the degree of support each team member demonstrates for a project. The easier part of this is the delivery of their own elements of any plan, which can be dealt with in terms of individual accountability.

What becomes much more elusive is the degree of informal support each of the team's members gives to a decision or project. Do they speak up to promote and defend the work? Do they move resources around in their own area to support it? Or do they undermine it by what they say and do?

Collective accountability is about the relationship of each member of the team to a decision. Working with this requires a new and different approach.

Individual vs Collective Accountability

	Individual Accountability	Collective Accountability
Scope	Breaks work down to focus on its elements	Mostly concerned with the interrelationships between elements and with other work
Focus	Primarily tasks or specific responsibilities	The quality of, and individuals' relationships with, decisions
Appears as	Usually recorded as targets and objectives	Intangibles – especially better decisions and changed behaviour
Application	Generally works best within departmental boundaries	Most important for issues with organisational impact, which are essentially cross-functional in nature

When team members genuinely take Collective Accountability and are fully aligned and committed, something amazing happens. Difficult tasks become easier. Things move fast. Individuals are ready to push themselves, to take personal risks. People's energy is focused on getting the work done. Mountains can be moved.

In this state of alignment, no-one needs to be appointed to police team members' behaviour. The team has an integrity, discipline and direction of its own. It knows what it is doing and why, and almost anything can be achieved.

The Ladder of Ownership

Leadership Team members need to be fully aligned with the decisions the team makes. They need to feel a sense of ownership. This is not easy to achieve, because it must apply to team decisions that individual members disagree with or have doubts about, as well as those that are unanimously welcomed.

But collective accountability is not an optional extra. Without this alignment, the team will not unleash its potential and realise its ambition. Miles Kierson has a shockingly blunt way of putting it that certainly rings bells with me.

'Successful implementation,' he says, 'is more about ownership than the quality of the decision.'

That sounds like a heresy. Surely the most important thing is for Leadership Teams to take the right decisions and choose the very best of the available options?

'No,' says Kierson. And I agree with him.

There are frequently several 'right' decisions that can be made in response to a particular business situation.

'Successful implementation is more about ownership than the quality of the decision.'

In practice, it is more important that everyone is aligned and prepared to take ownership of the decision that is made than that it is the right decision. Even a 'mostly-right' decision can sometimes produce spectacularly successful results, if the team gets behind it and acts on it with wholehearted commitment and purpose.

At the other extreme, a correct, perfectly judged decision that fails to win the active engagement and support of the team is unlikely to lead to the hoped-for results. Initiatives that don't have this unqualified support may fail completely, move ahead too slowly, consume too many resources or simply wither on the vine.

Kierson describes a range of relationships to any decision (Kierson, 2009). I call it the Ladder of Ownership:

The Ladder of Ownership

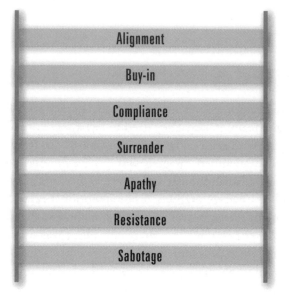

Most of these levels of ownership are self-explanatory and all too familiar. We have all seen plenty of situations where Leadership Team decisions have been grudgingly accepted ('compliance' or 'surrender') by one or more of the team members. Resistance, apathy and sabotage are less common, but by no means rare.

Unfortunately, on the most important issues, nothing short of alignment will do.

Even buy-in ('Yeah, OK, I'm on board') is not enough of a commitment. The purpose of Accountability Conversations is to arrive at genuine alignment, in which every member of the Leadership Team agrees to accept full accountability for the team decision, support it, speak up for it, live it and own it, whatever the challenges and obstacles it encounters.

That's why Accountability Conversations can be protracted and difficult. By the time the final decision is taken, any doubts and differences of opinion must have been raised and discussed within the team, and team members – even those who originally disagreed – must be prepared to accept full and committed collective ownership of the team decision.

Accountability for the intangibles

Leaders need to hold Accountability Conversations about two main areas.

The first is obvious. It is to do with tangibles – results, tasks or delivery. These are specific things that need to be achieved by a certain time.

The second is about behaviour and ethos – the standards by which the team operates and the values that are embodied in its behaviour.

By the time the final decision is taken, any doubts and differences of opinion must have been raised and discussed within the team, and team members – even those who originally disagreed – must be prepared to accept full and committed collective ownership of the team decision.

This begins with the commitment of each aligned Leadership Team member to stick up for and champion the collective decision, even if he or she did not originally agree with it. It also includes the need for Leadership Team members to continually support and challenge one another on how they can get to, and maintain, the standards of leadership required to deliver on the ambition.

Why teams struggle

Making decisions in groups isn't something that comes naturally to most of us. It's inherently difficult. And most members of Leadership Teams have arrived as team members by being leaders in their own areas where they can make decisions themselves.

Without a clear way to make decisions together and take shared responsibility for making them work, Leadership Team meetings can feel like Groundhog Day. At least one issue spins out into a much longer discussion than necessary, but even then, fails to provide a decision with the level of clarity and/or support required. A long agenda means the team has to move on to something else and everyone knows that they will have to return to it at a future meeting to go through the same routine again.

Leadership Teams suffer when accountability issues aren't fully understood and actively managed. At best, they often focus on the individuals involved and neglect the key issue of collective accountability. When this happens, a number of negative symptoms are all too familiar.

Alignment has not been achieved

Alignment may sound like an abstract concept, but it's something we all know and feel at a visceral level. Every Leadership Team member knows the feeling of being in a room when a decision has been taken, supposedly on behalf of the whole team, but one individual (maybe more) is tacitly opposed to it.

The team leaves the meeting thinking it has the green light for a new project, but everyone knows something's wrong and private conversations afterwards confirm the existence of a problem. 'Did you see James' face? There's no way he's going to back this up with his team. We'll never get this to fly. It'll be just like the last time.'

Whatever James really thinks, this is a disastrous way to start any new initiative. It sounds obvious, but we have all seen teams duck out of the difficult conversations that are necessary to understand and deal with the resistance or opposition that's in the room.

...we have all seen teams duck out of the difficult conversations that are necessary to understand and deal with the resistance or opposition that's in the room.

Failure is handled inconsistently

Companies are often inconsistent in their response when tasks are not attended to or are carried out incorrectly. I've lost count of the number of team members who have complained to me that people accept accountability for particular actions or projects but aren't held to account when they fail to fulfil their side of the bargain.

If it's recognised that responsibility for a particular failure lies in many places, no-one may be held accountable – and the organisation misses the opportunity to learn from its mistakes.

Many companies go to the other extreme and make a big thing of holding individuals accountable when they don't complete tasks successfully – even if the failure is clearly due to circumstances beyond their control, or, indeed, directly caused by lack of support from their colleagues.

The reward system sends the wrong signals

To make sure that team members deliver on their own areas of responsibility, they are often highly rewarded (and not just financially) for these achievements.

This produces an over-reliance on individual accountability at the expense of collective accountability. The danger is that this becomes self-reinforcing, with the failures of individual accountability producing a desire to resolve problems with yet more individual focus. Unfortunately, it's the lack of trust and cohesion that's the problem. Trying to address this with yet more individual accountability just makes things worse.

Collective rewards are harder to make work and to measure – particularly in teams where the members don't trust one another. As a result, many teams turn a blind eye to the tricky issues involved in assessing team performance and giving appropriate collective rewards.

Meetings seem to go nowhere

Most Leadership Team members will have experienced the frustrations of useless, repetitive meetings, overstuffed agendas and the endless tendency to cycle back, month after month, to the same few thorny issues, which never seem to move ahead.

When meetings feel like trench warfare, slogging backwards and forwards over the same ground, it's often partly because the Leadership Team has failed to have proper Accountability Conversations, right back at the beginning, and was never fully aligned behind the key decisions.

> *The seeds sown by a failure to achieve full alignment at the start mean that initiatives don't move ahead as fast as they should, because progress is undermined by hidden opposition or partial and half-hearted support.*

The seeds sown by a failure to achieve full alignment at the start mean that initiatives don't move ahead as fast as they should, because progress is undermined by hidden opposition or partial and half-hearted support. The frustration this causes leads to finger-pointing and recriminations which get in the way of understanding the true causes of the underperformance.

Most Leadership Teams we have worked with are unaware of missing the disciplines of collective accountability. They recognise the symptoms but don't see where the problem arises or how they should deal with it.

They don't know how much they don't know. As a result, Leadership Teams are typically far more confident than they should be about their ability to make aligned decisions. They are usually aware that they could do better in dealing with individual accountability, but they don't realise how far they fall short in relation to taking true collective accountability.

What do good Accountability Conversations look like?

They hold to the highest standards for decisions

Accountability Conversations are not group brainwashing sessions. They can't descend into 'groupthink', in which agreement is sought even if that means it's on the basis of the lowest common denominator. They are brought to a successful conclusion only when the Leadership Team takes on unanimous and collective responsibility, with every team member fully aligned.

When a decision is made, each and every team member must be committed to owning the decision, supporting it in word and deed, speaking up for it when necessary, and doing whatever it takes to make it work.

> *When a decision is made, each and every team member must be committed to owning the decision, supporting it in word and deed, speaking up for it when necessary, and doing whatever it takes to make it work.*

There is a cost to having the explicit and sometimes difficult conversations that are needed to reach this point. Asking each team member: 'Where are you on this decision?' implies a commitment to working through a number of possible objections. It takes time. It will also take a conscious effort to avoid a slide towards lowest common denominator solutions in the attempt to please everyone.

But it's a price worth paying. As EasyJet founder Stelios Haji-Ioannou said about airline safety: 'If you think safety's expensive, try having an accident.'

If you think Accountability Conversations are costly, just try getting the big things done without them.

That conclusion needs to be at the highest level possible, using all of the collective experience, insight and expertise within the team.

Each member will play a part here in setting the bar high and holding firm to both the transformational intent derived from the team's earlier Ambition and Priority Conversations and the need for full alignment. When, and only when, both of these requirements have been satisfied, the organisation will have the quality of decision it needs to go forward.

They work through all the issues fully

Everything relevant that needs to be raised is brought out into the open, discussed and resolved. Some people will inevitably lose some parts of the argument.

Each Leadership Team member has a duty to say whatever needs to be said to help the team see the issues fully and clearly and come to an aligned decision.

Each team member needs to be ready to explore further actions and options in order to get themselves aligned.

The team will always benefit from continuing to work at the issues involved in the attempt to resolve individuals' doubts and reservations. This may be time-consuming, but it almost always leads, eventually, to full alignment – and to better decisions.

Team members are prepared to contribute doubt

A good Accountability Conversation does not just focus on the decision itself. It requires the Leadership Team to talk explicitly about each team member's relationship with the decision. If there are two or three options on the table, there may be disagreements or open conflict. There may be people in the room whose reaction to a proposal is potentially down near the bottom of the Ladder of Ownership, in the realms of resistance, apathy or even sabotage.

> *When Accountability Conversations are at their best, people contribute everything they have that's relevant, including their doubts.*

Bringing these reservations out into the open is an essential part of the process. They need to be discussed and worked through to arrive at a decision that will have the full weight of the team's effort and commitment behind it.

Talking about your reservations is usually seen as a negative thing. But raising issues that need to be addressed – either for the team to be successful or for one individual to be aligned – is a positive part of the process of arriving at full alignment. When Accountability Conversations are at their best, people contribute everything they have that's relevant, including their doubts, and the team welcomes them as positive inputs towards arriving at the best possible decision.

They keep working towards real alignment – even when it gets tough

Crucially, at the end of the Accountability Conversation, each individual must be ready to let go of his or her original ideas and preconceptions in the interests of becoming fully aligned with the team decision.

The willingness to offer and accept views that make arriving at a decision difficult is crucial. This will require cycling back around and resolving reservations until everyone can be aligned. While it may take longer, the quality of decision that emerges will be much higher. Contributing and addressing doubt is, therefore, a positive part of the process. In my experience – and to many teams' surprise – it almost always results in both full alignment and a better decision.

That can also be hard. Sometimes a team member speaks up about a reservation and the entire team explores it fully and concludes that it cannot be accommodated, but the individual still won't let go of his or her objection. At this point, the person concerned has to choose whether to fully align with the decision or continue to oppose it. If he continues to oppose it, the leader will have to make a judgement about how that is going to be handled. Can the organisation accept a lower level on the Ladder of Ownership, or is a tougher conversation called for?

The willingness to offer and accept views that make arriving at a decision difficult is crucial.

Sometimes a failure to align is because the odd-man-out is being either stubborn or arrogant. If this happens repeatedly, with the same individual unable to get in line with the team on several occasions, the Leadership Team member may need to start thinking about his or her future (Sheard, Kakabadse, and Kakabadse, 2009). There is no place in an aligned team for one person who is always out of step and marching to a different drum. The question then, for the CEO and for the team member, is whether this person is capable of operating effectively as part of a true Leadership Team.

People accept accountability readily

When the team has good Accountability Conversations, Leadership Team members start accepting accountability, even when they aren't completely clear about how the desired results will be achieved, rather than feeling they must wait until they know all the answers. Organisations always have to operate on incomplete information. If the decision is made to launch in a new market or territory, people are ready to get on board to make sure it happens, even before they have figured out the practical details.

The conversations that occur during and after the decision look deeper into the issues and become more challenging and more successful at unblocking obstacles. The explicit contracting means that individual issues can be directly addressed and that the team can quickly move on to look at underlying barriers. The focus becomes unpacking and resolving problems, rather than pinning responsibility for them on individuals.

Team members start offering to take accountability, rather than simply accepting it when it's pushed onto them. They lift their own standards and the collective bar is raised higher. They are more willing to volunteer to take responsibility if they feel they will have the entire team behind them, and more willing to support others if they know this is likely to be reciprocated.

In any given decision, there will be some team members who are more deeply involved than others. Instead of merely looking on, and only later responding to requests for help and resources, the less involved team members actively anticipate how they might be able to contribute – including how they will respond to the challenges, resistance and problems that always accompany any worthwhile decision or action.

The explicit contracting means that individual issues can be directly addressed and that the team can quickly move on to look at underlying barriers.

Direct support may be needed. Other tasks may have to be shuffled around or reallocated to free up resources for the new priority. Even if Leadership Team members don't have a practical contribution to make, they will still have a role, which they can explore and expand, as leaders and advocates.

Conversations about accountability are focused on the future

All too often, the call for accountability in business is a sign that something has gone wrong and people are looking for someone to blame. But organisations that only focus on accountability when they are seeking scapegoats are missing the point.

The emphasis on accountability that emerges after a mistake or disaster is usually a destructive force. It may help with the forensic analysis of what went wrong, but it is often far too close to a witch hunt. The time for Accountability Conversations is beforehand, when a clear understanding of both individual and collective commitments can help ensure that every joint activity is set up for success.

The best Accountability Conversations are forward-looking. Collective accountability needs to be negotiated and accepted before any action is taken.

The benefits of Accountability Conversations

The central benefit of having effective Accountability Conversations and implementing their conclusions is that the team becomes better at delivering on its biggest and most important commitments. Consistency is improved, and anxieties about failure are lessened. A virtuous circle is established, with greater confidence leading to better results, better performance and consistent on-time delivery.

The team makes better decisions

The members of a Leadership Team are there for a reason. Each brings experience, insight and knowledge to the table. Working decisions through to full alignment, even when this is difficult and time consuming, ensures that the full benefit of the team's collective wisdom can be brought to bear. The decisions that are made are more robust and complete and have a better chance of being successfully implemented.

Each project and decision delivers more, faster

It is always much cheaper and easier to invest in resolving differences and gaining team alignment early on than to grapple with the problems later, when the project is three months behind schedule, people are feeling defensive, the pressure is on and everything is getting messy.

Ensuring that all the members of the team are fully behind the most important decisions, both in terms of practical support and in their role as leaders, ensures that many problems are avoided entirely. When further difficulties and barriers emerge, as they inevitably will, these too will be resolved more quickly and easily by an aligned team.

The culture of the team changes

Good Accountability Conversations soon begin to change the culture within the Leadership Team for the better. Conversations about commitments and responsibilities acquire a much sharper focus and automatically feed into new conversations about co-operation and collaboration. Team members develop a new confidence in each other's intentions and abilities and become braver about taking on the personal risks of signing up for ambitious and challenging transformational goals.

Team members set themselves higher standards

In the best teams, people hold themselves to higher standards because of their sense of obligation and loyalty to the team. They become more ambitious for the organisation as a whole, less tolerant of their own shortcomings and more ready to roll up their sleeves and do what it takes to make each project a success.

The organisation notices – and starts to shift

In most organisations, Leadership Team dysfunction is an open secret. This sends out negative signals, reinforcing frictions and encouraging siloed thinking and a lack of co-operation between departments.

When the Leadership Team achieves alignment, the mood music changes and a more positive message is sent out. The Leadership Team's example is echoed across the whole organisation and the ethos improves. People who work collaboratively begin to thrive and those who resist working across functions are exposed. There is nothing that promotes cross-functional efforts across the organisation more effectively than clear evidence of collaborative working within the Leadership Team.

Are Accountability Conversations needed in your team?

Accountability Conversations are needed for teams who want to:

▲ Get beyond circular discussions which carry on for a long time without a resolution.

▲ Consistently ensure that team members leave the room with the same understanding of what has been decided, and that decisions don't need to be revisited.

▲ Have confidence that when a decision is made, members of the team are sufficiently aligned with it, that any disagreements have been properly aired and processed and that everyone will fully support it.

▲ Close discussions down quickly as soon as the key elements of agreement are present, rather than continuing to circle round unnecessarily.

▲ Ensure decisions are made which strike the right balance between exploration and rigour on the one hand and speed and clarity on the other.

If this is what's needed in your team, you can see tools for developing Accountability Conversations, the Ladder of Ownership and Collective Decision-making, on pages 284-295. ▲

CASE STUDY

Signing up to 'less is more'

One client, a large British-based consultancy with significant operations in Europe and the US, was facing a huge strategic dilemma.

Although the firm had offices outside the UK, a large proportion of the experts needed for client assignments had to travel from the UK. The marketplace had become increasingly crowded, with more and more local competitors joining the traditional international players. Price competition had intensified and it had become difficult to recover the ➤

significant travel, accommodation and other costs associated with flying consultants around the world. The firm was having to pay premium rates to recruit and keep experts who were prepared to be away from home for months at a time.

Margins on work outside the UK had become wafer thin and some jobs were being taken on at a loss, just to utilise the expert staff and bolster turnover.

At the time I was involved with the company, a couple of poor years had meant that its managers were prepared to examine previously sacrosanct choices. The future of the firm's operations outside the UK ('exUK', as they were called) was being seriously debated. Some 30 per cent of the firm's turnover was coming from operations outside the UK, but these were generating an overall loss of about £5m.

There had been discussions about it before, but they had only led to a variety of sticking-plaster solutions, such as cost-saving measures (which made a small difference) and rules about the profitability of new contracts (which were regularly bent when bids were being submitted). The firm had stopped short of ceasing to bid for exUK contracts for many reasons, but the biggest was one of scale and credibility. Those at the top of the firm knew that retrenching to operate only in the UK would reduce turnover significantly and be seen by the industry, and particularly by clients, as a sign of weakness and a clear retrograde step.

The head of international operations, Geoff, had been tasked with looking at a possible exit. He knew he'd been handed a poisoned chalice and the first time he presented his findings and plan to the team, it didn't go well.

Objections and questions came thick and fast. Pretty soon he was on the defensive, besieged by the rest of the team. Many felt that pulling back would be admitting defeat and that presenting the change to clients, investors and the press would seriously undermine the organisation's credibility – and perhaps even its viability.

The CEO, Julian, finally stepped in. He reminded the team why they had agreed to consider the exUK withdrawal so seriously. He asked each team member to respond to an interesting question. ➤

'What would be needed to enable you to be fully aligned with a decision to pull out of exUK?' Each team member responded in turn and a long list of objections emerged. Julian suggested that they should return to the subject, to hear and discuss Geoff's responses, at their next meeting.

The next meeting was not easy, but Geoff did successfully address some of the objections – and went some way towards dealing with many of the others. After some discussion, Julian asked the same question again and they revised and updated the list of remaining objections.

It took two more meetings before Julian put his question again, this time in a slightly different form. 'Are you now ready to be fully aligned with the exUK exit?'

.This time, every team member agreed.

The message to both staff and the market had changed significantly as a result of the discussions. The firm was now able to present the exit as a bold move, ahead of the trends in the market, and produce market data to show how others would soon be forced, however unwillingly, to follow suit. It showed the change of emphasis to be the key enabler for an exciting new UK strategy in which the firm would be opening up two new areas of its offer.

A huge communication plan was put into effect. Shareholders, clients, the press and their own staff all had to be told the news in a carefully choreographed sequence. Every member of the team had a part to play and every person had to be able to speak with 100% conviction.

The communication plan worked. The consultancy retained all its key clients and had no important staff losses. Interestingly, the press covered it as a debate about the future of the industry, rather than seeing it as a retreat by one company.

Today the firm operates only within the UK. The withdrawal from overseas operations reduced its losses and the new offerings are growing well. While turnover is still significantly lower, profitability is higher and the increased focus on the UK has meant that the firm's growth is now well ahead of its projections. ▲

ACCOUNTABILITY
conversations

| 0 | 1 | 2 | 3 | 4 | 5 | 6 | 7 | 8 | 9 | 10 |

How often does your team get to full alignment on decisions?

| 0 | 1 | 2 | 3 | 4 | 5 | 6 | 7 | 8 | 9 | 10 |

How often does hidden resistance or inadequate exploration of issues undermine effective delivery?

| 0 | 1 | 2 | 3 | 4 | 5 | 6 | 7 | 8 | 9 | 10 |

How well do you balance the quality and speed of decision making?

| 0 | 1 | 2 | 3 | 4 | 5 | 6 | 7 | 8 | 9 | 10 |

Is your team leading by example on cross-functional collaboration?

| 0 | 1 | 2 | 3 | 4 | 5 | 6 | 7 | 8 | 9 | 10 |

How much do you hold one another accountable for behaviour as well as results?

OVERALL ASSESSMENT FOR ACCOUNTABILITY CONVERSATIONS

| 0 | 1 | 2 | 3 | 4 | 5 | 6 | 7 | 8 | 9 | 10 |

What is your overall assessment of the Accountability Conversations in your team?

Please mark your overall assessment, and then transfer this score to the assessment summary for your team on pages 240-241.

11 DELIVERY
conversations

> *Most organisations think of delivery as being about processes and documentation. But while an element of methodology is necessary, it is not sufficient. If the human factor is missing, process alone will not be enough to bring about successful delivery. Delivery happens through people, not paperwork.*

A TALE FROM THE MAASAI

A Maasai without cows is like a leopard without spots

The Maasai are an ancient tribe. Their culture dates back hundreds – probably thousands – of years. In that time, they have shown a remarkable ability to adapt to a changing world. Their approach to evolving their culture is quite different from the way we think about changing culture in the business world, and I think we have much to learn from it.

We're all familiar with the bright red shawl (the shuka) and fantastically coloured beadwork that appear in every image of the Maasai. Both of these, however, are relatively recent adaptations. The shukas are wool or cotton and are made in Bangladesh. The tiny glass beads that are threaded together to make the typically Maasai necklaces, bracelets, headdresses and earrings are manufactured in the Czech Republic. Most creatively of all, the Maasai's shoes are made from recycled motorcycle tyres!

Traditionally, both shoes and shukas would have been made of leather. The shukas were coloured with red ochre, which is abundant in the savannah soil and which they still use to colour their hair. Their jewellery was originally made of a mixture of bones, stones, seeds and parts of plants.

The decorative tradition that was so important to their identity has remained intact. But as new materials have become available through industrialisation and globalisation, the Maasai have embraced new ways to express that tradition. ➤

The world the Maasai live in, however, is changing more rapidly than ever before. The economy that used to be based on barter is becoming more monetised. The new roads, which bring many benefits, also bring with them land speculators, disease, crime and many other challenges. Western cultural images and advertising are changing the role models and aspirations of the younger generation. With more and more of the children at school, the work of a Maasai parent is changing dramatically.

Profound as all these changes are, the biggest challenge facing the Maasai comes from climate change. In the West, we worry when we have a warmer winter than usual and wring our hands about the risk of global warming over the next fifty years.

For the Maasai, climate change is already here. The equatorial rains arrive in blocks of just a few days in April and October. In between, there is nothing. These rains used to be reliable, but they are now much more unpredictable – and sometimes don't arrive at all. Missing just one rainy season is a devastating disaster for both wildlife and the Maasai.

In 2009, the October rains did not come. The rain didn't arrive in April 2010, either, and the eighteen-month drought left the savannah parched and devoid of grass. Animals died in their hundreds of thousands. Among the dying animals were 90 per cent of the goats and cows herded by the Maasai families.

Cows have a central place in Maasai culture. The very earliest Maasai made the significant shift from a hunter-gatherer lifestyle to become semi-nomadic herders. The golden thread of herding cattle has become the core of the Maasai's identity, along with their philosophy of 'community first'. As their proverb says, 'A Maasai without cows is like a leopard without spots.'

Cattle provide food and drink. They are the wealth of any Maasai family. Strange as it may seem to us, they also provide companionship. Every warrior has a favourite cow, with whom he has a special relationship. Cattle matter more than money. If a Maasai sells a cow, the money earned from that sale is more valuable than other money – and it will be used highly selectively. You would never, for example, lend someone else the proceeds of selling a cow.

Losing 90 per cent of your cattle, then, is utterly devastating. It's like one of us losing 90 per cent of our wealth, and some family members, too, at the same time.

While the length of the drought of 2009/10 is, thankfully, still exceptional, every year now brings the very real possibility of missing a single rainy season. Even one missed season means twelve months with no rain, and that can leave a family with just half a herd.

In 2009, Ntiato, a warrior with a modest herd, made an extraordinary decision. When the first rainy season failed, he reasoned that the condition (and the value) of his cattle would only deteriorate over the coming months and that a significant number were likely to die. Although prices were low, he decided he should sell every single one of his cows.

➤

The reaction in the community was a mixture of astonishment, amusement and pity. Clearly, Ntiato had lost his mind. Our equivalent would be responding to a downturn in the property market by selling your house, putting down your pets and taking your family to sleep in a tent.

When the April rains failed as well, Ntiato, his wife, Nyoleng, and their children started to fare much better than everyone else. As well as being able to sustain themselves, by carefully using some of the money they had raised from selling the herd, they were also in a position to support some of the other families and children in nearby bomas. They took in the children of other families so that the parents could walk for days with their cattle to seek out pasture.

By the time the rains returned, the community was on its knees. Ntiato and Nyoleng used their remaining money to buy a new herd of cows (at very low prices, as no-one else had any money). From being an ordinary family in Merrueshi, they had become one of the wealthiest.

Today the example set by Ntiato is widely accepted. Most Maasai have a more flexible attitude to holding some of their assets in cash when necessary. Yet again, the Maasai have demonstrated how they can retain and enhance even the most important aspects of their culture, by innovating to adapt it for the world they now live in.

Culture change is something that concerns the Maasai deeply – just as it preoccupies every Leadership Team. The difference is that the Maasai are constantly thinking about preserving and progressively evolving their culture, whereas leaders, in my experience, are often almost exclusively concerned with correcting the faulty culture of their organisations.

Culture change in organisations is notoriously difficult, and all too often unsuccessful. I wonder how much easier and more successful organisational cultural change would be if we learned from positive cultural exceptions and exemplars (Pascale, Sternin, and Sternin, 2010), in the way the Maasai have learned from Ntiato's experience, rather than always trying to 'fix' our organisations and people, as if they were broken. ▲

What are Delivery Conversations?

Delivery Conversations are how the Leadership Team ensures that big, transformational changes actually happen. They are about what is needed to successfully carry through the kind of complex, cross-functional initiatives that will move the whole organisation forward, towards achieving its Ambition.

When Delivery Conversations are working well, something changes. You can feel the difference. Like the Americas Cup boats that lift up and fly along on hydrofoils with their hulls high out of the water, the organisation suddenly finds itself facing less resistance.

As momentum builds, people start to see the first signs of change. A virtuous circle is created. Early wins encourage greater efforts, and enthusiasm becomes contagious. Energy levels improve. People work harder, gain in confidence, take on more personal risk and help each other out, leaving behind old demarcation lines in the pursuit of a common aim.

Delivery Conversations focus on the human dimensions of making the work happen. Beyond project management tools like Prince2 and all the systems and processes organisations adopt, these are the areas where business transformation projects succeed or fail. Most organisations think of delivery as being about processes and documentation. But while an element of methodology is necessary, it is not sufficient. If the human factor is missing, process alone will not be enough to bring about successful delivery. Delivery happens through people, not paperwork.

> *Delivery Conversations focus on the human dimensions of making the work happen. Beyond project management tools like Prince2 and all the systems and processes organisations adopt, these are the areas where business transformation projects succeed or fail.*

Delivery needs as much attention as strategy

Strategy is the glamorous end of business, and conversations about strategy have dominated business thinking and writing for decades. Many organisations hire professional consultants to help them devise their strategies. This can be a big investment and it often results in a set of intelligent, well-designed recommendations for the future.

But these strategies are often doomed to sit in a dusty binder on a shelf, simply because they have failed to take account of the dynamics and complexities that will necessarily be involved in getting them delivered.

Strategy consultants are seldom interested enough, or patient enough, to get involved in the complexities and nuances of stakeholder management, leadership capability development and cultural change. I remember one of them blandly declaring on the second page of his presentation: 'We have assumed perfect execution' – an assumption that's roughly on a par with assuming it will never rain.

Delivery is the difference

More recently, though, analysts have recognised that an organisation's ability to deliver successfully is at least as critical as its strategy. There has been a huge upsurge of interest in execution and delivery.

There is plenty of detailed research that confirms that when organisations fail, it's much more likely to be because they haven't executed the strategy than because they have chosen the wrong one.

When organisations fail, it's much more likely to be because they haven't executed the strategy than because they have chosen the wrong one.

One of my favourite articles on this subject was published more than fifteen years ago in *Fortune* magazine. The title of the study, by consultant Ram Charan and journalist Geoffrey Colvin, was 'Why CEOs Fail' (Charan and Colvin, 1999) and its conclusions are still as relevant today.

A core theme of the article was that it was much more difficult to deliver on a good strategy than to come up with one in the first place.

Seventy per cent of failed CEOs blew it, they estimated, because of bad execution. It wasn't 'lack of smarts or vision' that did for them. It was simply a failure to drive delivery in the relentless way competitive businesses need.

Leadership Teams develop their strategies in their Ambition Conversations and Priority Conversations. Delivery follows on by creating results based on the outcome of these conversations. In fact, looked at one way, this whole book is about executing strategy, for strategy creation and delivery are inextricably bound up with each other.

Without a strategy, people don't know what they are supposed to be doing. Without delivery, the strategy is just a document on the CEO's desk.

Delivery Conversations have two parts

Getting individual projects delivered is, of course, an essential part of a Leadership Team's responsibilities and forms a part of Delivery Conversations. This is the part that is mainly concerned with methodology and process. I like to distinguish this, more familiar, element of Delivery Conversations with the term 'execution management'.

There are, however, bigger, broader things that only the Leadership Team can do to ensure that delivery, across the board, is faster, more effective and requires less effort to sustain.

Delivery Conversations are also, therefore, about creating the right conditions to give all projects positive momentum and to sustain the progress that is being made. They address both the need to impart pace at the outset and the task of maintaining progress as the project proceeds. I call these 'delivery imperatives'.

How execution management differs from delivery

	Execution management	Delivery imperatives
Focus	Process	People
Concerned with	Documentation, disciplines, rigour	Stakeholders, leadership resources, culture
Challenge	Solution easy – compliance hard	Multi-dimensional, with many right answers
Succeeds when	Simple, consistent and sufficient	Underlying issues, about where people are and what they need, are addressed

Execution management

Execution management is a hot topic these days. There are any number of different project management systems, from the widely recognised Prince2 to in-house systems developed in organisations and the proprietary methodologies championed by hundreds of different strategy firms and consultants. Most of these process-driven systems can potentially be made to work well, if carried through properly, but there are very few organisations that use them well or consistently.

Many of them are far more complex than they need to be, and the extra work they entail creates resistance. Alongside all the everyday pressures bearing down on the organisation, they are simply too cumbersome. The result is usually a half-hearted approach to the methodology or little execution management at all.

We have developed a quick and easy one-page methodology (see Project Charter and PINS, page 296) that – despite its simplicity – is sufficiently rigorous and comprehensive to provide a sound basis for getting the mechanics of execution management right. Unlike many methodologies, it is straightforward enough to help and encourage users, making it more usable and effective.

Execution management is a relatively straightforward and well-understood discipline. Few Leadership Teams completely overlook the need to follow some process to move their initiatives forward. Doing it well is difficult, but it's not complicated.

Three Delivery Imperatives

When I first get involved in working with Leadership Teams that really want to change and do great things, the same three subjects – stakeholder engagement, next-tier bandwidth and culture – almost always come up early in our conversations.

There are never enough good people for them to turn to, team members tell me. One or other of the key stakeholders is proving very hard to handle. Attitudes within the organisation are making it more difficult than it should be to make the changes that are needed. The story is almost always the same.

Delivery Conversations also need to deal with making the organisation fit to execute and deliver the results that are needed. And it is quite clear to me, from long experience of these situations, that the teams that achieve the best outcomes are those that are prepared to put the most effort into tackling these three vital issues.

Three Delivery Imperatives

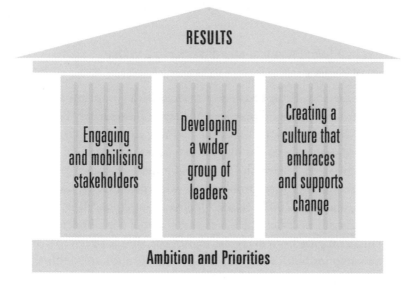

RESULTS

Engaging and mobilising stakeholders

Developing a wider group of leaders

Creating a culture that embraces and supports change

Ambition and Priorities

Imperative One: Engaging and mobilising stakeholders

The first essential for sustainable delivery – engaging and mobilising stakeholders – is more complicated than it seems.

Identifying the full range of stakeholders whose attitudes and actions will have an impact on a major change initiative is not always a simple task.

Identifying the full range of stakeholders whose attitudes and actions will have an impact on a major change initiative is not always a simple task.

In the outside world, there will be customers and key suppliers. Closer to home, there may be directors on a parent company board, as well as the CEO and his Leadership Team. But the stakeholders will also include all the departmental leaders and section heads who report to the Leadership Team members – the crucial next tier of management that every organisation relies on to break the big plan down into tasks and projects and make sure the work gets done.

Within this group, there are always a few individuals who have specialist knowledge or on whom there is a particular dependency. These people are key stakeholders in their own right. Without their engagement and co-operation, the desired changes will not happen.

Stakeholder management is hardly a new concept, but dealing with the wide range of people and their needs, practical as well as emotional, is something few teams manage well. It lies right at the heart of many of the problems they report in making change happen.

Imperative Two: Engaging and developing a wider group of leaders

Every Leadership Team I have ever worked with complains that there aren't enough good people in the layers immediately below them in the organisation. This issue has only recently begun to be researched, but early results suggest that issues of capability, mutual mistrust between Leadership Teams and middle managers and systemic communication problems are widespread (Raes, Glunk, Heijltjes, and Roe, 2007), (Raes, Heijltjes, Glunk, and Roe, 2011).

Within this next tier, there is always a mixed bag of talents and potential, ranging from energetic high-flyers who are keen to take on new responsibilities and help shape the organisation's destiny, to placid quiet-lifers whose instincts are always to lie low, keep things ticking over and stay out of the limelight. There may also be people who are in the wrong job or who simply don't have the skills to perform at the level that will be required as the organisation changes. There may be frightened passengers. There may even be saboteurs.

Execution improves when teams increase the management bandwidth that's available to make change happen

Whatever the strengths and weaknesses within this group, this is the raw material you have to work with in order to improve the organisation's capacity to deliver.

The second imperative for sustainable delivery is, therefore, to develop the capabilities of these next-tier managers, recognise and promote people from lower down the ranks and, where necessary, reposition or weed out those who can't or won't make the contributions that are needed.

Execution improves when teams increase the management bandwidth that's available to make change happen, so that they don't always have to rely on the same small pool of talented but overworked individuals. In addition to their role in getting things done, the people in this group usually have a critical part to play in sharing the load of leading the organisation.

It is often hard for a member of the team to make a frank, unbiased assessment of people he or she sees every day and may have worked with for years. Other Leadership Team members may be painfully aware that there is a weak link near the top of a team member's department, but are sometimes inhibited about raising this as a problem for fear of being seen to encroach on the responsibilities of their colleagues.

This need for increased management bandwidth is virtually universal. I've never yet come across a Leadership Team that is doing enough, fast enough, to get the people in that next-tier group moving forward and developing new capabilities.

Transformation initiatives can only maintain their progress towards successful delivery if the Leadership Team can keep the hulls up out of the water and keep the project riding above the organisational noise.

If you want the boat to go faster, it needs a more powerful engine. Developing a bigger, better leadership cadre is the way to add that extra horsepower. The sooner you start, the more effort you put in and the more decisive you can be, the sooner delivery will improve.

Imperative Three: Creating a culture that embraces and supports change

The third imperative – developing the right culture to support transformational change – is a challenge that has no straightforward, process-based solutions. It is partly a question of leadership, the ability to enthuse and inspire a whole organisation to move towards a positive future. It also includes communicating the vision, the goals and the rationale to the people most closely involved, to others who aren't directly involved and to all those who need to contribute.

> *Above all, it is about nurturing positive attitudes and helping people overcome their apprehensions and embrace change.*

Above all, it is about nurturing positive attitudes and helping people overcome their apprehensions and embrace change.

This kind of cultural shift can only happen one way. It has to start with the CEO and the Leadership Team and ripple out through the whole organisation. It cannot be mandated, and it invariably involves a lot more showing than telling. It begins with Ambition Conversations, is focused by Priority Conversations and is manifested in the organisation through the Leadership Team's Delivery Conversations.

It ends with a shared focus, across the whole organisation, on the need for everyone to co-operate, collaborate and think, from hour to hour and day to day, about what can be done to realise the Ambition and to deliver on the priorities.

Not three but one

It's easy to see that the Three Delivery Imperatives are heavily interdependent. There are so many stakeholders that you need the support of your wider leadership group to manage them. Equally, though, that extended cadre of leaders is a huge part of today's culture, so you will need these people to lead any change of culture by example.

You also need enough leaders around the team who can be trusted to successfully drive the execution of your key change initiatives. This is necessary to enable the Leadership Team's involvement in execution management to be minimised.

Once these three foundations are in place, the more familiar part of the delivery process – the execution management phase – will run smoother, faster and more successfully.

Why teams struggle

When Delivery Conversations aren't working, the big things just slow down. Sometimes they slow down so much they lose all momentum. The hulls drop into the water, the boat has to butt its way through the waves, progress becomes imperceptible and people lose their optimism and sense of purpose.

As the focus starts to drift, but the imperative to change things remains, people feel the need to start something else. Many businesses are littered with the zombie remains of ambitious projects that started with lots of drive and enthusiasm, and then ground to a halt. It is hard to keep big

Many businesses are littered with the zombie remains of ambitious projects that started with lots of drive and enthusiasm, and then ground to a halt.

transformative changes on track and forging ahead if the agenda is cluttered with stalled or unfinished projects, especially when no-one is quite sure which of them are actually dead and which are still worth working on.

People talk about delivery, but aren't able to deliver change

The leaders I work with often tell me that their Leadership Teams already talk a great deal about delivery. To find out what that means in practice, I ask them two questions:

1. Delivery of what?

2. How is that working out for you?

These questions almost always flush out the same experiences. The first is that the teams are mostly talking about delivery of business-as-usual. That's hard enough. What most Leadership Teams have even more difficulty with, though, is delivering transformational and cross-functional change.

The second question often unleashes a litany of woes. Delivery on the ground is not going nearly as well as it needs to. There are too many things going far too slowly. And because big cross-functional change is always the slowest and most difficult thing to deliver, it is hard to see the impact on business results – which leads to an often irresistible temptation to add yet more initiatives.

Almost all teams start more initiatives than they finish.

The talking Leadership Teams do about delivery is almost always about solving today's problems – all too often at the expense of dealing with the underlying causes.

Too much is started, but too little is finished

Most of the organisations I see are awash with initiatives. I've met Leadership Teams that have lost count of the initiatives they are working on.

This is partly because there are so many, and partly because there is no central place where they can see and assess the big picture. I know one organisation that employs someone just to keep track of these things on a huge spreadsheet. The spreadsheet is updated monthly, but it's never actually consulted because it is so daunting and complicated.

Almost all teams start far more initiatives than they finish. They begin with good intentions, but the initiatives are often abandoned halfway through. They may tail off into nothing, get forgotten or not be properly executed from start to finish. Very few go on to deliver what was originally intended.

Even the most important transformational initiatives are often compromised and watered down until the change that's delivered falls far short of what is wanted.

Bad habits develop

When this happens, opportunities are missed and people get into bad habits.

The natural desire of team members to tick items off the to-do list often leads them to quickly conclude that a project is complete and move on, without assessing whether the initiative has delivered what it was supposed to. They do not measure whether the money and time invested have delivered the expected results.

There is no concerted effort to look at the initiative analytically, compare it with the problems encountered in other projects and learn the vital lessons about how to improve delivery more broadly.

Repeated disappointment breeds cynicism and it becomes hard to approach the next new initiative with quite the same enthusiasm

Repeated disappointment breeds cynicism and it becomes hard to approach the next new initiative with quite the same enthusiasm. People start to assume today's big thing will end up going the way of all its predecessors.

Work migrates upwards

A well-known business fable, first published in the *Harvard Business Review* forty years ago in an article by William Oncken and Donald Wass (Oncken and Wass), gives a graphic reminder of how easy it is for a leader, or a team, to end up doing work that should be in the hands of others.

It tells the story of a CEO who gives his employee an ugly little monkey and asks him to make sure it stays on his shoulder all day and every day. It sounds like a simple enough task, and the man agrees to take it on.

A week later, the boss and the employee have a catch-up meeting to see how the monkey project is getting on. The employee mentions that the task is harder than he thought and that paying for all the bananas the monkey needs is causing a problem.

'OK,' says the CEO. 'Let me see if there's a cheaper way to feed the monkey.'

The conversation ends and, as the employee walks away, the boss catches sight of himself in a mirror and sees the monkey is now perched, grinning, on his own shoulder.

It's all too easy for leaders to allow responsibility for delivery to shift back to them and away from their subordinates. There are a lot of CEOs and Leadership Teams, around with a lot of ugly little monkeys clutching firmly onto their shoulders.

Projects and decisions, even those which have been delegated to other managers, have a habit of percolating back up the organisation to the Leadership Team. Problems that should be solved by subordinates and decisions that should be made lower down are constantly floating up to the Leadership Team, clogging up the agenda and making it hard for the team to focus on the right things.

Because it's quicker and easier to deal with these problems in the Leadership Team than to explore why they percolate up, or to push them back down, many monkeys arrive, and stay, in the boardroom, making it noisy and crowded. Getting anything done is tough, and finding the time and space to address the themes underlying consistently weak delivery becomes ever harder.

Leadership Teams grapple with symptoms, not causes

When Leadership Teams meet to discuss delivery, overcrowded agendas often mean there's no time to discuss everything properly. The serious underlying causes are rarely addressed, so symptoms proliferate, cluttering the agenda and leading to a rash of new sub-initiatives.

Later on, there will probably need to be another initiative to address the problems that should have been dealt with this time around. Meanwhile, unresolved issues can often cause damage throughout the organisation.

Leadership Teams find their agendas become hopelessly cluttered, with less and less time to address the big ideas and the challenges of transformational change.

The role of Delivery Conversations is first to understand, and then find solutions to, the human issues that almost always underlie problems with the pace or effectiveness of delivery – and to find ways of solving the systemic challenges, as well as the immediate ones.

What do great Delivery Conversations look like?

Execution management takes up less of the team's agenda

Leadership Teams will always need to attend to the successful execution of some projects. The difference in high performing teams is that the range of projects they are attending to is more narrowly focused on those that only they can drive.

When the team members talk about these key projects, their involvement is more light touch. Even within the narrow focus on the key projects, they focus their attention and expertise on the issues that can't be solved outside the team. These issues are identified in advance of meetings and the background material is deliberately brief, providing only the information needed to get to grips with them.

This allows the valuable expertise of team members to be brought to bear on the most complex and critical issues facing the organisation. Agenda time is freed for other things that only the top team can handle – the Three Delivery Imperatives.

> *Failure to identify and engage all the interested parties is understandable but often fatal.*

Stakeholders are in the room

Failure to identify and engage all the interested parties is understandable but often fatal. It takes time, thought and discussion, and there are so many stakeholders, with such diverse needs, that it's easy to miss some or misread them. Some of those needs are rational and directly relevant to the task. But being human means that stakeholders also often have needs which are more emotive and it is every bit as important to understand these, too.

Some successful teams regularly invite key stakeholders to join the Leadership Team to work together on important issues. Even when they are not physically present, though, their voice is heard in the room. Their needs and perspectives are consistently and clearly articulated by members of the team.

When the relationships with stakeholders are good, they are referred to as partners rather than challenges to manage. Discussions are more often concerned with how the stakeholders can be recruited to accelerate progress than with removing roadblocks.

The capability of the wider leadership group is actively managed

Every organisation has weaknesses at the level immediately below the Leadership Team. Typically, when it comes to making transformational changes, it becomes painfully obvious that there is not enough leadership talent of the right calibre, in the right places and in the right numbers. There are a few strong leaders, but not enough to do what has to be done.

Leadership Teams find these weaknesses hard to tackle. Individual members find it hard to do within their own teams. Often team members don't have the relationships and confidence to hold their colleagues sufficiently accountable for dealing with the weak links in their own departments.

> *Typically, when it comes to making transformational changes, it becomes painfully obvious that there is not enough leadership talent of the right calibre, in the right places and in the right numbers.*

The challenge, of course, is that everyone seems so much better at spotting the underperformers and troublemakers in other people's departments than in their own. Personal loyalties, defensive attitudes and memories of good past performance can all get in the way.

The best teams see the next tier of leaders as a shared resource for the organisation. They manage the capability, deployment and performance of these people together. By investing time today, they build capacity for the future.

There are regular reviews of the performance of existing members of the wider leadership group and of the gaps in actual and potential capability and numbers.

These discussions lead to addressing problems with underperformers by sensitively but firmly grasping the nettles that need to be grasped. The team actively creates gaps to make it possible to recruit new people, brings in new energy and perspectives and pushes the bar higher for the expectations of leadership at this level.

Culture is what the Leadership Team does, not something it imposes on others

In the absence of the right culture, any change effort will soon sink in a swamp of unhelpful attitudes and destructive behaviours. The Leadership Team can see it, but can't see a way through it. Culture becomes the ultimate insoluble problem, and the very mention of it provokes rolling eyes, deep sighs and a sense of hopeless resignation.

Research by the Hay Group has suggested that 70 per cent of organisational culture is driven by senior leadership behaviour. Put simply, people in the organisation take their cue from what they see the leaders do, not what they say.

The best Leadership Teams understand this. They spend time deciding and articulating the culture that will be needed to meet the challenges facing the organisation and deliver on its Ambition. Unlike the less effective majority, they follow this through, not with posters and screensavers, mouse mats and slogans but by challenging themselves and each other to lead by example.

Once the desired culture is clearly defined, they give one another feedback on what each can do to live the culture in the way he or she operates. They make and share plans for the changes each will personally make. They continually support one another and challenge their colleagues about how they are behaving and what more they could do to model the behaviours that are required.

Once they have wrestled with the challenges of changing their own behaviour, they can begin to work with others, usually starting with the wider leadership group.

Once they have wrestled with the challenges of changing their own behaviour, they can begin to work with others, usually starting with the wider leadership group. Because they now have direct experience of how hard it can be, and what may be needed to help each person make changes, they are far better equipped to do it. Their approach changes from marketing and broadcasting messages to working with each person, providing feedback, support and challenge.

Execution management becomes slicker

Every business, like every army, needs a plan. But, as the Prussian general Helmuth von Moltke famously said, 'No plan survives contact with the enemy.' Plans need to be changed to reflect changing circumstances – anything from an economic downturn or a new competitor to an abruptly altered deadline or the loss of a key employee.

Great Leadership Teams occasionally do the planning themselves, but they usually only do so on the very biggest projects or change programmes. More commonly, they will review plans created by others.

To ensure consistency, there must be a commonly understood framework and approach to plans which is both rigorous and simple. When plans are brought to the Leadership Team, the members will know, therefore, that these will be good and consistent enough for the team to be able to focus its time on understanding, testing and improving what is put before them. Those preparing the plan arrive knowing that the team will engage deeply with it and that they will leave with the support they need to make delivery possible.

This approach extends throughout the life of each project. Those running the project bring simple, clear and thorough updates to the Leadership Team. They have clarified in advance the key issues the Leadership Team needs to understand and the decisions or support that are required. Review sessions are focused and efficient, using up as little of the valuable agenda time as possible and ensuring that the project leader gets what's needed to drive the plan forward.

All this brings a sense of pace and direction, making it far easier to keep change moving forward at speed.

The benefits of Delivery Conversations

Show, not tell, shifts behaviours

In practice, the key to getting the next tier of leaders engaged in changing the overall culture of the organisation is to take others on the same journey the Leadership Team has travelled. When people understand the story that lies behind the change initiative, they can tell the same story themselves to their colleagues and those who report to them.

When they can see and explain in their own words why major change was needed, how the ambition and priorities came into focus, why the vision matters and how attitudes towards working together need to change, they are ready to engage with the effort that follows – and to play their part in leading other employees to do the same.

All the Three Delivery Imperatives shift quickly

All of the Three Delivery Imperatives improve as the Delivery Conversations start to have an impact on the way the Leadership Team operates.

Relationships with stakeholders become easier, and there is a better understanding of their needs. The next tier of leadership is more engaged and offers more candidates with the capabilities to handle key projects. And the culture of the organisation, as it becomes increasingly positive and collaborative, stops being a source of frustration and a barrier to progress and turns into a positive enabling force.

What surprises the Leadership Teams I work with is how quickly these things move.

What surprises the Leadership Teams I work with is how quickly these things move. Shifting the culture and upgrading the capability of the wider leadership group are tasks that will each take some time to complete, but small changes in these things can make a big difference.

Stakeholders' attitudes change when they see the Leadership Team's genuine intention to work with them. They are more prepared to support the team, and more forgiving when things don't go to plan.

The best leaders appreciate it when they see the Leadership Team genuinely starting to grasp the nettles of underperformance, resource allocation and capability. Each small change comes to be seen as evidence that the top team is properly addressing the things that really matter.

People in the organisation are remarkably sensitised to the behaviour and tone set by the Leadership Team and its members. They know and see when that is changing and they follow suit.

Equally significantly, members of the Leadership Team start to feel more positive. The big issues they have known to be underlying so many of their problems are now on the table and being addressed. Frustration and resignation are replaced by optimism and energy. These changes, too, send signals out to the rest of the organisation and create their own positive ripples, further contributing to the momentum.

The nature of the Leadership Team's work changes

As these changes begin to bite, past frustrations give way to a feeling of progress and pace. There's less work for the Leadership Team to do to keep the hulls up and greater confidence the next time there is a key initiative.

The Leadership Team can switch its focus to new priorities and horizons, confident that existing initiatives are moving and will deliver. Less crowded agendas are limited to things that genuinely need the team's input – usually trimming the sails, rather than plotting new courses.

People in the organisation are remarkably sensitised to the behaviour and tone set by the Leadership Team and its members. They know and see when that is changing and they follow suit.

Because there is real clarity about what has to be done, leaders are empowered to deal with the tasks and initiatives they are accountable for without having to discuss every problem with the whole team.

Other members of the Leadership Team can play the role of emergency trouble-shooters, staying in the background but ready to offer their support and expertise if a project looks like running into difficulties.

The whole organisation knows what it's doing

When the Leadership Team is tackling the right things related to delivery, people outside the team, in the next tier of management and further down the chain of command, start to notice that it's getting easier to get things done.

They feel they have the support of the Leadership Team, when it is needed, but that they are also being given more opportunity to use their own initiative. Instead of the traditional meetings where next-tier managers face questions about every aspect of delivery – 'What's going on with this? Tell me about that. Give me every last detail. Why don't we do this? Why don't we do that?' – they find they are expected and trusted to work without this kind of micromanagement.

People respond well to this change of style, and it tends to filter down through the organisation, changing the culture in ways that encourage more creativity and engagement at every level.

Results get better, and the Leadership Team enjoys work more

As the increased focus on execution starts to feed through into better results, the Leadership Team is scrutinised less and challenged less frequently. Stakeholders trust the team more and demand fewer reports and explanations.

The team gains in confidence and becomes less sceptical about future initiatives. Team members are able to look up and focus on new priorities and new horizons, knowing that the existing initiatives are on course for successful delivery.

The working environment and the culture both improve as the team becomes a real joint endeavour, in which the members are mutually supportive, rather than a group of people with separate, sometimes conflicting, responsibilities.

Because the team functions more effectively, the issues that place strains on Leadership Team members' home and family lives – long hours, frustration and disappointing outcomes – all change for the better.

Are Delivery Conversations needed in your team?

Execution Management is needed for teams who want to:

- ▲ Get alignment on all of the key aspects of a project at its inception.
- ▲ Empower the project's leader and team by providing a clear brief and parameters within which to operate.
- ▲ Manage project updates quickly and succinctly – in a way that is most supportive and helpful to the project team.
- ▲ Do all of this with the minimum of paperwork and bureaucracy.

You can see tools for Developing Execution Management, The Project Charter and PINS, on page 296.

If you need to:

- ▲ Assess the team members both for what they deliver and how they do it.

- ▲ Separate those who are, or can be, team players from those likely to have a continuing negative effect on the team's functioning.
- ▲ Decide who to persevere with and support – and where a more direct and decisive solution is required.

See the tool, the Leadership Audit, on page 302.

Accountability Conversations focused on behavioural and cultural change are needed for teams who want to:

- ▲ Set the tone for the culture you want to see in the organisation and to lead cultural change by example.
- ▲ Improve the behaviours in, and functioning of, the Leadership Team.
- ▲ Learn by personal experience what it takes to change behaviour – and what is, therefore, needed to support and accelerate it in others.

If this is what's needed in your team, see the tool, Contracting for Cultural Leadership, described on page 310.

CASE STUDY

Lipstick on a bulldog

A frozen food company had decided on a dramatic change of strategy, aimed at repositioning its familiar breaded-fish products (fish fingers, goujons and fillets in breadcrumbs) to emphasise the health benefits of fish oils and fatty acids. Instead of selling a product that was seen as a cheap and cheerful alternative to a trip down the road to the chip shop, it wanted to be known as a purveyor of healthy, attractive convenience meals.

The Leadership Team approved the plan and assigned accountability for various elements of its execution to specific individuals. ➤

Several departments had to work together to rebrand the new product and make sure it would appeal to a more upmarket customer segment. Operations was busy working to improve the processed fish meals to bring them in line with the needs of a more health-conscious public. Marketing created new packaging, new POS materials for the supermarkets and a range of shiny new brochures and recipe cards, extolling the virtues of eating more fish. Sales focused on ensuring all the major retailers would give the new product freezer space among the premium products, rather than the basic economy lines. The plans made sense, and the Leadership Team settled on a date for delivery.

A couple of months before the deadline, reality dawned. The team suddenly realised it was nowhere near ready to launch successfully. Among other items of bad news, worrying reports from marketing's focus groups indicated that customers were actually less likely to buy the new, revamped product than the old one.

The problem was simply that there had never been a committed, co-ordinated approach across the organisation. There had not been enough – or good enough – Delivery Conversations to lay the foundations for a successful launch.

The Leadership Team had not effectively communicated the decision to rebrand through all the levels of the organisation, and this had created a glaring disconnect between what was promised and what was being delivered.

At the heart of the problem was the fact that the product, the basic frozen breaded fish fillets, seemed to have hardly changed at all. The fish looked and tasted much the same. Though many small improvements had been made, they were undetectable to the customer. Cynical focus group participants simply assumed that the new logo and packaging were the usual marketing hype, bringing no real benefits. A lack of true collaboration between the departments responsible for creating and launching the new product had created a range of issues from inaccurate communication of the product concept to inadequate quality control, and from poor packaging to unimaginative recipe suggestions. ➤

When the storm broke, there was an angry executive team meeting, with raised voices and a lot of finger-pointing. But it was the financial director, to everyone's surprise, who took the lead in turning the team onto a positive track.

'Look,' he said. 'The thing is, we've got lots of different stakeholders involved in this, inside the company and out in the outside world, with a lot of competing requirements. Let's really focus on mapping out who they all are and then see what we can do to reconcile their needs.'

Gradually, the picture became clearer. There were the consumers, of course, who would ultimately decide if the new product was a hit or not. There were the parent company's directors and their financial expectations. And there were the individual departments. The product development people were deeply involved. Production needed to know how much would be needed and when. Marketing needed to be able to plan the media campaign. Sales needed to sell the product in and distribution needed to load the supply chain and get the product out to the supermarkets. What's more, many of these tasks were interdependent.

After an hour, the Leadership Team members realised they really needed to start again from scratch. Diaries were cleared and the team spent the rest of the day in a long, candid Delivery Conversation, based on a collective sense of accountability for the success of the project. A number of key leaders from outside the team were called in to contribute their ideas.

The afternoon's discussions quickly moved beyond getting the original project back on track. It was clear that repackaging and rebranding products that seemed essentially the same was at the heart of the problem. As one team member memorably put it, 'All we're doing here is putting lipstick on a bulldog.'

The team members began to devise a new way of relaunching the company's products. Instead of providing cheap and quick packaged food, they would exploit the trends towards healthy eating and quality home cooking that were being promoted by celebrity chefs and cooking ➤

programmes on TV. They decided to take the best of their products (quick, healthy and easy dinners for busy families) and adopt a premium, restaurant-style approach, positioning them in a completely new way. They would put freshly frozen fish with unusual pre-prepared sauces in a single packet, using a celebrity chef endorsement to add to the impression of quality.

A special cross-functional delivery team was set up, board updates were scheduled for the next three monthly meetings and an energetic communication plan was put in place to make sure everyone in the company was clear about what was going on and how important it was.

The next day, the hard work started. Teams of people were brought together across the organisation to work on packaging, recipes, production, sales and marketing and to find the right celebrity chef to front the campaign and appear on the product packaging. In a huge last-minute effort, the resources of all the organisation's departments were channelled into delivering a high quality product that was clearly different from the original offering.

The product was launched successfully and quickly became a central, and highly profitable, product line, going on to win the company a new customer base of more upmarket (and less price-sensitive) buyers.

Equally importantly, the revised approach to development and launch has become a celebrated template for how to get things done in the organisation. The old culture of isolated work in departmental silos, stitched together by the Leadership Team, has been replaced by one where cross-functional working is the norm on projects of all sizes. The Leadership Team agenda now includes far fewer project updates and far more work on people and culture.

Truly transformational projects like this are very rare. But for these team members, and their organisation, life has never been the same again. ▲

DELIVERY *conversations*

| 0 | 1 | 2 | 3 | 4 | 5 | 6 | 7 | 8 | 9 | 10 |

How consistent and rigorous is your approach to Execution Management?

| 0 | 1 | 2 | 3 | 4 | 5 | 6 | 7 | 8 | 9 | 10 |

To what degree do you have the support required from your stakeholders to make the changes you need?

| 0 | 1 | 2 | 3 | 4 | 5 | 6 | 7 | 8 | 9 | 10 |

How strong is the leadership group below the Leadership Team compared to that needed to deliver your ambition?

| 0 | 1 | 2 | 3 | 4 | 5 | 6 | 7 | 8 | 9 | 10 |

How much does the culture in your organisation facilitate consistent delivery?

| 0 | 1 | 2 | 3 | 4 | 5 | 6 | 7 | 8 | 9 | 10 |

How well does the Leadership Team model the behaviours and disciplines required for quick and efficient delivery?

OVERALL ASSESSMENT FOR DELIVERY CONVERSATIONS

| 0 | 1 | 2 | 3 | 4 | 5 | 6 | 7 | 8 | 9 | 10 |

What is your overall assessment of the Delivery Conversations in your team?

Please mark your overall assessment, and then transfer this score to the assessment summary for your team on pages 240-241.

LEARNING
conversations

Learning Conversations lead to a profound and dramatic transformation in the way the team works. They are the mechanism through which the team is able to explore assumptions and bring together the data, experience and knowledge of all its members.

A TALE FROM THE MAASAI

Learning conversations with the Maasai

Beyond the challenge of day-to-day survival in a harsh, unforgiving environment, one of the main problems facing my Maasai friends is how to preserve their core traditions and culture in the face of rapid and unstoppable change. The elders are well aware of this. The building of a road, the advent of mobile phones, the spread of HIV/AIDS and the tendency for the brightest youngsters to be drawn away to Nairobi by the attractions of education and new career prospects are all posing challenges to the traditional way of life. The Maasai cannot hope to resist the waves of change. But the elders continue to think carefully about when the community should adapt to change and when it should hold out against it.

One of the long-standing traditions of the Maasai warrior culture is the hunting and killing of lions. For a young man to earn his status as a fully-fledged warrior, he has traditionally had to prove his strength and valour by going out alone with his spear and shield and killing a lion, returning in triumph with the lion's mane, tail and claws as proof of his victory.

In the past, when lions were plentiful and were a major threat to the Maasai's cattle and goats, lion hunting served a useful practical purpose. These days, the human population has increased and the number of lions has declined dramatically, falling from an estimated 200,000 a century ago to fewer than 40,000 today.

The continuation of the tradition of solo hunting threatened the lion's continued existence in the Maasai's lands and the elders recognised that a new approach was ➤

needed. The problem they faced was how to preserve the age-old traditions without wiping out the lions completely. Wildlife conservationists have campaigned for the killing of lions to stop and it has been banned by the Kenyan government. These external pressures have caused resentment among the Maasai, who often feel their time-hallowed way of life is under threat.

After much thought, the elders decided they needed to find a way to adapt their hunting traditions to today's realities. They tackled the problem through gathering as many perspectives as they could. This wasn't easy. The lion hunt is a deeply embedded part of Maasai culture, with roots going back many generations.

What has allowed the Maasai to follow this difficult road from tradition to modern pressures has not been a forced or imposed solution. Instead, it has been an alternative approach that handles this delicate discussion as a series of Learning Conversations. All perspectives are valued and explored with respect and understanding. By talking about their ideas in an inclusive and understanding way, the Maasai have been able to make real and sustainable progress.

A solution has taken shape which preserves the rite-of-passage significance of the lion hunt in Maasai culture, while dramatically reducing the number of lions that are killed. These days the young men carry out the lion hunt in groups of ten. One lion is killed and everyone in the group is credited with it.

Further progress is being made, including the creation of other tradition-based rite-of-passage ceremonies that dramatise and celebrate the transition from boy to man and fulfil some of the functions historically associated with the lion hunt.

Among the Maasai today, lion killing is on the wane. It is on the way out because meaningful, constructive, non-confrontational Learning Conversations were held about the practice. Little by little, these helped the Maasai elders and people relax their views, discover the range of different opinions within their own community and discuss new ideas and alternatives. Gradually, the lion hunt is coming to be seen as a celebrated feature of the past, but something that is no longer a fundamental cornerstone of the Maasai culture.

The debate about the lion hunt is obviously very different from the sort of Learning Conversation most Leadership Teams have. But the point is the same, whether in the boardroom or the boma. When it comes to discussing difficult, contentious subjects, the style of the conversation really matters. When members of any group of people decide to talk to each other in an open, exploratory way, entrenched positions can be broken down and new solutions can be found to even the most intractable problems.

Change happens most easily when we get beyond positional, right-and-wrong debates to really understanding and learning from different perspectives. Only then can we create something genuinely new and transformational and move forward together into new futures that were invisible to all at the outset. ▲

What are Learning Conversations?

A Learning Conversation is an exchange in which new insights and understandings are created through exploration, with the potential to create genuinely new options for action.

Learning Conversations call for special attention. They don't just happen. For most leadership groups, conversations that lead to real exploration and creative options are rare.

In fact, conversations within Leadership Teams are usually full of assertion and certainty, even when neither is warranted. As a friend of mine once put it about a colleague of ours, 'He's sometimes right and sometimes wrong, but he's always certain!'

Opportunities for learning – for better understanding, new insights and different options for action – are undervalued, overlooked and often completely missing.

Discussion and dialogue

There are two distinct types of learning conversation, both important and constructive in different ways:

- ▲ Conversations in which there is an attempt to understand something new, to seek new knowledge or insight and to find new options.
- ▲ Conversations in which people actively reflect on what they can do to enhance their own effectiveness or that of the team.

Both types are founded on alternative ways of interacting (Senge, 2006).

What distinguishes Learning Conversations from most of the discourse in Leadership Teams is best understood by the difference between discussion and dialogue:

Discussion occurs when different views are being put forward. They are usually presented as the 'best' or 'correct' answers and are usually met with counter-assertions that also claim to be 'best' or 'correct'. Views are stacked up against each other and competing positions are taken. Talking like this about important issues can be useful, as it can get all the points of view out into the open.

But when all conversations are like this, opportunities are missed. There is no chance to reflect on assumptions underpinning views or experiences that might be relevant. As a result, there is no opportunity to combine different perspectives into a richer and more powerful understanding that is a synthesis of all the knowledge and experience present.

Instead, the outcome is usually a 'win/lose' scenario in which one existing view prevails and the value in the others is lost.

Dialogue takes place when people engage in a creative exploration of subtle or complex issues, or things they don't yet know enough about. In dialogue, participants invite exploration and alternative views, rather than just defending their positions or assertions. Instead of opposing each other, people collectively explore the matter in hand and their respective understandings of it.

This is a much more uncommon form of discourse in Leadership Teams. Most of us have some experience of it, however brief or infrequent. How many times have you been in win/lose discussions in your team? How does that feel? How often does dialogue emerge – and how does that feel by contrast?

> *'He's sometimes right and sometimes wrong, but he's always certain!'*

'I told you so'

How we each experience reality – as individuals and as teams – is always a product of our past and current thinking.

If a Leadership Team believes that a particular market is extremely competitive, for example, its members are almost bound to fall prey to what psychologists call 'confirmation bias', seeing proof of their hypothesis everywhere.

How they examine any situation and address it when they launch new products and deal with their suppliers and customers is all informed by their view that the market is competitive. This, of course, becomes self-fulfilling as they seek and notice further 'evidence' that it is a difficult environment, with few new opportunities to be explored.

But if team members believe they see opportunities and market gaps that are not well catered for, their discussions, questions, research activity and organisational focus will be quite different. They are likely to find what they are expecting to find – that the market does indeed offer inviting opportunities.

I've frequently seen Leadership Teams talk themselves into certainty about 'facts' which are not objectively true and which limit or eliminate the possibility of new thinking or different solutions.

In *On Dialogue*, the physicist David Bohm explains the distinction between dialogue and discussion: (Bohm, 1996)

Bohm points out that 'dialogue' comes from the Greek word dialogos. With 'logos' meaning 'word' and 'dia' meaning 'through'. Thinking about the word in this sense emphasises the communication and creation of meaning or ideas through the flow of words that passes between people.

This kind of generative interaction has the capacity to lead to new insights and thinking, which may not have been the starting point at all. These outcomes are, by definition, creative.

Bohm contrasts this with the word 'discussion,' which has the same root as 'percussion' and 'concussion'. It emphasizes the idea of people presenting a range of different views which are colliding with one another and competing for supremacy.

The emphasis moves to evaluation and analysis of each idea to see which has the most merit. This has benefits in some situations but doesn't help us get far from the understandings and ideas we had at the outset.

These range from blaming financial performance on the weather to dismissing whole segments of the market as inherently unprofitable or concluding that there are no good people anywhere in the organisation who can be brought in to work on a project.

Conversations that assume the immutability of a particular situation lock the team into a fixed position, making it hard to see beyond the current perspective.

Feeling defensive

Learning Conversations get beyond our psychological instinct to defend our views. Indeed, there is convincing research that shows we only have to choose to adopt a particular opinion to become doggedly

CONFIRMATION BIAS

Most of us like to believe our beliefs are the result of years of objective analysis of the information we have available. The reality is that we are all susceptible to the problem known as a confirmation bias. While we like to imagine that our beliefs are rational, logical and objective, our ideas are actually often based on paying attention to the information that supports our ideas and ignoring anything that challenges our existing beliefs.

A simple example would be a person who believes left-handed people are more creative than right-handers. Whenever they encounter someone who is both left-handed and creative, they will place great importance on this 'evidence' in support of the existing belief. The person led astray by confirmation bias may even actively seek out 'proof' that further backs up this belief, while discounting examples that do not support the theory.

committed to it – even if we were initially quite undecided. The fanaticism of the convert is potentially present in all of us.

It's in our nature to want to defend our perspectives. When people challenge our opinions, we're inclined to respond defensively, without understanding how our reaction limits the available options (Argyris, Chris, 1991). We don't reflect on our assumptions, explore what others think and why, or open up our thought processes. As a result, we become trapped in our current understanding, with access to only a limited and static range of solutions.

> 'No man ever steps in the same river twice, for it is not the same river and he is not the same man'
> Heraclitus

Reacting defensively is a simple by-product of how we have adapted to our complex environment. To function effectively, we reduce the cognitive strain, building a simplified picture of the world to make it easier to navigate. Most of the time this is very helpful, allowing us to handle familiar challenges with little thought or effort. We see people and situations as stereotypes, which makes them easier to understand.

Argyris' Ladder of Inference

But while this gives us crude guidelines on how to respond in different situations, it narrows our options by inhibiting us from exploring situations in more detail. No situation is, of course, exactly like any other. These simplifying stereotypes stop us exploring, or even being aware of, the complexities and subtleties of this situation that make it different.

Defensive behaviour can operate and create self-fulfilling prophecies at all levels.

Business theorist Chris Argyris has developed a model called the Ladder of Inference that explains why people get into conflict so often, and why resolution can seem so difficult (Argyris, 1990). Our brains absorb torrents of information all the time, impatiently jumping to conclusions based on this data before they have had any time to analyse it properly.

Once we understand how inference works, and how destructive it can be, we can begin to dismantle the inferences we have made, understand our situation better and find new ways forward.

In Leadership Teams the malign influence of inference takes two main forms. It prevents genuine exploration and synthesis of views of situations and it corrodes cohesion by building up suspicions about other team members and their motives.

I once worked with a client where two of the Leadership Team were constantly falling out. Darren felt that Rosemarie was political and manipulative. He had become entrenched in this position and, unconsciously, defensive of it.

The way he reacted to her elicited behaviour from her that seemed to confirm his view. When they had to work together, he was reluctant to share his viewpoint, worrying that she might steal his ideas or use things he said against him.

Rosemarie, in turn, picked up this lack of openness, and formed her own suspicions about Darren's motives. Because they were reluctant to communicate openly with each other, they would discuss one another with other team members to try to understand what was happening and to express their frustrations.

Inevitably, both would hear on the grapevine about elements of these conversations, and this would increase their frustration and irritation. It was a difficult cycle to break. Even when they began to discuss the issues as part of the team development programme, both initially interpreted the other person's attempts to be open through the lens of the negative motives they had already assumed. Even honesty was seen as potentially devious and manipulative.

Only as they developed their relationship and were able to examine their own prejudices and assumptions together were they able to see the part they had played in the antagonistic relationship. Through doing this they were gradually able to allay their entrenched suspicions, build trust and improve the quality of their work together beyond all recognition. ▲

Learning Conversations in Leadership Teams

Individuals are psychologically predisposed to drawing conclusions by inferring them from data that they colour with their existing beliefs and prejudices. Without being conscious of it, they systematically seek and find evidence to further cement those beliefs.

When they come together as teams, this tendency to seek confirming evidence for what people already believe is magnified. Finding new ways to understand and respond to the complex and changing situation that Leadership Teams have to deal with is limited by their existing beliefs – which are at best incomplete and often inaccurate.

Finding new insights and options for action is then made more difficult by the propensity of any group – and particularly a Leadership Team that's full of strong personalities with strongly held views – to interact by debating, rather than exploring. Discussion, rather than dialogue, tends to be the dominant form of discourse. The result is that instead of new ideas or knowledge being created by synthesising the expertise and experience of the entire team, one of the competing views comes out on top.

Learning Conversations are the antidote to these risks. When they are successful, teams deliberately introduce more dialogue to combine the wisdom present into new conceptions of the problems they face and creative alternatives for how to address them. As well as leading to better consideration of the external issues, Learning Conversations also help the team members reflect on and continually improve the way they work together.

> *Once we understand how inference works, and how destructive it can be, we can begin to dismantle the inferences we have made, understand our situation better and find new ways forward.*

Why teams struggle

When Learning Conversations are missing, team discussions become, as one client once described it, 'like a group of TV screens around a table. Each broadcasting to a row of deaf and unresponsive other'. Trying to manage those kinds of interactions is exhausting. What's worse is the knowledge that so much more should be possible.

Every team member knows that both they and their colleagues have so much more to offer. Surely it ought to be possible for a team with such diverse talents, experience and knowledge to do better to create new insights and fresh options. Why does that seem so difficult?

'Facts' are traded and arguments flare up

Conversations often turn into verbal battles because of the defensive mechanisms that kick in when people feel their positions are threatened. Each member is wanting to win the argument, rather than engaging in a more creative dialogue and finding a better understanding or solution.

Conversations can become a series of exchanges of views, all presented as 'facts' or 'truths'. Nobody recognises that each view is subjective, so new perspectives and explorations of the team's assumptions and prejudices are not encouraged.

The team can end up with increasingly polarised views, with no common ground and no way to reconcile the opposing positions. Some views are advanced so strongly that other team members feel there is no point in arguing, even if they are unconvinced, and react by becoming passive. This can lead to lengthy, sometimes repeated, exchanges that don't reach a conclusion or which reach a less than optimal answer.

Teams fail to understand the entire elephant

Teams miss opportunities by relying on different but incomplete assumptions, data and experience.

You probably know the old Indian story about five blind men trying to describe an elephant. Each of them feels a different part of the animal. When they compare notes, it leads to a furious argument.

'An elephant? It's like a thick canvas fire hose!' cries the man who felt the trunk.

'It is hard, cold and shiny,' claims the man who felt a tusk.

'It grows on a single thick, rough bough, like the mighty devil tree,' says the man who felt a leg.

'It is like a piece of rope,' insists the man who felt the tail.

'Nonsense,' says the man who felt an ear. 'You're all wrong. An elephant is flat and leathery and flaps from side to side.'

Like the blind men, the members of Leadership Teams often have to rely on incomplete evidence. They could combine their knowledge and expertise and maybe get to see the bigger picture. But pressures of time, old habits, poor relationships and defensive reasoning get in the way.

Both the internal environment (the organisation) and the external one (markets and stakeholders) are so fantastically complex that they require the most complete synthesis of understanding from all of the team to grasp and respond to. Anything less is not enough – but anything less is what most Leadership Teams settle for most of the time.

Leadership Teams can start to make sense of this complexity only when their members successfully exchange information about all of the parts of the elephant that are within the grasp of each person.

Defensive positions lead to a lack of learning

Consciously or unconsciously, team members are led by their desire to find conclusions (usually their own) quickly. Exploration makes things more complex and confusing and increases discomfort. It also extends the length of the discussion – and time is always at a premium.

Each person, therefore, presses for a quick resolution, and this leads to competing resolutions being argued ever more forcefully. This, in turn, leads to defensive positions being adopted, making genuine exploration and understanding even more difficult – compromising the final conclusion.

All this creates a series of problems that hamper the quality of exchanges within the Leadership Team.

> *Consciously or unconsciously, team members are led by their desire to find conclusions (usually their own) quickly.*

- ▲ People don't reflect on their own assumptions or examine where they are coming from and why. What are the past experiences that have led me to this conclusion? Where are those experiences relevant to this issue? In what way does this issue differ from them?
- ▲ Team members don't explore why others think the way they do. Why do others hold those views? What do my colleagues know about this that I don't? How might that be valuable?
- ▲ Team members present their own thoughts in ways that don't invite exploration. The approach is often 'This is the way it is', rather than 'It seems to me that…because…What do you think?'

Some issues become no-go areas

In many Leadership Teams, members know from bitter experience that some topics just can't be discussed. They learn that some issues trigger difficult reactions from one or more people in the team, and that it's easier not to go there. Sometimes these 'undiscussables' are based on real past experiences, and sometimes they are founded on myths and supposition. Either way, it's often these very issues that most urgently need to be explored and understood, so that the team can find new ways to address them.

It is all too easy for leaders themselves to create a situation where key issues become no-go areas for the Leadership Team. Peter Senge tells a story in his book, *The Fifth Discipline* (Senge, 2006), that illustrates the point perfectly.

One forceful CEO recently lamented to me about the absence of 'real leaders' in his organisation. He felt his company was full of compliant people, not committed visionaries. This was especially frustrating to a man who regards himself as a skilled communicator and risk-taker. In fact, he is so brilliant at articulating his vision that he intimidates everyone around him.

Consequently, his view is rarely challenged publicly. People have learned not to express their own views and vision around him. While he would not see his own forcefulness as a defensive strategy, or as a cause of the problems that frustrate him, if he looked carefully, he would see that it functions in exactly that way. ▲

(Senge, *The Fifth Discipline*, 1990)

It's easy for leaders who are short of time and under pressure to get results to push too hard or be dismissive of other viewpoints. But this may leave them seeming isolated and dictatorial. When they look around for help, support and alternative viewpoints, they are unlikely to find them. They will inevitably reduce the capacity and inclination of those around them to think critically or creatively or challenge bad ideas, and many of the most important benefits of true Leadership Team co-operation may be lost.

No business leaders are likely to see themselves as browbeating or dismissive and many of these problems are invisible to them. They will be visible to others, though. Being able to discuss and explore them in the team offers the prospect of first bringing them into awareness and then finding new and better ways to work with each other and with the rest of the organisation.

People settle for poor compromises and the biggest problems are left unresolved

Most organisations are held back by a relatively small number of underlying issues, yet most teams spend most of their time dealing reactively with the multiple symptoms of each. Performance inevitably suffers when the Leadership Team fails to understand or address these deep-rooted challenges.

It is all too easy for leaders themselves to create a situation where key issues become no-go areas for the Leadership Team.

Teams that don't hold effective Learning Conversations tend to have unproductive meetings that get bogged down in heated discussions that are never resolved or in which the same issues are raised over and over again.

Debates are often settled (if at all) by defaulting to an easy decision, or by the leader deciding or deferring the issue. The result is that the team leaves the room frustrated, with a conclusion that doesn't address the underlying problem.

These outcomes are profoundly unsatisfying. People are left wondering why the team needs to spend so much time to achieve so little. Team members know the issue needs resolution for the organisation to genuinely take a step forward, and they feel frustrated when they know this has not been achieved. As well as its impact on the decision at hand, this also undermines the motivation and willingness in the team to get to grips with future issues.

What does a good learning conversation look like?

Leadership Teams hold conversations all the time, so how can you recognise a genuine Learning Conversation? Let's look at the key characteristics.

Views are presented in ways that invite exploration

There's a different intensity when a Learning Conversation is going on. Instead of the ferocity of a debate, with competing solutions battling for supremacy, thought and reflection bring a different tempo.

Most team members, if not all, are engaged with the issue. Even if it's not a subject they know about, they are able to make a contribution by asking questions.

Discourse tends to be either slower and more thoughtful or, later, rapid and energetic, with ideas tumbling out in quick succession.

What makes this possible is the way all the team members add their own perspectives, expertise, experience or ideas as contributions to the conversation. Rather than being offered as answers or solutions, these are introduced as additions to the collective pool of knowledge that may help others understand the situation.

Most of all, Learning Conversations feature more questions. In order to understand the issue, team members, and the team collectively, actively seek new ideas, perspectives and input to expand the resources that are available to help in addressing the problem at hand.

Teams build understanding together

Learning Conversations increase awareness and understanding of what is happening, in the organisation and outside, and how the team might respond. This involves exploring and comparing the knowledge and assumptions of everyone in the meeting.

> 'When you change the way you look at things, the things you look at change'
> Max Planck

When team members all have the same information in front of them, but are reaching different conclusions, Learning Conversations explore how their experiences and assumptions are leading them to these different points of view. They determine what is useful in individuals' perspectives and what will help the team and the organisation move forward. Through this exploration, the team creates and embraces new opportunities for change, which in turn lead to a different set of outcomes.

Learning Conversations spark meaningful dialogue. When they are working well, team members are able to challenge their own assumptions, change their perspectives, examine their conclusions and modify the actions they take.

This happens when team members are willing to let go of the need to be right or to have the answers. When this is happening, you hear comments like, 'I might have been wrong' or 'I see now that my view was incomplete' or even just 'There's more to this than I thought.'

This might sound straightforward, but it can be hard. It takes conscious effort for individuals within the team to reframe their views of the others and see those who disagree with them as colleagues with different points of view, rather than adversaries.

When the blind men are able to accept that they only have partial information and begin to share what each of them knows about the elephant, they can piece together a much more complete picture of the enigmatic beast.

Conversations are kept on track

In every conversation, there are two elements. The more familiar element is the content of the conversation – the subject matter being discussed. The less obvious element is the process of the conversation, the approach being taken by the group to tackling the task at hand.

Within a successful Leadership Team, it is often the element of conflict that sparks fresh insights and understandings and creates a stimulating, rewarding environment.

Effective Leadership Teams recognise the role and value of process. There are a variety of ways of managing process from using a dedicated facilitator (external or internal), using the meeting 'chair' to manage it or sharing the responsibility of attending to process.

Each approach has its advantages and disadvantages, but recognising and actively managing the process produces more purposeful and productive interactions.

Honesty and directness sparks productive conflict

Effective learning conversations are built around a healthy, productive examination of different ideas, information and perspectives.

Within a successful Leadership Team, it is often the element of conflict that sparks fresh insights and understandings and creates a stimulating, rewarding environment. There is a considerable body of academic research that demonstrates that conflict is valuable, as well as inevitable, within Leadership Teams (Eisenhardt, Kahwajy, and Bourgeois, 1997).

Critically, however, that conflict is about how ideas collide and spark new possibilities or questions, rather than being about the expression of interpersonal hostility or ideas competing for victory.

The process of conversation has many dimensions, but can be simplified to include just five key elements:

Sequence. What is the best order to address each component of the issue?

There are many models for this, but we use a variant on the GROW model: What is the Goal we are seeking to achieve? What do we know (and not know) about the current Reality? What Options do we have? What are the merits of those options? Which option Will we choose? (Whitmore, 2002)

Contributions. How are we making sure that all the relevant inputs have been heard?

Who has spoken? Who hasn't spoken? Who needs to speak or has an important contribution?

Emotions. What's going on in the human dimension?

Who is engaged and who isn't? What unspoken dynamics are at work? Who needs what if a successful conclusion is to be reached?

Time. Are we going to get the job done in the time that's available?

How much time should we take? Where are we in the intended sequence, in relation to the time we have left? If we're off track, should we pursue the issue that has emerged or divert back to the original plan?

Decision. What mechanism is the group going to use to reach its conclusions?

Is a decision needed? If not, what is the right way to conclude? If a decision is required, how will that be made? (See also Collective Accountability on page 137.)

In the best conversations within a Leadership Team, team members co-operate with real honesty and directness.

When team members trust each other to challenge one another candidly and constructively, the Leadership Team is able to bring all its experience and brainpower to bear on deciding what is needed to resolve the issue at hand.

The boardroom becomes a classroom

Too often, Leadership Team meetings are seen as a bear pit – a place where people must fight for survival and do battle to win support or resources for their own priorities.

In high performing teams, the exchange of perspectives and the deep examination of issues and members' assumptions makes the experience of meetings very different. While difficult debates are both important and inevitable, Learning Conversations are common and new insights, understanding and ideas are generated.

Too often, Leadership Team meetings are seen as a bear pit – a place where people must fight for survival and do battle to win support or resources for their own priorities.

Team members experience the time spent together as important, insightful and generative. They emerge with more confidence, more energy and more capability to deal with whatever is put before them in the future.

The benefits of learning conversations

Learning Conversations lead to a profound and dramatic transformation in the way the team works. They are the mechanism through which the team is able to explore assumptions and bring together the data, experience and knowledge of all its members. Learning Conversations are the key to recognising new possibilities and options for action.

The team can see the big picture

Learning Conversations help the Leadership Team explore and synthesise the vast amount of expertise its members possess. They help team members make sense of the immensely complex set of data that's available about the organisation, the marketplace, the customers and the competition.

A Leadership Team that can understand the elephant by taking data and turning it into actionable information through the expertise and experiences of all its members is already on course to develop a significant edge over its competition.

Positions are held more flexibly and skilfully

Members of Leadership Teams can't help bringing their own assumptions to meetings. They bring with them a variety of positions – including some on which they are open-minded and others where they may feel compromise is not an option.

By engaging in Learning Conversations, they can manage these positions more skilfully and flexibly. As the language shifts from 'Here's how it is…' or 'Obviously, we must…' to 'Well, the way I see it is…' and 'Here is my analysis…', the way is opened for new and more creative ways of thinking and working.

New possibilities emerge

Fresh approaches and solutions take shape and are brought into focus as Leadership Team members piece together the many understandings and insights available within the team.

Dialogue and respectful discussion free the individuals to explore everyone's views and synthesise from them new and imaginative ways of addressing underlying issues that have seemed impossible to resolve.

> *Learning Conversations help the Leadership Team explore and synthesise the vast amount of expertise its members possess. They help team members make sense of the immensely complex set of data that's available about the organisation, the marketplace, the customers and the competition.*

Understanding leads to trust

As members of the team get to understand each other better, their relationships become closer and more trusting. As Corinne De Staël put it two centuries ago, 'To know all is to forgive all', and simply having more insight into each other's motives and concerns makes potential adversaries more welcoming of different viewpoints.

Getting to know each other better also helps team members

recognise one another's complementary strengths, value them more highly and use each other in new ways.

Even tough conversations make the team stronger

As we saw earlier (see page 196), simply being a Leadership Team means that there are many forces which tend to push team members apart, set up one person against another and diminish the team's ability to work powerfully together (Oshry, 2007).

When Learning Conversations become characteristic of the way the team works together, trust between members of the team builds. Individuals feel that board meetings are a place where important problems get solved and where they can find support and solutions for the issues facing them.

Are Learning Conversations needed in your team?

Learning Conversations are needed for teams who want to:

- ▲ Develop a deeper, more complete and more insightful understanding of issues, find better solutions and decisions and deliver improved results.
- ▲ See the big picture and take full advantage of the range of experience, knowledge and insight that's available across the team.
- ▲ Have meetings that build shared meaning, rather than leading to collisions that foster disagreement, frustration and confusion.
- ▲ Find a quick and systematic way to reflect on and continually improve the way members work together.
- ▲ Lead by example, by consistently seeking to learn and improve.
- ▲ Adopt a single simple review tool that has a wide variety of applications and can be used to get better results on a range of other issues.

If this is what's needed in your team, you can see tools for developing Learning Conversations, Structured Dialogue and Good, Tricky, Do Differently, on pages 316-329.

The team that learned to learn

A company I worked with that produced kitchen equipment for independent takeaway food outlets had been struggling for years, missing its profit targets with wearying predictability.

At the beginning of each year, the directors told the parent company how much they realistically felt they could make. Each year, they were told 'Not enough' and presented with a new, much higher, target. When they duly failed to hit the revised target, they would come under pressure from the parent to cut costs. So they'd cut costs, and that, of course, made it hard to invest in making any effective change for the better. The company was stuck in a downward spiral of decreasing profitability.

Conversations at team meetings tended to start from a defeatist position.

'We can't go on like this,' someone would say. 'We'll have to cut back. We can't sustain this cost base with sales at this level.'

This negative but apparently logical perspective was presented each year as inescapable fact, the only possible starting point. But eventually the sales and operations team came up with an impassioned counter-argument.

'We can't cut costs any further,' the sales director lamented. 'We're already struggling to service the customers we've got – and we won't be winning many new customers if we have to cut the sales force any further.'

Again, this was stated as blunt fact. Shoulders slumped and energy drained away.

We'd been working on Learning Conversations and the CEO, Sabine, consciously tried to set the meeting on a better course.

'OK,' she said with more than a little frustration in her voice. 'Our sales and service costs are too high for the revenue we're producing, so there's pressure on us to bring ➤

them into line. But if we take money away from sales and customer service, things will just get worse. Let's think about this. How can we reconcile these two facts? What other data can we consider?'

The two perspectives – the parent company's and the CEO's – were actually describing different parts of the elephant, different aspects of the organisation. Each of these points of view was largely correct, as far as it went. But neither of them was the whole story.

Exploring the CEO's question led to a discussion about the wasted costs and inefficiencies in the ways different departments worked together. A number of processes that involved the whole organisation were identified and the team started by looking at two of them, new product development and order fulfilment. Both were regular sources of friction between departments and all agreed that there was huge scope for better outcomes, as well as reduced costs.

The Leadership Team started to spell out the challenge in a new way. Members would have to find ways to get their people to work together to resolve the issues, despite the poor relationships that had hampered co-operation between departments. They did this by working as a close-knit team and involving leaders from the next level, so that they could demonstrate the collaborative and constructive ways that they had learned to work together.

As these conversations continued, a bigger plan was taking shape. It took several off-site events in which the Leadership Team members talked, compared notes, explored possibilities and practised increasingly cross-disciplinary thinking before they were able to formulate a new plan for breaking out of the cycle of underperformance.

By the time the idea was ready to present to the parent company, the plan was strong. It was also radical, and required some investment support, so there was some trepidation in the air ahead of the presentation.

The team's plan was to break out of the accepted boundaries of the industry. Rather than being just a supplier of commercial catering equipment, the plan was to work in partnership with a food manufacturer to develop a range ➤

of very high quality ready meals that could be prepared and presented attractively in the cramped environment of their customers' premises, using the company's standard equipment.

This would help the company's customers respond to a number of the challenges facing them. By enabling them to offer interesting new menus for their less price-sensitive diners, it would help their margins and add extra value to the supplier relationship. It also simplified the buying process for the operators, who had previously been restricted by the fact that many products they would have liked to sell were hard to store and prepare with limited kitchen facilities.

The proposal clearly had potential and it soon won the support and investment it needed from the parent organisation, becoming the first successful step in rebuilding the company's market position. It had only emerged because of the shift to a Learning Conversation prompted by the CEO's question. ▲

WHAT MAKES A HIGH PERFORMING LEADERSHIP TEAM?

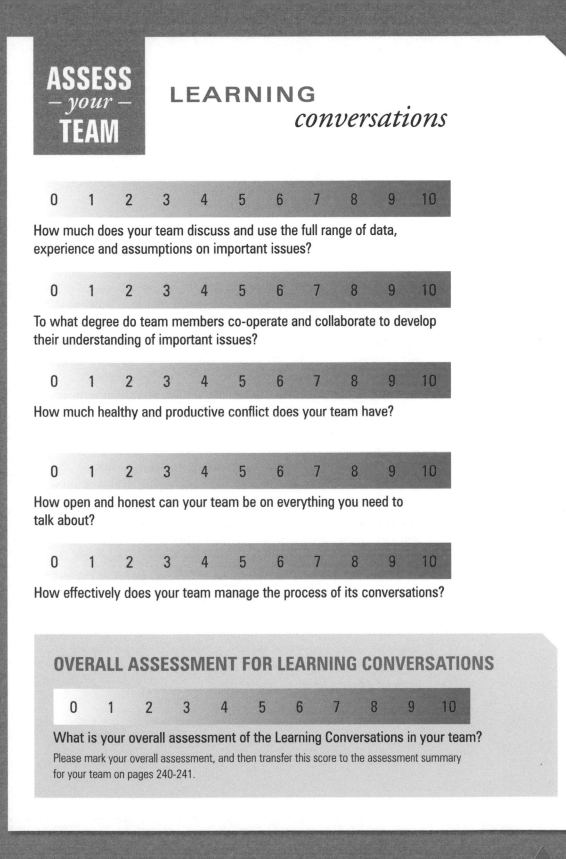

ASSESS
— *your* —
TEAM

LEARNING *conversations*

| 0 | 1 | 2 | 3 | 4 | 5 | 6 | 7 | 8 | 9 | 10 |

How much does your team discuss and use the full range of data, experience and assumptions on important issues?

| 0 | 1 | 2 | 3 | 4 | 5 | 6 | 7 | 8 | 9 | 10 |

To what degree do team members co-operate and collaborate to develop their understanding of important issues?

| 0 | 1 | 2 | 3 | 4 | 5 | 6 | 7 | 8 | 9 | 10 |

How much healthy and productive conflict does your team have?

| 0 | 1 | 2 | 3 | 4 | 5 | 6 | 7 | 8 | 9 | 10 |

How open and honest can your team be on everything you need to talk about?

| 0 | 1 | 2 | 3 | 4 | 5 | 6 | 7 | 8 | 9 | 10 |

How effectively does your team manage the process of its conversations?

OVERALL ASSESSMENT FOR LEARNING CONVERSATIONS

| 0 | 1 | 2 | 3 | 4 | 5 | 6 | 7 | 8 | 9 | 10 |

What is your overall assessment of the Learning Conversations in your team?

Please mark your overall assessment, and then transfer this score to the assessment summary for your team on pages 240-241.

CONCLUSION

From ideas to action

I hope that by now you feel you've developed some insight into the significance of Leadership Teams and the relationship between their effectiveness and the results they achieve.

I hope, too, that thinking about the Six Conversations has helped you reach some conclusions about where your own team is strong and where the emphasis needs to be placed for it to move forward.

I'm sure that you'll have been reflecting on your own team as you've been reading this book. If you've got this far, I'm pretty sure you'll have recognised that there is room for improvement in how it operates.

My greatest aspiration for you, then, is that you are sufficiently inspired by what you have read to take some action to change things.

If you want to change the way your Leadership Team works, so that it helps you deal more effectively with the real issues, so that you can achieve great things together and take the organisation to a new level, you're probably itching to know how you might do that.

The next section takes these ideas and shows how you can get started on developing your own team. I'll set out the steps you need to take, and the order to tackle them in, to embark on the journey.

Section 4 takes these ideas further by providing a set of tools to employ in the programme to learn, embed and sustain the Six Conversations, and to move the organisation forward towards achieving better results.

A parting imperative from the Maasai

You may be thinking that my references to an exotic community from a distant and incredibly different place have little to do with modern business life in your boardroom.

But is that really true? The environment that businesses are operating in is every bit as brutal – and the weakest can and do die. Organisations that constantly struggle to squeeze out a percentage point or two of growth each year are operating in subsistence and survival mode, rather than thriving.

The key issue that stops many organisations successfully addressing their problems – including those that stand in the way of real progress – is the prevalence of dysfunction in their Leadership Teams. What's needed is a way of operating together that makes the most of the extraordinary power of groups of people to deal with huge, even existential, challenges.

If your Leadership Team was able to genuinely operate in the interests of the collective good, and make individual and departmental needs a secondary consideration, just how far could you go?

That is exactly what the Maasai excel in, and we can learn from them. It is the key to unlocking the door to a better future. If your Leadership Team was able to genuinely operate in the interests of the collective good, and make individual and departmental needs a secondary consideration, just how far could you go? ▲

SECTION 3

Changing your team

13 UNDERSTANDING
the journey

Knowing there's a problem in the way our Leadership Teams work together is not enough. Creating and – equally importantly – sustaining the changes is a matter of changing the ways team members interact with each other.

In Section 1, I explained the nature of Leadership Teams and what makes them different. In Section 2, I went on to explain each of the Six Conversations, why they don't always happen, what they look like when they go well and the benefits that flow from them.

I hope that you have found this grounding interesting and illuminating. Even if you have, though, that's not enough. The theories and ideas for us, as for you, are only valuable if they make it possible to make real changes in teams.

This section of the book is dedicated to explaining the techniques and methods we have developed and refined at OneThirdMore, so that you can understand them and use them in your own team.

Before we get into practical steps though, we need to understand some things about the changes we're trying to make.

Creating a high performing team requires behavioural change

Most members of Leadership Teams know what they need to do to be more effective as individuals. But that isn't the same as doing it. If knowledge was all it took to change behaviour, nobody would ever smoke cigarettes or be overweight.

In the same way, knowing there's a problem in the way our Leadership Teams interact and work together is not enough. Creating and – equally importantly – sustaining the changes is a matter of changing the ways team members interact with each other. It's about their behaviour. And anyone who has tried to give up smoking or lose weight knows how hard that can be.

Alan Deutschman's modern classic on behavioural change, *Change or Die*, identifies what he calls the Three Rs of change – Relate, Repeat and Reframe.

> *It's about their behaviour. And anyone who has tried to give up smoking or lose weight knows how hard that can be.*

CHANGE OR DIE

According to change guru Alan Deutschman (Deutschman, 2007), patients who have had major surgery find it extraordinarily hard to shake off their old, bad habits, even when they are told that it is, literally, a matter of life and death.

Deutschman points to research about patients needing coronary bypass or angioplasty operations. These people are told that the procedure will resolve the immediate issue but that if they don't change their lifestyle (stop smoking, eat better and take more exercise), the condition will return and it will kill them, probably quite quickly.

Even faced with this blunt choice between changing their behaviour or dying, 90 per cent of these patients do not manage to make and maintain the necessary changes.

Deutschman describes this approach to change as the Three F's – Fear, Facts and Force – and says that this example is powerful evidence that it simply doesn't work when it comes to human behavioural change. If even the threat of death won't persuade us to mend our ways, what chance do we have of making changes with less mortal consequences?

If this is a dispiriting message, he goes on to describe a more successful approach to persuading heart patients to save their own lives.

There have been some well-documented trials in recent years that have shown that dramatically different outcomes can be achieved, and with patients who suffer from the very same conditions. ➤

In these trials, the doctors took quite a different tack. They assembled the patients in groups that met regularly. As well as getting the benefits of mutual support, they were taught relaxation techniques, healthy cooking and a range of other methods to support their changes.

The difference was spectacular. An impressive 85 per cent of the patients in these groups achieved sustained behavioural change.

Deutschman goes on to discuss a number of other successful examples of behavioural change techniques, with the psychological theories underpinning them, and demonstrates how these all share common characteristics. He calls them the Three Rs.

Relate

All change is made in relationships. By introducing new relationships and involving those with whom individuals already have relationships, people start to believe they can change. The previously existing relationships will also have played a part in sustaining past problems, so the new and changed relationships help by altering the environment to one that gives better support for the changes.

Repeat

Sustained success requires the individual to learn, practise, refine and master the new habits needed. A lot of repetition is required before these changes feel easy, natural and comfortable.

Reframe

Through the new relationship, and the repetition of new habits, individuals learn new ways of thinking about the issues and themselves. Ultimately, they start looking at things in ways that would have been completely alien to them before the process began. ▲

In a Leadership Team context, the three Rs required for sustained change imply:

Relate

Everyone in the team, and some who aren't a part of it, will need to be involved since they are all involved in sustaining the present situation and need to make changes to create an environment that supports change for each individual.

There is also significant benefit in introducing new people or relationships to the team as this will automatically shift the personal dynamics. This is one of the reasons why it is so much easier to use a facilitator, rather than trying to manage the process within the team.

Repeat

The team will need to learn, practise and master new processes, habits and ways of interacting. These will feel awkward and unnatural at first, so it is vital to sustain, and learn from, these efforts over a period of time.

Without a sustained effort and the repetition and practice this permits, any positive changes will quickly decay. This is why one-off awaydays, or sporadic team events, never produce lasting results.

Reframe

Gradually, often imperceptibly, people learn to think differently about what it means to be a Leadership Team, the part they should play in it and how they can contribute. They begin to see the team and their meetings, for the first time, as a positive place that helps solve the problems facing them personally as well as dealing with the bigger issues that the business needs to resolve to move forward.

It is easier to act yourself into a new way of thinking, than it is to think yourself into a new way of acting.

To accelerate and embed this new way of seeing work and the changes that have been achieved requires continuous cycles of action (which generates new and different experiences) and reflection (which allows you to see how those differences translate into the better outcomes that are being achieved).

What is keeping you stuck?

Successful Leadership Teams create their own momentum and tend to carry on achieving great things. Unsuccessful teams tend to get bogged down in a tangle of frustrations and conflicts, where even the members' best efforts and intentions seem doomed to disappointment.

The self-reinforcing pattern of success is one of the key benefits to be realised by becoming a high performing team. The place to start, though, is by understanding how the negative spiral of performance and team effectiveness keeps teams stuck – and why a breakout plan is essential.

Underperforming teams: the vicious circle

As we established earlier, there are a lot more underperforming Leadership Teams than successful ones. This is inevitable, because there are systemic problems that affect all Leadership Teams. A team that is not working well is not a great tool for solving complex problems – and that includes the complex problem of Leadership Team underperformance.

Failing teams get locked into a vicious circle of underperformance, and it takes concerted action to break the pattern and escape.

When I have talked to members of underperforming teams over the years, they have consistently described to me a wearying and predictable cyclical pattern with startlingly similar features.

This cycle goes a long way to showing why underperforming teams tend to get stuck and struggle to break out. Each element of the pattern is not only continually reinforced by the others but also frustrates efforts to improve effectiveness.

Busy meetings mean, for example, that team effectiveness never gets time on the agenda. The team members' tendency to focus on their own responsibilities means that even when it is discussed, little progress is made.

High performing teams: the virtuous circle

The good news is that when Leadership Teams do manage to make the shift to high performance, the same kind of cyclical factors apply, reinforcing the positives sustaining progress and driving both effectiveness and results continually upwards.

The vicious circle of underperformance

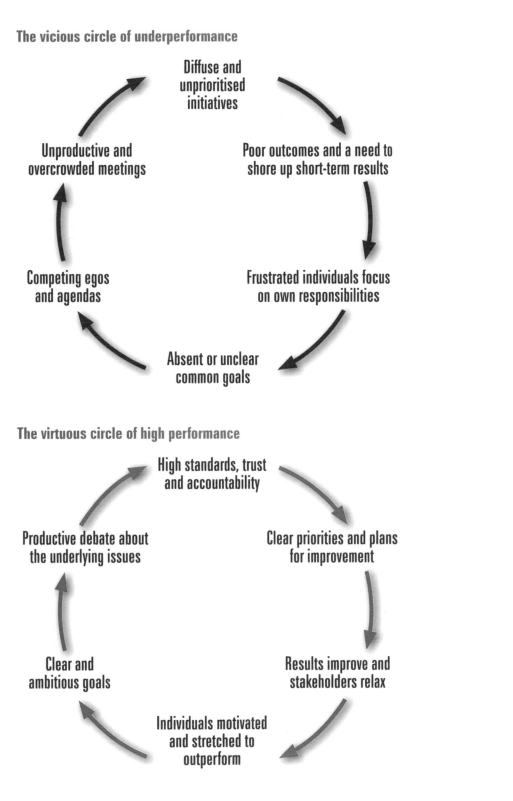

Diffuse and unprioritised initiatives

Poor outcomes and a need to shore up short-term results

Frustrated individuals focus on own responsibilities

Absent or unclear common goals

Competing egos and agendas

Unproductive and overcrowded meetings

The virtuous circle of high performance

High standards, trust and accountability

Clear priorities and plans for improvement

Results improve and stakeholders relax

Individuals motivated and stretched to outperform

Clear and ambitious goals

Productive debate about the underlying issues

The result is a virtuous circle in which the healthy functioning of the Leadership Team becomes self-perpetuating. High performance becomes a habit. Team members work together well, trust each other and regularly achieve results they thought would be impossible. The Leadership Team is carried forward by a momentum that can survive personnel changes, external crises and even, in many cases, a change of leader.

Just as underperformance and an ineffective team replicate themselves through their effect on the leaders around them and the rest of the organisation, so the effects of a high performing team are magnified by both the positive example they set and the new ways they interact with those around them to get things done. ▲

DO YOU HAVE THE RIGHT PEOPLE ON YOUR
Leadership Team?

14

Bringing together the right mix of roles and personalities and the right size team is also vitally important.

The question I am most commonly asked by leaders thinking about developing their teams is 'When is the right time to review the membership?'. There's no simple answer to this question, as there are two competing needs that have to be reconciled.

The first is that some teams have members who will always undermine efforts to change. These 'blockers' can have a damaging and corrosive effect on the way the team functions. In my many conversations with leaders over the years, by far the most common cause of regret is the failure to address or remove these blockers early enough. Most CEOs I speak to already know which of their team members aren't part of the future they want or who aren't going to be able to make the journey.

The second need, and the most common reason for failing to confront these disruptive team members, is the desire to give them a chance to change. This is a noble motive, but it is also important to set the tone of the organisation as one which makes the best of its people and seeks to support people to make changes – which is difficult for us all.

Genuine team development also often reveals unexpected outcomes in the way individuals respond. Those who were once seen as critical team members and allies can find that they are uncomfortable and out of step with the new ways of operating. Others, who had perhaps been seen as peripheral or even obstructive, may become converts and powerful supporters of the new approach.

> *Most CEOs I speak to already know which of their team members aren't part of the future they want or who aren't going to be able to make the journey.*

Decisions about individuals must, therefore, be based on the circumstances and history and whether efforts have already been made to support them in making changes. There is, though, a simple way to sort those who can change to become better team players and those who are likely to continue to hold the team and organisation back. The Leadership Audit tool on page 302 provides a way to think about each team member and to make the distinction between those who need to be tackled early and those who should be given a chance to change.

Who should be represented on your team?

Bringing together the right mix of roles and personalities and the right size team is also vitally important. Your Leadership Team should also be a manageable size – ideally with no more than seven or eight members. It must also represent all the parts of the organisation that will be most involved in the transformational changes ahead.

Look at what needs to be done

The make-up of the Leadership Team should be defined by the range of tasks and challenges its members must tackle. But that may not become clear until after successful Ambition Conversations and Priority Conversations have taken place. In the meantime, you may have to make some intelligent guesses about who will be needed.

For example, if the biggest challenge for the organisation is geographical expansion, the head of the international division should be on the team. If cultural change is needed, the head of HR must be involved. If quality has become a burning issue, both production and customer service will need to be properly represented.

Pick people with complementary skills and personalities

It will also be important to take account of the mix of personality types and skills within the team. The most successful Leadership Team I worked in was led by a quiet, thoughtful and understated CEO. But he deliberately brought in an inspirational, charismatic, lead-from-the-front communicator whose ability to put the team's ideas across complemented the boss's own more cerebral skill set.

Don't let the Leadership Team get too large

Getting the actual size of the team right is vital. Most bosses will find that, for historical and political reasons, the Leadership Teams they inherit are too big and unwieldy. Cutting down the numbers may call for sensitive management, but dodging the issue will slow the pace of change and may stall it entirely.

A key issue here is the number of interpersonal relationships that exist within the team. Every member must develop a good working relationship with each of his or her colleagues. And that is a matter of simple arithmetic.

If you are working with a streamlined, pared-down Leadership Team of just seven people, there will be twenty-one strong individual relationships to be created and maintained between the members involved. With a team of twelve, that number rises to sixty-six. With thirteen, it's seventy-eight separate relationships, so you can see that the numbers go up fast.

There is an enormous difference between working with a team of seven (twenty-one individual relationships) and a team of twelve (sixty-six relationships). More relationships means more complexity – and that, in itself, is a good reason to strip the Leadership Team down to those who are essential to the work that needs to be done.

5 team members	=	10 relationships
6 team members	=	15 relationships
7 team members	=	21 relationships
8 team members	=	28 relationships
9 team members	=	36 relationships
10 team members	=	45 relationships
11 team members	=	55 relationships
12 team members	=	66 relationships
13 team members	=	78 relationships
14 team members	=	91 relationships
15 team members	=	105 relationships

This arithmetic is supported by research that suggests an optimum size for executive teams, striking the best balance between diversity and efficiency, is usually just six to eight people (Hay Group, 2001).

Each extra person also means there's another perspective to be brought into the conversation. If you have twelve people, rather than seven, and each member contributes equally, there will be 70 per cent more information to take on board. Either, therefore, each person must contribute less – or you will need to extend the amount of time you spend together.

Logically, you have a choice each time you extend the team. Either meetings will be longer or you will have to make do with less quality input from each participant.

> *Logically, you have a choice each time you extend the team. Either meetings will be longer or you will have to make do with less quality input from each participant.*

In general terms, a smaller Leadership Team is always likely to perform better and be easier to develop and manage. 'Less is more' is a good rule of thumb.

Even if personal and political factors make it difficult to adjust the size and composition of the Leadership Team immediately, CEOs should have a clear idea of their ideal number and mix of roles and personalities. Most teams change frequently as people leave or take on different roles, and clarity on the desired end state will help create and exploit opportunities to move towards the ideal line-up. ▲

SEVEN STEPS
to breaking out

The virtuous circle described at the end of chapter 13 is clearly a desirable and attractive place to be, but reaching it means breaking out of the pattern of self-reinforcing challenges described in the vicious circle.

There are many ways to develop a team, and different approaches to sequencing the steps. Over the years, my colleagues and I have experimented with many variations, and we have found that there is one sequence that consistently generates the best results.

Even so, this sequence of steps needs to be adapted to reflect the particular needs and context of each organisation and set of leaders. Even if you decide to do it a little differently, whichever way you choose needs to include all of these elements.

STEP ONE
Commit, and begin

This may seem obvious, perhaps patronising, but even when we know things would be better if we made changes, we often act as if change isn't necessary. We can duck out of the big decisions and hope we can get by with more familiar solutions that are less disruptive and challenging.

Like the smokers who know the grim facts about their habit but still light up, we resort to denial and other psychological mechanisms to avoid tension by rationalising conflicting information and beliefs. When we put up with poor performance from a disillusioned or disorientated team, we do it

> *This may seem obvious, perhaps patronising, but even when we know things would be better if we made changes, we often act as if change isn't necessary.*

by convincing ourselves that things are not so bad – or even that it can't be changed and so is beyond hope.

The team may be hurting the organisation and affecting the wellbeing of all its members, but until some sort of crisis forces the issue, it's often tempting just to let things slide.

Being honest with yourself and the rest of the team about the scale of the problem – and the opportunity – is the first step in this change, as in any other.

There is never a right time to start. Or at least, there is always some reason to delay a little longer. In fact, there are many reasons, including misconceptions about the purpose and goals of team development.

You are bound to come across some scepticism, in yourself as well as from others. The table opposite shows some of the most common limiting beliefs about team development, and some appropriate and positive responses to each of them.

Change will only begin once you step over the threshold. 'Just do it,' as Nike says. Rather than waiting for the perfect moment to initiate change, which may never come, the best approach is to make the decision and choose to start now.

STEP TWO
Clearly articulate the rationale

As a leader of a team, if you're going to make the investments of time and effort required, you need to be clear about the reasons for making the change. It's often a new situation, whether externally imposed or internally created, that creates the conditions for a group of executives to make the shift to becoming a true Leadership Team (Katzenbach J. R., 1998).

While there are as many reasons for change as there are teams, in my experience they usually fit into five broad categories:

▲ **A new boss.** A new CEO can put old habits behind him or her and set the scene for a fresh chapter in the organisation's development. With no history to refer back to, or past mistakes to explain away, the new leader can call for a new commitment, new ideas and a new approach to collective effort and responsibility.

10 limiting beliefs about team development

Limiting beliefs	Reasons to act
A Leadership Team isn't a true team and doesn't need to be developed.	Most Leadership Teams don't operate as true teams. The goal of team development is to change that.
Team development is only needed when the team first forms.	Every team can, and needs to, improve – throughout its life.
Team development only needs to happen when things are getting difficult.	If the first time you address relationship issues is in the divorce court, you have left it too late!
The only way to improve the team is by changing the personnel.	A team can perform as more than the sum of its parts or less than the sum of its parts. Which do you want?
Team development is about helping the team members relate better to each other.	Team development is about all the Six Game-Changing Conversations – including the 'hard stuff', as well as the 'soft' human aspects.
Team development is about helping the team members trust each other.	Absolute trust between human beings is an unrealisable goal. Team development will create enough trust for members to disclose and deal with any mistrust.
Team development is about reducing conflict.	Teams need conflict, of the right kind. Too much or too little conflict are both unhelpful in a team.
Team development only happens off-site on awaydays.	Team development can be assisted by off-site awaydays but the core development happens in the heat of working together on the tasks you face.
Team development is about having better meetings.	Better meetings will follow, but what counts is the quality of the work you do, the decisions you make and the results that flow from both.
Team development is an end in itself.	Team development is only valuable when it is clearly and explicitly linked to improving business performance.

Adapted from the work of Peter Hawkins (Hawkins, 2011).

▲ **A shift in team membership.** When the membership of the team is altered significantly, either in numbers or because key roles change, this always changes the dynamics. These dynamics will grow and develop of their own accord over time, but the team can take this opportunity to ensure they develop in the way that is most helpful, and that this development is accelerated.

▲ **An external challenge.** A change in the market, a shift in customer needs or a new set of demands from a parent organisation can provide the stimulus that demands new ways of thinking and acting from the team.

▲ **Team dysfunction.** We have found this is less common as a rationale for investing in the change than people imagine. It certainly can be the case, though, that it becomes so hard to make progress on the issues facing the organisation that changes have to be made.

▲ **A new narrative.** Even when there has been no obvious external or internal change, a CEO will often instigate change by offering a new account of the organisation's situation. By recasting the story of where it has come from, where it stands, the challenges facing it and what it must do to succeed, a CEO can galvanise it into action on a variety of fronts – including team development.

While this is very common when someone arrives as a new leader of a team, it is also a powerful tool for an incumbent CEO to use to reinvigorate the organisation or change its course.

As well as being the key to getting enough support for the changes to begin, wholehearted backing from those the team is accountable to is important for every Leadership Team that is going through change.

The rationale provides clarity about the purpose and benefits of the change. It will help provide the impetus to begin and will be an important touchstone as the work continues – especially when the going gets tough.

Improvements in team function may take a little time to show up in improved results. Resources, and particularly the team's time, will need to be invested initially and sustained over time.

The people responsible for those resources also need to believe that change is necessary. The rationale provides clarity about the purpose and benefits of the change. It will help provide the impetus to begin and will be an important touchstone as the work continues – especially when the going gets tough.

STEP THREE
Decide who will manage the change

Get the right expertise and support

The leader of the team must lead the change. I have never seen a Leadership Team development programme work where this has not been the case. Sometimes the idea will be introduced by another team member, but it must be picked up, owned and led by the CEO or MD.

Very few leaders of teams are well equipped, however, to manage the change. They are likely to be skilled in other ways, but even if they have the capability, they won't have the time to give it the focus it needs and carry out the necessary steps.

In my experience, the team leader also usually wants to be able to participate fully in the programme. It is very difficult, if not impossible, to do this at the same time as being responsible for managing the process.

The leader will, therefore, need the help of someone who can run the programme and work with the team. This person will need the skills to facilitate and coach, as well as being equipped to manage the project.

The right person will depend on the team and its situation.

But this person will need to be able to:

'Senior Leadership Teams, like other teams, need expert help in learning how to become better at working together over time. Coaching such teams is often more challenging than coaching front line teams. High-spirited, independent-minded thoroughbreds are often convinced of the rightness of their ways and are not responsive to correction – even from the lead horse'

(Wageman, Nunes, Burruss, and Hackman, 2008)

- ▲ Create and manage a sustained programme of work that unites the many perspectives inside and outside the team.
- ▲ Collate a range of thinking and articulate a collective position, while also working effectively with the team leader, as the principal client.
- ▲ Work well with individuals on a one-to-one basis and have the coaching skills to support each of them in making behavioural changes.

▲ Manage the stresses and dynamics of team interactions, in the demanding environment of the boardroom. This requires a high level of facilitation skills.

▲ Gain and maintain the trust and confidence of all members of the team.

External facilitation

Using an external facilitator offers a number of benefits. An outsider who comes into the organisation and asks all the relevant parties for their insights and opinions has the advantage of starting off with a clean sheet. There will be no prior preconceptions or relationships with anyone on the team. The external facilitator can bring both actual and perceived objectivity.

Skilled external facilitators cost money, though, and a Leadership Team that's already under financial pressure may see taking on outside help as a luxury it cannot afford. Even financially impoverished teams should think very carefully about trying to make cost savings here, as they can't afford not to use the right help. The value available from creating successful change is so much higher than the cost that it's almost always a false economy. There are reasons why considering alternatives to external facilitation is valid, but cost considerations are a dangerous basis for that decision.

Internal facilitation

There are examples of successful Leadership Team development using internal facilitation, but these are comparatively rare.

Choosing a facilitator from within the organisation presents its own problems. If the team leader tries to take on this role, he or she has ownership of the project and a demonstrable interest in its successful completion, which can be advantageous. But most CEOs are already overloaded – and team members will always find it hard to be completely candid if the facilitator is also the boss.

Giving a Leadership Team member the job of facilitator can cause difficulties, too. The process may benefit from the individual's detailed knowledge of the organisation and its workings, but other team members may feel that objectivity has been sacrificed.

When an internal facilitator is chosen, it is often the HR director. Again, this can be problematic. The head of HR already has relationships with the other team members, but even if this individual has had training as a coach and facilitator, he or she is unlikely to be using and honing these skills regularly.

The HR director's involvement with the CEO in hire and fire decisions is also likely to get in the way of frank and open discussion with other members of the team. This will make it very difficult to win the complete trust and confidence of team members, who may feel unable to say what they really think, for example, about their relationship with the CEO.

> *The HR director's involvement with the CEO in hire and fire decisions is also likely to get in the way of frank and open discussion with other members of the team.*

It may be possible to bring in a facilitator with the right experience and skill set from another part of the company. Some organisations have skilled facilitators available in a central function. This can be a good option, but they must have the specific experience and skills needed to deal with the people and dynamics of Leadership Teams.

STEP FOUR
Win support

Winning support for radical change calls for a business case that will convince everybody whose support matters. A clear business case will be required that shows the value of the outcomes that are envisaged and which helps convince these stakeholders – including potential sceptics – of the need to invest in improving the team's performance.

Start by asking the right questions

Most leaders say, unprompted, that the value of these interventions massively exceeds the cost, so the return on investment from achieving a high performing team is huge. Creating the business case is about helping to articulate this in a credible way and getting all stakeholders to support that analysis. The best way to do this is by getting them to help build it.

To understand exactly what needs to be different, and to build this business case, it is necessary to bring together many opinions and views and recognise what everyone wants and needs. A process of consultation is required that focuses on a number of questions. These are best asked on a confidential, one-to-one basis.

We have seen many Leadership Team members struggle, initially, to articulate their own views on the case for change, even when they are thoroughly committed to the need for it. Leadership Team members are not in the habit of examining their own observations of the team's functioning and their own needs and aspirations in relation to it. The experience of exploring the answers in depth can be very powerful.

We have seen many Leadership Team members struggle, initially, to articulate their own views on the case for change, even when they are thoroughly committed to the need for it.

Time needs to be set aside for each team member and stakeholder to think, reflect and explore.

The six questions that need to be explored are:

1. What do you really want for the organisation, for yourself and for the team?

This is the $64,000 question. Answering it, and coming up with a collective destination that honours each individual's point of view, creates a new clarity around the Leadership Team's goals, together and as individuals.

Perversely, this is the question most leaders find hardest to answer. It tends not to be discussed amid all the debates about budgets, strategy and plans – and it requires people to talk about what they really care about. Helping them explore and articulate this is critical.

2. If this success is realised, what benefits and opportunities will follow?

This question forces people who have been immersed in today's difficult, complex and ambiguous situations to think about the long game. It encourages them to give themselves time and space to explore what would happen if their ambitions for the organisation came true.

The focus on the payoffs and opportunities that would be unleashed adds depth, colour and motivation to the individual's picture of the future for the organisation and the team.

3. What do you see as the main barriers to achieving your goal?

Team members usually start by identifying one or two market challenges and financial or external barriers. But they soon move on to the softer issues within the organisation. The ones that almost always come up are:

- ▲ We're trying to do too much, overloading ourselves and others and failing to fully deliver the benefits of what we do.
- ▲ There's conflict in the team which hampers the delivery of today's solutions and gets in the way of properly understanding our underlying problems well enough to find real answers.
- ▲ Processes that run across the organisation are broken, because we operate too much in silos and many of the most important things require cross-functional solutions.
- ▲ The quality of leadership available outside our team, and particularly in the next layer of leaders who report to us, is extremely mixed. We have a few good people that we always go to and too many people who create problems or don't contribute enough.
- ▲ The culture of the organisation gets in the way of responding to customers, delivering at pace, working cross-functionally and getting the most out of our people.
- ▲ Our team meetings are overcrowded and ineffective. They are failing to help us to get to grips with the big issues that we need to address.

The answers to this question begin to forge the crucial link between each individual's desired future and the human issues in the organisation and the team. They also bind the full range of barriers and issues into the formation of the business case for the team development work.

4. What are the implications and costs of not reaching the goals you have described?

This question prompts realistic thinking about the future. Can the team ever reach its goals if it continues on its current path? If it falls short of these goals, what does that mean for the organisation? What will it cost in terms of revenue and lost opportunities? How will it feel to work in that team and organisation?

Getting team members to think about these issues begins to direct the answers on the previous page towards hard financial and other measures that will form the foundation of a robust business case.

5. How is the team currently functioning?

The earlier questions helped team members imagine a future in which change has already happened. This question invites frank exploration of the current work within the Leadership Team. How successful is it? What is working and what isn't? How does the current situation impact on the team's ability to achieve its goals? How successfully is the team addressing the underlying issues and avoiding the costs of failing to do so?

> *Getting team members to think about these issues begins to direct the answers on the previous page towards hard financial and other measures that will form the foundation of a robust business case.*

By working through this, each team member will come to see more clearly the gap between the team as it is and the team that is needed. Synthesising these views into a collective picture of the team functioning can lead to a powerful articulation of the necessity for change.

6. How would the team need to work in order to meet its goals?

If the team is not working in a way that helps it achieve its goals, how could it work differently? Team members often know, intuitively, what needs to be done.

This question draws on their experience of past powerful teams they have been a part of. By doing so, it helps them articulate what really matters to them about the team they want to create that would allow them to contribute at their best. The aggregated answers from this question play an important part in forming the sequence and agenda for the programme to follow.

STEP FIVE
Collate views and assemble the case for change

By the time these interviews are completed, the process of change is already under way. Two critical outcomes will have been achieved.

First, every member of the team will know that his or her opinion and needs form part of the agenda. People's confidence that they are being listened to is being developed, even before the process of change begins. They become engaged and curious and believe that change will be done *for* and *with* them rather than *to* them.

Second, by gathering the views of the most important people in the organisation on where the team is now, what its goals should be and how these could be reached, a powerful body of data has been collected.

Because these people all have unique knowledge about their own parts of the organisation, and of the functioning of the team, their combined insights can be used to create a programme of change around which the team, the organisation and its stakeholders can rally. Each person sees part of the elephant. Helping the whole team see all of it is a powerful intervention in itself.

Collating the answers to all of these questions is the first step in formulating a business case. We always produce a document which includes both the areas on which everyone agrees and those where there are significant differences of perspective. Both of these become important areas for exploration at the launch workshop, where the team will discuss the business case together for the first time.

STEP SIX
Win the support of your boss

One particular challenge for many leaders wanting to embark on the development of their team can be the person they report to. Their 'boss' may be a group chief executive, chairman or owner. They will at least need to be convinced of the case for investment and may also see developing the team as the leader's responsibility.

In our experience there are three lines of argument that are helpful to win over their support:

Frame it in terms of the deliverables they are most interested in

You will already know what your boss most wants from you and the team. You will have, from the team interviews, some very clear linkages between improvements in team functioning and the speed and effectiveness of delivery of these priorities.

Highlight the benefits of succession and of reducing exposure to individuals

Your boss will know that the organisation is heavily dependent on you, and probably on other key individuals in the team. A well-functioning team, and investment in development, is the best way to reduce these risks because it both accelerates the development of successors and also ensures that more people are involved in the key projects.

One particular challenge for many leaders wanting to embark on the development of their team can be the person they report to. Their 'boss' may be a group chief executive, chairman or owner who may also see developing the team as the leader's responsibility.

If you or other important team members were to leave, the team will be in a much better position to maintain momentum in the very short term and make quick appointments to plug the gaps.

Explain the value of external expertise

They may believe that developing the team is your job, but Step Three on page 223 explains why you can't develop the team without help. You can use the rationale both for the value of expert support and also to articulate the benefits of the chosen alternative – whether external or internal.

STEP SEVEN
Start with a launch workshop

By now the Leadership Team and other stakeholders should be engaged in the agenda for change and be at least curious as to whether it can really move them to the next level. Now it is time to start the work that will make change happen.

Purpose

Making change within a team requires, among other things, a number of personal behavioural changes. By definition, every team member is playing a part in the way things are today. It follows that all the team members will need to make some alterations to their own approaches and attitudes if they are to contribute to improving the functioning of the team.

These behavioural changes will take time, effort and perseverance. The programme of change that's needed will involve working with both the team as a group and with individuals separately. It's most unlikely, however, at this point, that everyone who needs to sign up will be ready to make the necessary commitment of time, effort and money. The role of the launch workshop is to develop this shared commitment.

The workshop provides the opportunity for team members to make real progress, become truly involved and move beyond curiosity to believing that this is a process that will help them fulfil their goals.

Duration and venue

We have found that the launch workshop works best if it is spread over a day and a half. A day isn't enough to do all that needs to be done and the overnight stay provides invaluable social time together as well as time for shared processing of the first half day.

Part of the reason why the Six Game-Changing Conversations have not been happening so far within any Leadership Team is due to habits that have developed within the group and the organisation as a whole. Most Leadership Teams have a tendency to slip into well-worn ways of doing things, even when these are not effective in helping them reach their goals.

Every team member is playing a part in the way things are today. It follows that all the team members will need to make some alterations to their own approaches and attitudes if they are to contribute to improving the functioning of the team.

There are many such habits, and many reasons why they develop, but our experience is that the pressures and norms in Leadership Teams that lead to these ways of doing things are often similar. They include long agendas, rushed conversations, insufficient time for stepping back to look at the big picture and interactions consistently dominated by the same voices.

Creating a new way for your Leadership Team to work is about introducing more choice in terms of behaviour and applying a degree of flexibility to the challenges ahead. Getting out of the rut is part of this and I, therefore, strongly recommend that you hold the launch workshop, and subsequent events, at an external venue. This also has the added benefit of escaping from the interruptions and distractions of the office.

Environment and tone

Change the physical environment. Small changes can make a big difference. Rather than sitting around a table, sit team members in a circle of comfortable chairs, allowing everyone to see each other properly.

Taking the table away can make a surprising difference to how people interact. The implicit hierarchies disappear and it becomes easier for people to move away from well-worn behavioural patterns and routines. At a very practical level, every person can see everyone else – allowing much better understanding of when people have something to say, facial expressions, body language and when important things may be unspoken.

Opening the door to new thinking is helped simply by making the session feel different from the usual Leadership Team meeting. Just creating a Day Zero atmosphere, in which nothing is assumed and taken for granted, is an important first step. Altering the physical surroundings and broadening the agenda to escape from the usual litany of firefighting issues and admit many different ideas and points of view will encourage the team to approach its role differently.

Change the physical environment. Small changes can make a big difference.

A launch workshop agenda is shown opposite. There are many ways of setting up and facilitating each of the elements and there are a variety of tools for doing this in the next section, starting on page 236.

By the end of the launch workshop, team members will feel the investment of their time has been well worthwhile, and that further investment is both necessary and desirable. They will be developing a new confidence that they have the power to move the organisation forward by making the changes they've identified.

The facilitator has a key role to play in this process. He or she will need to design the event, formulate questions and summarise responses, manage the conversations and provide the framework around which constructive discussion can develop.

Outcome

This initial investment of just a day and half will not magically resolve all the underlying issues that are stopping the Leadership Team from achieving all it could. But the launch workshop can help to make everyone concerned feel interested, committed and confident enough to allow the team leader and facilitator to create the business case and plan for the sustained programme of work that will be needed.

THE LAUNCH WORKSHOP AGENDA

DAY 1

Understand the leader's rationale for developing the Leadership Team. Debate and agree how the team functions and what it should be focussing on.

Begin to create a shared ambition for the organisation that all the Leadership Team members feel passionately about (Ambition Conversation).

Take the first steps towards developing greater trust and understanding with other team members (Relationship Conversation).

DAY 2

Reflect on the progress and discussions made on the first day.

Agree a set of priorities that will lead towards the team's shared ambition (Priority Conversation).

Work together on clarifying each of the priorities and agreeing next steps for each of them (Delivery Conversation).

Make commitments to each other about what individuals will do next to sustain and build on the progress made (Accountability Conversation).

Reflect together on how team members have worked differently together and how they will take that back to the office and into other team meetings (Learning Conversation). ▲

Designing a programme

After you've run the launch workshop, the person chosen to manage and facilitate the programme should work with the CEO or team leader to create the business case and plan.

The choice and sequence of tools will depend very much on the outcome of your first seven steps and your launch event. Some of the tools can be planned into the programme from the outset. Others can be picked out and used as the programme evolves. The initial plan will always need to be flexed and adjusted as the programme progresses and additional needs emerge.

The flow of outcomes for a typical programme run by OneThirdMore would be as shown opposite.

Do you need help?

In this book I have included as much detail as possible about the tools we use to develop teams, so that you can apply them to make changes to yours. Whilst I hope you can use the techniques yourself, our years of experience with them enable us to adapt and combine them into powerful programmes that will deliver the best results.

If you don't feel confident in creating your own programme, or if you would like to understand the options for best applying these techniques in your situation, we'd be happy to discuss this with you. We understand that you will probably still be at an exploratory stage, and that you certainly don't want a hard sell. As a starting point we, therefore, offer a complimentary Strategy Session.

This takes the form of a 90 minute conversation in which we jointly explore your context and objectives, and discuss the options for using our approaches with your team. By the end of it, whether you decide to work with us or not, you will have:

- ▲ A clearer business case for developing your team, including the benefits of making changes as well as the costs of inaction
- ▲ A better understanding of what a programme might look like for your team, and some options for first steps
- ▲ A good feel for us, and our approach to the work, to help you decide whether you could work with us
- ▲ Most importantly, a renewed sense of excitement about what is possible for you, your team and your organisation

There's absolutely no obligation and you can arrange your Strategy Session by visiting www.onethirdmore.co.uk/contact.

Programme design – the sequence of outcomes

LAUNCH EVENT

Decide the destination

A clear and shared understanding of the destination

Agreement on the key challenges to reach goals

A sense that this is a group each can travel the journey with

An appetite for the next stages – which will involve more personal work

Ambition

STAGE 1

Prepare for the journey (2 months)

New ways of working are agreed and put into practice

Each person knows, and shares, what they will have to do to be fit for the journey

Unspoken issues have been raised and addressed. The group is open and trusting

Relationship and Priorities

STAGE 2

Forge the path (4 months)

Plans have been executed

Major setbacks and emerging challenges have been overcome

A wider group of key leaders have been engaged and tested

Deep bonds of trust and confidence within the team

Accountability and Delivery

STAGE 3

Guide others (2 months)

Work to embed and sustain the changes is passed to the wider group of leaders

Improved results are evident, stakeholders relax and pressures reduce

Team are focused on the agreed 'next summit' to exploit the possibilities from their achievements

Learning and Enrolling support

SECTION 4

*Tools for developing
Leadership Teams*

Moving on to the 'how'

If you have begun to glimpse the untapped potential of your Leadership Team, you will already understand the 'why' of transformational change.

We have discussed the kind of changes that are likely to be necessary and explored the Six Game-Changing Conversations you can use to bring the performance of your team to new levels. We have also examined the steps required to set a programme in motion. Now we need to look at the detailed methods you can employ.

In this section of the book I have assembled a series of tools – a workbox, if you like – that your team can use to improve its effectiveness. My colleagues and I have tried many different techniques over the years, and these are the ones that have proved most useful in helping teams make radical, lasting changes in a relatively short time.

With my colleagues, I have used this toolkit to address the problems and missed opportunities in the Leadership Teams of many organisations, large and small, in many different industries. The tools are powerful, but also simple and accessible. Some can be used without specialist facilitation; others require more expertise. I will highlight which fall into each category.

Just as the world's top sprinters use training routines that specifically target upper-body strength, alongside the more obvious focus on the leg muscles, Leadership Team members need to build up a broad range of new capabilities. You can think of each of the tools as a training programme for a particular muscle. Real success will come only as all the newly bulging muscles begin to be used together.

I have selected two or three tools that focus on each of the Six Game-Changing Conversations. There are also a few that are almost always useful and benefit more than one conversation.

The results you get will depend on the tools you choose, the way you use them and the order you use them in. That's going to need some careful thought and discussion both before you start and as you go along.

The approach that's best for your team will depend on your people and your circumstances. I can't give you a recipe to follow, but I can give you a great set of ingredients that will cover the vast majority of situations. The quality of the final product will depend on the skill with which they are combined and used.

Whether or not you decide to use some of these techniques yourself, the set of tools detailed in this section will give you a good idea of what a comprehensive approach to team development looks like. Each tool is powerful in its own right. But the most profound and sustainable change will be achieved by working on developing all of the conversations, using a range of different tools.

Among these techniques, you may see versions of methods that you have come across before. If so, it will help if you can reflect on these past experiences and consider:

- ▲ Which tools and conversations did you focus on?
- ▲ How effective were the tools, and why?
- ▲ Which conversations were not addressed?
- ▲ What impact did not addressing those other conversations have on the ultimate success of that team development effort, and on the business results it delivered?

YOUR TEAM ASSESSMENT
summary

1. Please populate each of the axes on the diagram opposite with the scores from pages 99, 117, 133, 153, 179 and 203.

2. Mark your overall assessment of the team from page 71 in the box below.

3. Join the points on the spider diagram.

4. Add a point on each axis of the spider diagram for where your team needs to reach to deliver what you really want.

5. Join up the 'needs to reach' points on the spider diagram.

6. Add your assessment of the performance uplift if the team was fully effective.

You now have a graphic representation of where your team is and where it needs to be, together with an estimate of the value at stake for developing it.

The following section includes tools and techniques for improving aspects of your team performance.

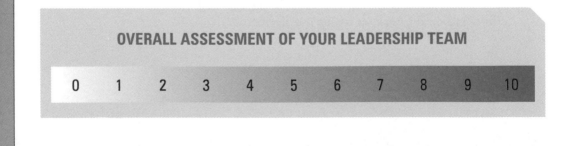

OVERALL ASSESSMENT OF YOUR LEADERSHIP TEAM

| 0 | 1 | 2 | 3 | 4 | 5 | 6 | 7 | 8 | 9 | 10 |

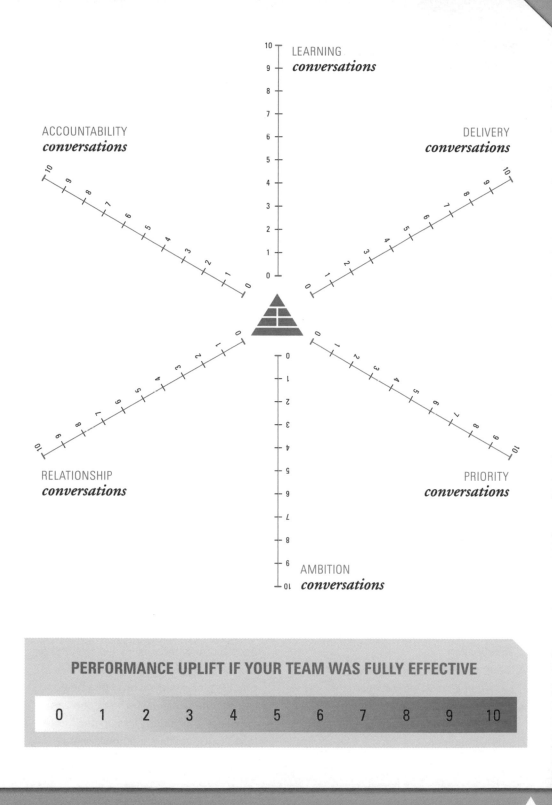

10
9
8
7
6
5
4
3
2
1
0

LEARNING
conversations

ACCOUNTABILITY
conversations

10 9 8 7 6 5 4 3 2 1 0

DELIVERY
conversations

0 1 2 3 4 5 6 7 8 9 10

RELATIONSHIP
conversations

0 1 2 3 4 5 6 7 8 9 10

PRIORITY
conversations

0 1 2 3 4 5 6 7 8 9 10

0
1
2
3
4
5
6
7
8
9
10

AMBITION
conversations

PERFORMANCE UPLIFT IF YOUR TEAM WAS FULLY EFFECTIVE

0   1   2   3   4   5   6   7   8   9   10

AMBITION
conversations

The ambition line

❓ Why you need it

Leadership Teams work incredibly hard towards goals, targets and plans which are tough to achieve. But they often mistake this hard work for ambition. The things they are working on often deliver little more than survival, and rarely represent the sort of change they truly want to deliver.

The purpose of this tool is to get the Leadership Team members talking about their own highest aspirations for the organisation and to form these together into a single, shared ambition for the team. It starts a dialogue about what would be needed to achieve something that's truly worthy of their efforts, that will inspire them and others, and that will lay the foundations for all the other conversations.

The Ambition Line is a tool for teams that want to:

▲ Uncover and address differences in the team about direction and destination.
▲ Shift the organisation's ambition to a higher level of aspiration.
▲ Re-energise themselves and others to move beyond today's challenges and limitations.

🔧 The tool

Making something as abstract as ambition visible can be very powerful in understanding where people are relative to one another. It can open up important conversations about where aspirations are shared and where differences lie.

The Ambition Line is quite a simple tool to use, though the best conversations and outputs will only be achieved with the help of an expert facilitator.

The facilitator starts by drawing an imaginary line across the floor. One end of this line represents the current baseline for the team, the point that will be achieved over a chosen horizon (usually three to five years), if the team keeps going as it is. The other end of the line represents a position where the team has achieved something genuinely transformational.

👉 How to use it

Each team member is invited to stand on the line at a point that represents the organisation's current level of ambition, and then to explain why he or she has chosen that position. This, in itself, often leads to interesting and unexpected

The conclusion of the exercise is to find a simple and powerful way to articulate what they want to deliver together, the legacy that they want to leave.

insights, by bringing all the different perspectives on the current situation into view.

It usually brings out the fact that working at full throttle, as most teams already are, is not going to be enough to produce a transformational outcome. If this point doesn't emerge spontaneously, the facilitator should draw it out.

The facilitator encourages the dialogue to go where it will, as people focus more on ambition – a subject that may never have been discussed at all in some Leadership Teams. The facilitator should encourage team members to ask each other questions. What interests them? What surprises them? What are they curious about? What is missing?

When all the issues and questions arising from this have been explored, the facilitator asks people to reposition themselves on the line, this time at the point where they think the organisation's ambition should be pitched. Few of those taking part are likely to stand exactly where they stood before.

Where individuals have moved along the line, they are invited to talk about where they are now and why they have

moved. Again, the facilitator should encourage team members to explore the perspectives on view. What do they notice? What has changed? What hasn't changed? What are they seeing or understanding that's new or different?

After the new positions have been explored and explained, the facilitator asks those whose stated levels of ambition are lower what it would take for them to move further up the line towards those who are at the higher end. Those at the higher end are asked how they would address the doubts and reservations expressed by the more cautious members.

As this dialogue broadens out, a skilled facilitator will gradually encourage the Leadership Team members to generate a greater understanding of how the level of ambition that is now being discussed differs from the goals and targets that they are currently working towards. The facilitator will also lead team members to think about the importance within ambition of talking about what they really want, as well as what seems achievable.

The conversation will evolve into a discussion about what the ambition should be, for the team and the organisation.

The ambition line

The conclusion of the exercise is to summarise this, if only in a crude form, for further refinement and discussion.

✔ The benefits

The Ambition Line provides an engaging, visual way for the whole team to see the differences between its members. People can see the team's centre of gravity, where the greatest number of opinions are clustered, and the outliers, the people whose levels of ambition stand out as different from the rest.

The exercise makes it possible to explore and discuss why and how the level of ambition could be higher, why that makes sense and how it would change what team members work on.

The final part of the conversation is essentially forward-looking. Through exploring what it would mean for the Leadership Team and the organisation to move to a different level of ambition, and the change this would require, team members begin to prepare the ground for powerful and genuinely transformational Priority Conversations.

This exercise will help produce a team in which people have a much better understanding of each other's motivation and where the members share a deeply felt and genuine alignment around a higher level of aspiration. ▲

Taking the leap across the ambition gap

A few years ago, I was called in by the newly recruited managing director at a company producing materials for the construction industry. The organisation had been tracking the cyclical ups and downs of the market for some time. When the industry was buoyant, it prospered. When the market was depressed, sales would dip alarmingly.

Even when it was doing well, though, the firm was never the top-performing company in its field. And when market conditions were difficult, it always seemed to do a little worse than its competitors.

In his early conversations with his executives, the managing director had quickly picked up on the fatalistic mood within the Leadership Team. The prevailing belief was that there wasn't much they could do when the market was poor. They just had to keep working hard and wait until, eventually, the market turned and things got better.

The managing director found this frustratingly defeatist, and wanted the team to raise its sights. I was brought in to organise an offsite meeting and the first thing we did was the Ambition Line.

The first part of the exercise produced a fairly strong level of consensus about the current level of ambition. The team members clustered around a point not far from the 'status quo' end of the line. But even these early discussions started to nudge the team's understanding forward, and the managing director was pleased to see that his Leadership Team members spontaneously started talking about how everyone in the company, including its leaders, habitually cast themselves as the helpless victims of market fluctuations.

The second part of the exercise – when people were asked to stand on the Ambition Line again to indicate where they thought the company's ambitions should be – produced some less predictable responses.

➤

TOOLS *– for –*

AMBITION *conversations*

The ambition line

A number of members of the team, especially those with operational responsibilities, remained pessimistic.

When we explored this together, it became clear that those who still stood near the bottom end of the Ambition Line were there not because they didn't want to aim higher but because they could not see a way to change the current situation.

There was a general sense of powerlessness. Team members who couldn't visualise a path forward were willing to contemplate alternative futures, but unable to see how the company could move towards them.

'If you can tell me what needs to be done to break out, I'll do it like a shot,' one director said. 'But I just can't see it.'

There was also anxiety about what might happen if they committed themselves to aiming for ambitious targets and then weren't able to achieve them.

The finance director, though, had placed himself in a surprisingly bullish position. Indeed, he was even more ambitious than the managing director.

When he was asked about this, the finance director's explanation was based on quite a different view of the company's past experience.

> *'If you can tell me what needs to be done to break out, I'll do it like a shot'.*

'I've been around a long time,' he said, 'and there have been occasions when we've managed to outperform the market because we've been prepared to innovate with our products and take some risks. Some of these succeeded and others failed, but we have, at times, led the market by doing this.' He gave some examples.

'I know it's possible,' he said, 'because I've seen it happen.'

The discussion shifted. Team members began by talking in general terms about new possibilities, but quickly moved on to specifics. They discussed how they could make better use of new construction technologies and become a company that led the market, rather than trailing behind and following the lead of others. They talked about how aiming high could sit alongside working towards everyday performance targets, and how people could be reassured that thinking big would not expose them to the risk of failure and personal criticism.   ➤

As the conversation widened out, even the more pessimistic members of the team started to edge up the Ambition Line, until they were all at roughly the same point. The pessimists were helped to shift by a discussion about emerging market niches that offered new opportunities. There was also evidence that technical and operational successes in other areas could be applied to these niche products to create something genuinely new and exciting for the firm's customers.

The Leadership Team members left the room far more positive after their day's work. They had pinpointed several areas in which the company could genuinely take a lead in the market, rather than simply waiting for things to pick up.

They had identified and agreed to address some of the organisation's major underlying problems and they had also developed the curiosity and appetite to want to start talking in detail about the ideas that had been raised.

Alongside the optimism, there was also a sense of sobriety and proportion. While the new ambition represented some exciting possibilities, it was going to be challenging to realise them.

> *As well as generating new focus and real excitement, the process had changed team members' beliefs about where they were and where they needed to go*

By the end of the day, though, the focus of the team and the organisation had already shifted.

Things that had been seen as interesting experiments and ideas, largely lying buried in peripheral parts of the organisation, had moved to centre stage. As well as generating new focus and real excitement, the process had changed team members' beliefs about where they were and where they needed to go – and given them a way to generate new levels of excitement in both their own staff and the parent organisation. ▲

TOOLS
— for —

AMBITION
conversations

Reimagining the future

❓ Why you need it

When Leadership Teams fail to see how the future can be different, it is usually because their thinking is limited by not knowing how a new future might be achieved.

Their conversations typically overemphasise the rational. They fail to engage people emotionally, as well as intellectually, with what would excite and motivate them, so the limitations that are identified become self-fulfilling.

Reimagining the future is for teams who want to:

▲ Break out of the current trajectory to something genuinely better.
▲ Free themselves from today's problems and obstacles to enable them to look at what is truly possible.
▲ Energise themselves and those around them with a renewed sense of purpose.

🔧 The tool

Reimagining the future frees people to talk about what they really, truly, deeply want – and would be prepared to make big changes for.

Our imagination, when it's let off the leash, is capable of going far beyond the boundaries of assumptions, rational self-checking, the 'art of the possible', and all the cultural conventions about how things are done and what it's OK to talk about.

To get to truly transformational ambitions, we need to move beyond these things, and this tool uses an approach designed to get straight to the unconscious – a part of our minds that's rarely deliberately accessed in a working context.

It can be challenging at first, because it is so obviously different from the way Leadership Teams usually approach things.

But that is its great strength. It takes Ambition Conversations – which should be exciting, stimulating and inspiring, but often get bogged down in market statistics and shared assumptions about the limits of what is possible – and brings them to life. It encourages people to park their assumptions and let the imagination take charge.

The tool is based on the use of a reflective script, which you may recognise as drawing on some of the techniques successfully used in Neuro-Linguistic

The conclusion of the exercise is to find a simple and powerful way to articulate what they want to deliver together, the legacy that they want to leave.

Programming (see box on page 86). It guides the mind to a specific area of focus in which it can be productively creative, while leaving spaces into which team members' own imaginations can insert images. The images and ideas that emerge combine real personal meaning with the wide range of implicit and explicit knowledge each person holds about the organisation and its environment.

☞ How to use it

Reimagining the Future is a tool that requires a skilled facilitator. While reading the script is easy, it takes someone with perceived expertise and authority to give people the trust and confidence to fully invest in what is a very unfamiliar process.

The facilitator begins by asking the team members to sit comfortably, put aside their pens, papers and iPads and close their eyes.

The facilitator then reads through a script, speaking slowly and steadily and pausing at the end of every line to leave time for the imagination to form images in each person's mind.

When everyone has opened their eyes, the facilitator asks them to jot down a few notes about what they saw and what changes seemed particularly significant.

Each team member in turn is then invited to outline the most important things this person saw on this trip to the future.

As descriptions are shared, common themes emerge – and interesting differences. The facilitator should help the team explore those similarities and differences and search for a picture, or theme, that brings together the best of what emerged from each person.

Teams will usually be in a hurry to seize upon something important that seems to have emerged from this discussion. But if they are allowed to jump to conclusions too quickly, it can often be at the expense of some of the richness, significance and energy in the individual accounts. It's important to restrain the desire to close down too quickly and to keep looking for what it is that brings all of the pictures together and, particularly, what captures the personal significance of the different pictures.

Part of the facilitator's skill here is to continue the exploration until something ➤

Reimagining the future

FACILITATOR'S SCRIPT

Imagine you are sitting in this room.

The sun is streaming in through an open window. The air is clear and still. It's a glorious day and all is well with the world.

On the table in the middle of the room is a calendar, with the top page showing today's date.

As you look at that calendar, a gentle breeze blows in through the window and turns the first page over, so that tomorrow's date is displayed. Gradually the wind strengthens and more pages begin to turn, slowly at first, and then with increasing speed.

You watch the days start to flick by, faster and faster, as weeks turn into months, until the pages are turning so quickly you can hardly see them move.

For a while they are almost a blur, but then they start to slow, eventually coming to a stop on a date that's exactly three years from today.

Take a moment to think about what is going on in your life and in the lives of the people around you on this day, three years from now.

What are the big issues and events going on around you?

What's going on in your life?

What's happening in the lives of your loved ones?

What are you looking forward to? What has recently happened?

Today, you have arranged to hold a celebratory reunion with the members of this team, because the last three years have gone incredibly well. It's been a transformational time for the organisation and you've had an amazing experience. You cherish the memories of the last three years as one of the highlights of your working life. Things have gone so well that you have since been promoted to a bigger and better job.

Although you're meeting the team this evening, you have decided to pop into the office to see some old colleagues, take a look around and see what's new.

➤

What do you see when you arrive at the offices?

What do you notice that has changed?

What is different now?

What can you hear?

What can you see on people's screens and on their desks?

What do you notice about the work they are doing?

What do you notice about the way they are doing the work?

You stop and talk to a few people. What do they tell you about the changes that have occurred over these last three, tumultuous, years?

What are they doing now, and what does it mean to them?

You bump into a couple of customers you know and you ask them about how they feel about the organisation today. What do they tell you?

It's time for your dinner with the old team. You pause at the door and look over your shoulder. How do you feel as you walk out of the building, perhaps for the last time?

What are your thoughts on what has happened and how you got there?

Take a mental snapshot of that moment. Compose it carefully so that it captures all of the things that matter – and everything you are most proud of.

When you're ready, allow your mind to return to this room. Notice that the calendar is still on the table.

A gust of wind starts to move the pages again, backwards this time, slowly at first and then more quickly, faster and faster, until they slow down and it finally settles back at today's date.

Take a moment to gather your thoughts and reflect on what you saw in your visit to the future.

What seemed most significant to you about that image of a time three years hence?

Revisit your snapshot of it. Re-check and record it carefully for yourself.

Take your time, but when you are ready, open your eyes again. ▲

emerges which captures the essence of the future all the participants are seeking. This can take many forms, but it often coalesces around a particular word or phrase that strikes a chord with several members of the team. It's like a crystal forming. Once this seed emerges, the ambition builds and grows around it until it forms the basis of a first draft of a description of what the team wants to aim for – something that everyone can get excited about and that will eventually develop into the final, finessed statement of the team's ambition.

Discussing the gap between this desirable future and the current situation is the start of profound change for any team. It changes what they understand their joint work to be. It changes what the priorities are. It changes what they work on and how they work on it. And it changes how they feel about the people with whom they have decided to embark on this quest. ▲

✔ The benefits

This tool elicits an ambition for the organisation that's very different from the one the team members know. It can help people renew the emotional connection with what they came into their roles to do and give them new clarity about what they really want for the organisation – and for themselves.

Reimagining the Future provides a mechanism for team members to visualise and describe the future they really want to see and to bring this together as a clear and shared ambition. It also builds trust and cohesion by enabling team members to discover and understand more about the motivations and aspirations of all their colleagues.

Imagining £30m into £70m

A manufacturing plant in England's industrial northeast, a division of a major multinational, had been in decline for many years. The Leadership Team had narrowly escaped the threat of closure by some radical cost-cutting, reducing the workforce by over a third. Against the odds, the company had struggled back to break-even profitability.

It had been an exceptional effort and the team was rightly lauded for this achievement. The CEO knew, however, that the bigger challenge was yet to come. The division was still making no profit and working out how to grow was proving even harder than finding the cuts that had to be made to stem the losses.

Despite some initial scepticism, the team agreed to use Reimagining the Future. When we went through the exercise, they surprised me with the key theme that emerged.

'I saw a future in which this company could be like it used to be,' said one executive, summing up the feelings of most of his colleagues. 'We once again had a great place in the community, not just as a big employer but as one of the major elements in people's lives.'

> *'I saw a future in which this company could be like it used to be,' said one executive, summing up the feelings of most of his colleagues. 'We once again had a great place in the community, not just as a big employer but as one of the major elements in people's lives.'*

The plant and the local community had grown up together over decades. It had once been the place where every man had a job and every son wanted to work, which funded every housewife's spending and which filled the pay packets that drove every local business.

Years of underperformance and cuts to the workforce had undermined this symbiotic relationship with the community. The plant now employed a ➤

Reimagining the future

fraction of the numbers it did at its peak, and there was no disguising the resulting decline in the town.

Times change, though. The industry was contracting and the Leadership Team members quickly realised that it would be difficult, if not impossible, to recreate this situation. Nevertheless, the what-if scenarios started to emerge.

What if we could attract new investment, focus on more specialised steel products and actually start to grow again?

What if more jobs could be created, bringing new money and life into what had been seen as a dying community?

What would have to happen for the global organisation to feel confident that this kind of revitalisation could be made to work? What would need to be true for the parent company to make the investments needed?

> *The company's Leadership Team scrapped its modest but already difficult ambition of making £30m in three years and set itself a new target of £70m.*

The outcome of this discussion was genuinely transformational.

The company's Leadership Team scrapped its modest but already difficult ambition of making £30m in three years and set itself a new target of £70m – a dramatic decision that immediately ruled out any approach based on incremental growth and challenged the team to go for radical, aggressive new ideas.

The team arrived at this figure not by arbitrarily choosing a larger number but by a logical line of thought that stemmed directly from the ambition to get back to the role the plant had historically played in the community.

To grow the staff the company employed would require major investment in the plant, which had been neglected for years. New equipment costing tens of millions would be needed to replace machinery that was outmoded, beyond its useful life and unable to produce what new markets and opportunities demanded.

To convince the parent company of the viability of these investments would require profit levels significantly above those they were currently targeting.   ➤

The team members estimated they'd need to be at £30m within a year and that further investment, and the resulting access to new markets, would need to get them to £70m for the investment to pay off.

Now the Leadership Team could start to explore every decision it made, using as its touchstones the twin ambitions of making £70m and returning the company to the standing it once had in its community.

Within a year, the company reached its £30m profit level and successfully made its case for the new investments. Today, it is about to commission the new equipment and is preparing itself for the big push on to £70m – and, incidentally, for a major recruitment drive. ▲

RELATIONSHIP
conversations

Speed feedback

? Why you need it

Many of the challenges that face Leadership Teams can only be properly discussed and resolved when there are strong and trusting relationships between team members.

Yet, as we have seen, teams rarely choose to invest time in talking and relationship building. Most Leadership Teams simply do not communicate often enough, or in the right way, and team members often don't understand the impact they have on others, or what more they could be doing to help and support each other.

Speed Feedback is for teams who want to:

▲ Be able to talk about even the most difficult subjects without worrying about defensiveness, antagonism or politics.
▲ Dissolve personal tensions and replace them with robust and trusting relationships.
▲ Create a unity that will support each of their members as they tackle the many challenges facing each of them.

✗ The tool

Speed Feedback is a simple tool that offers a quick and powerful way of focusing on the essentially collaborative nature of Leadership Team work. It is based on the work of Roger Harrison (Harrison, 1971).

The aim is for team members to give each other direct and practical feedback on what each colleague has done that has helped them carry out their work effectively, what has made it more difficult, and how they could help more by doing things differently.

The format of the questions follows the 'Good, Tricky, Do Differently' (GTDD) formula, which is described in more detail on page 324.

☞ How to use it

While the mechanics of Speed Feedback are simple enough, team members are being asked to do something that feels new and even intimidating. An expert facilitator can help by giving people the confidence to step out into this unfamiliar territory.

The initial response to this exercise is sometimes one of apprehension, as team

Fantasies about great difficulties between people usually prove to be just that when they talk together properly about how they can help one another.

members worry about the feedback they receive or how they themselves will give difficult messages. One of the responses to this can be suggestions to modify the exercise.

If this happens, the facilitator must gently but firmly insist – and explain that the exercise is designed as it is for good reasons. The apprehension is entirely normal, but it rapidly melts away as soon as team members get started. In our experience, participants often not only get a lot out of the process but also really enjoy it.

Each person is asked to prepare for the session by making notes for each of their colleagues on:

▲ What you do that helps me most in doing my job.
▲ What you do that can make my job more difficult.
▲ What I would like you to do more or do differently to help me more.

Team members are asked to make brief but clear notes on this – with each person's feedback on a separate piece of paper, as they will be passing the paper to the person they are feeding back to at the end of each discussion.

The facilitator also needs to prepare in advance. The logistics of pairing each person with every other are not straightforward. There are a variety of sites online that will provide a schedule for this, usually based on systems for scheduling sporting fixtures. A search on 'fixture list generator' will quickly take you to a tool that will do this for any size of team.

The facilitator begins the session by publishing the pairings sequence and telling people what they need to do. Each pair will need to work together for half an hour, working to the same sequence:

▲ A gives all three feedback elements to B (10 mins)
▲ B asks any questions for clarification and then responds to the requests for changes (5 mins)
▲ B then gives his or her feedback to A (10 mins)
▲ A gets to ask any necessary clarification questions and then responds to the requests for changes (5 mins)

Speed feedback

Team members then move on to the next 'fixture' and each pairing follows the same process, until every team member has met with every other.

When all the rounds are complete, the facilitator invites the team to reflect together on the experience of the session. This is usually extremely positive. If they don't emerge spontaneously, three important points should be drawn out.

▲ Fantasies about great difficulties between people usually prove to be just that when they talk together properly about how they can help one another.

▲ The positive experience most people enjoy is driven by the affirming qualities of the positive feedback (which is all too rare) and the constructive discussions that emerge from mutual feedback about how people can help one another more. This is a simple enough idea, but just doesn't happen consistently or frequently enough in normal business life.

▲ The whole process took only 30 minutes for each pairing, so any two people can easily do it again whenever they like.

After the initial exercise, a follow-up session should be scheduled around two months later, to check on the progress that has been made and explore what still needs to be addressed. Many organisations find Speed Feedback so useful that they return to the tool regularly, every half year or year, as a way of updating their thinking and uncovering issues and opportunities that do not emerge in other contexts.

✔ The benefits

Speed Feedback provides a framework in which people are helped to move quickly to talking about things that allow them to make one another's jobs easier. The time-limited format nudges participants towards clarity, directness and simplicity.

Speed Feedback gives each participant a large amount of useful information – and leads to changes in colleagues' behaviour that will help the team in real and practical ways. Its mutuality also quickly builds trust and dissolves tensions.

In practice, despite any existing anxieties, individuals' experience of the exercise is almost always hugely positive. This is because:

▲ Team members provide positive affirmation for each other. Just hearing someone at work say 'I really value this about you – this is really what helps me in what you do' is a novel experience for many people. Hearing recognisably similar positive comments from several different team members is powerful and motivating. Being explicitly charged with finding positive things to say about each of one's colleagues helps team members practise giving affirmation.

▲ Well-framed criticisms of the less-than-helpful things people do are particularly powerful when an individual sees similar themes emerging in several people's comments. These are often relatively minor issues, but if the same niggle is raised by different people, it clearly adds weight to the imperative to make a change. In many cases, the destructive impact of individuals' behaviour is something they have been unaware of. When they understand the impact it has, they usually need little further persuasion about the importance of making changes.

▲ Most people aren't short of feedback, but simple, practical suggestions about the changes that need to be made are often in much scarcer supply. Positive ideas about changes the participants can work on make it far easier for them to respond. When this results in people working to improve their relationships with other team members, the payoffs ripple out across the Leadership Team and beyond.

Engaging in the Speed Feedback process – and discovering that, far from being scary or destructive, it can produce rewarding conversations and useful insights – alters team members' attitudes. By building trust and confidence in the value of giving and receiving feedback, it makes it much easier for them to hold similar conversations with colleagues in the future, even outside the context of formal sessions.

Most importantly of all, the behaviour of their Leadership Team colleagues is a big part of that environment. Improving the working environment for all the members of the team enables them to deliver more of their potential, more of the time. That generates both better results and less frustration. ▲

CASE STUDY

Speed Feedback turns foes into allies

A classic demonstration of the power of Speed Feedback came when we were invited to work with a company where the relationship between two key Leadership Team members had broken down and become a serious problem.

The financial director, a driven, logical and forceful technician, and the director of marketing, who was artistic, creative and tended to think in abstract terms, were locked in an antagonistic relationship that was harming the effectiveness of the entire Leadership Team. Factions had started to form around each person and discussions in the team regularly polarised around these two individuals.

The CEO had resorted to dealing with his executives in small groups to avoid the unpleasantness and gridlock that seemed to occur whenever the whole team met. He was also mediating between the two – both when they were apart and in meetings where both were present. It was enormously frustrating for the CEO and the team, but the antagonism was so bad that the relationship, and its impact, had become undiscussable.

I met the CEO and we agreed that, rather than focus only on these two individuals, we would arrange a Speed Feedback session for the whole Leadership Team. As usual, each team member would spend time sharing feedback with every other member, but there was no doubt where all eyes were focused.

> *What would happen when the time came for the two protagonists to give each other their feedback?*

What would happen when the time came for the two protagonists to give each other their feedback? The discipline of the tight time limit would necessarily force them to address the issues simply and directly, and there seemed to be every chance that confronting one another with their feedback might lead to some sort of explosion. ➤

To everyone's surprise, except mine, their interaction didn't erupt. It did start slowly, but soon became energetic.

The two directors began to see how they unintentionally rubbed each other up the wrong way. They were each surprised to discover how small and simple the changes were that the other was asking for. Having to think and talk about what they valued about one another helped them both remember how complementary their different skill sets were. The lightbulb moments of realisation came thick and fast.

In the end, we had difficulty stopping the two of them at the end of the allotted time. Their conversation carried on over lunch, when the two of them chose to sit together, talking animatedly, away from the main group.

Their conversation carried on over lunch, when the two of them chose to sit together, talking animatedly, away from the main group.

Since that conversation, the relationship between them has developed further. Each of them now sees the other as a valuable first port of call for different perspectives and ideas. They have worked together on an initiative to solve the problems with a key market launch, transforming it into a huge success.

Leadership Team meetings have been transformed. They have become a source of energy and creativity for the CEO and the whole organisation. Tensions between the two directors' departments have dissolved and the two former foes are now seen as an important axis of influence and a driver of strategy for the company.

Since that time, conversations between other members of the group have also led to many insights and agreements on how key issues can be addressed by working together better. The day of the Speed Feedback marked a decisive turning point for the CEO, his Leadership Team and the whole company.

The whole exercise took just four hours. In ROI terms, this was one conversation that paid for itself in the very next Leadership Team meeting. ▲

TOOLS
— for —

RELATIONSHIP
conversations

Seeing styles

? Why you need it

Every Leadership Team member brings a different set of personality traits to the table. Understanding more about the mix can help team members communicate better, use one another's skills better and work more effectively together.

Many of the misunderstandings and frictions that occur in Leadership Teams stem from the diverse personality types represented and the different ways they see the world. If these are not addressed, even small problems can escalate and lead to tension and dysfunction.

It is also valuable for a Leadership Team to know if there are personality type gaps in the team which might lead to collective blind spots. Action can then be taken to compensate by bringing in new team members with different characteristics, or by deliberately taking care to ensure that missing perspectives are addressed.

Seeing Styles is for teams who want to:

▲ Understand the different traits brought to the group by each member and how people's strengths can be used to best effect.

▲ Defuse tensions and build stronger relationships by deepening team members' appreciation of one another.
▲ Identify 'blind spots' in the team and gaps in the collective team make-up that need to be addressed.

⚒ The tool

There are hundreds of personality type assessment tools available. They vary widely in their degree of accuracy, research base and, most importantly, in the ease with which they can be used.

We almost always prefer to use the Myers-Briggs Type Indicator for three reasons:

▲ It is by far the best researched and most robust of all the tools available.
▲ The output is simple and clear and it's easy for people to remember and use.
▲ The range of supporting resources and information is far greater than for any of the other tests.

Myers-Briggs is a powerful tool for understanding personality types and how

The impact of using this tool is invariably profound. Most, often all, of the participants will have moments of genuine revelation – about themselves and others in the team.

these work together, originally derived from the theories of the early 20th-century psychologist Carl Jung.

It uses a questionnaire to identify four opposing pairs of personality preferences, which allow people to be classified into sixteen different personality types. The tests have been developed and refined over fifty years and it is, by a long way, the most reputable and widely used psychometric profiling system.

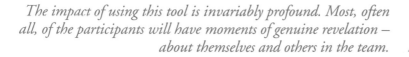 How to use it

The Myers-Briggs Type Indicator is a powerful proprietary system belonging to the Myers and Briggs Foundation. It demands training and experience and it can only be used by accredited facilitators certified by the British Psychological Society.

Each member of the team first completes the online questionnaire. This generates a report which describes the individual's preferences on each of the four dimensions, indicates his or her personality type and describes, in general terms, how this will influence the person's work and relationships.

Each team member then has a one-to-one debriefing with the facilitator. This takes 90 minutes, during which they are briefed on the meaning of personality types, discuss their own type, explore how this impacts on some real current issues and get answers to any questions they may have.

The team stage involves the facilitator drawing four lines on a flipchart, each representing the continuum between the pairs of opposing characteristics – E and I, S and N, T and F, and J and P (see overleaf).

Team members are asked to make a mark for themselves along each line, based on their personality types, and to share what they have found most useful and illuminating about the report and debriefing they have received.

Some aspects of the report may have been very familiar, reinforcing what the participants already know about themselves. Others will often come as a surprise or raise questions the individual has not considered before.

When each team member has made a mark on each axis of the chart and summarised his or her perspective, the facilitator invites the team to look at ➤

RELATIONSHIP *conversations*

Seeing styles

MYERS-BRIGGS

Myers-Briggs testing assesses personality by means of a questionnaire that asks ninety-three simple either/or questions. It uses the answers to rate people in terms of four dimensions, each based on an opposing pair of characteristics:

Extroversion (E) versus Introversion (I) Do you prefer to focus on the outer world or on your own inner world? Do you get your energy from being with other people or from time spent alone?

Sensing (S) versus Intuition (N, to avoid confusion with I for introversion) Do you prefer to focus on the basic information you take in or do you feel the urge to interpret and add meaning? Do you like to nail down the details or try to see the bigger picture?

Thinking (T) versus Feeling (F) When making decisions, do you look first for logic and consistency or do you look at the individuals and special circumstances involved? Are your decisions mostly based on analysis or values?

Judging (J) versus Perceiving (P) In dealing with the outside world, do you like to get things decided or do you prefer to stay open to new information? Do you instinctively want to plan ahead, or do you like to keep your options open and go with the flow?

The basic output from Myers-Briggs testing is a four-letter personality type, assigning the subject to one of 16 personality archetypes – ranging from ESTJ to INFP.

Nobody is all E and no I, or all S and no N, but everyone has preferences which are formed early in life. While the strength of these preferences often changes with age and experience, few people ever change preference from one side to the other.

If you are interested in finding out more about the Myers-Briggs Type Indicator – including the mass of research assembled over many years that validates its accuracy and value – there is a wealth of information available. Many books have been published about MBTI tool and its applications, and the Myers and Briggs Foundation's website, www.myersbriggs.org, provides a useful and informative starting point. ▲

the picture as a whole. There may be noticeable clusters, with some areas where the team members mostly have similar preferences and others where the team is more dispersed.

Seeing this graphic representation of the team's personality profile is always illuminating and invites exploration of a number of aspects of the team's functioning, including:

- ▲ Are there any areas which are underrepresented – and so are likely to be blind spots for the team?
- ▲ Where are there big differences between members? When do these cause friction and when do they enrich the team by bringing together diverse perspectives?
- ▲ What light does the team profile shed on the things you choose to talk about and those that are neglected?
- ▲ How does the team profile make itself felt in the way the team works together?

The facilitator should steer the discussion to help team members decide what actions to take in response to the answers to these questions.

There is also real value in the new understandings and insights for each individual. The facilitator should end the session by asking people to share their own key insights – and describe what they plan to do differently as a result.

✔ The benefits

Using the Myers-Briggs Type Indicator to reveal some of the hidden dynamics that drive the Leadership Team consistently leads to greatly increased personal understanding for each individual, as well as a more nuanced understanding of the relationships within the team.

The impact of using this tool is invariably profound. Most, often all, of the participants will have moments of genuine revelation – about themselves and others in the team.

These reactions fall into two main categories:

'Ah, THAT's why I always get into problems/really like those things. It's not that I'm mad, bad or incompetent. It's just that I'm different!'

'Ah, THAT's why I get on with X or don't get on with Y. It's because we're different. It's not that one of us is right or wrong – we just see and process things in very different ways.'

The Myers-Briggs tool helps people move towards a clearer view of the team's strengths and weaknesses and why it functions as it does. It uncovers insights and prompts conversations that lead naturally into fruitful, thoughtful discussions about how relationships and performance can be improved, for the team and for each of the individuals within it. ▲

Seeing styles

CASE STUDY

When the chair wasn't a chair and the back seat wasn't enough

I vividly remember one Leadership Team I worked with. When the Myers-Briggs reports came in, it was immediately apparent that, while the rest of the team members were quite closely grouped together along the four personality dimension lines, there was one individual who was clearly the odd man out. And that odd man out was Heather, the managing director.

Her results showed she was an outlier, with a very different personality type from any of her colleagues.

When we delved into this, it became evident that she was the sort of person who prefers not to rush decisions and to keep all the options open as long as possible. As she was responsible for chairing team meetings, this was often a problem. Like every other meeting she chaired, they tended to run on and on. Important conversations were often left unfinished because the team ran out of time before a decision could be made.

People had noticed this, of course, but they had not realised that it was a direct result of the personality preferences hardwired into the managing director's character. Recognising this, with the help of the Myers-Briggs process, meant that the team could take steps to do something about it.

To address the meetings issue, the managing director made a conscious decision to chair meetings much more decisively. She also asked her team to help by pointing out when she didn't, when she reverted to type, and to help her to ensure that the decisions arrived at in Leadership Team meetings were always clearly spelled out and understood.

Within a couple of weeks, feedback from the team members and other contributors confirmed that the MD's meetings were running more smoothly and decisions were being made much more quickly.

The members of this team also learned from Myers-Briggs that there was a ➤

strong group preference for logical analysis over empathy. This showed up in a number of places including their downbeat, cynical view of the capabilities and motives of the managers in the next tier down in each of their departments. They saw their subordinates as being underpowered and in it for their own gain, and this had a negative impact on how they worked with them, contributing to a lack of connection between the Leadership Team and the wider management group.

As the team talked through these discoveries, people were chastened to realise that seeing everybody else as problems and opponents had become a self-fulfilling prophecy.

> *The team talked through these discoveries, people were chastened to realise that seeing everybody else as problems and opponents had become a self-fulfilling prophecy.*

Happily, the team profile also helped the team recognise that it already had a largely untapped, undervalued resource on board, in the form of the HR director. He was more empathetic than the others, but his opinions were not expressed forcefully and they were often overlooked or brushed aside. He had got used to the comfort of a back seat role.

As a result of the post-Myers-Briggs dialogue, the HR director was encouraged to step up and offer his balancing perspective. He promised to be more proactive in voicing his views. The Leadership Team made it clear how much his perspective was needed and agreed that members would make a conscious effort to pay more attention to it.

By the end of the session, a number of important issues had been identified and practical solutions had been found. On top of the things they had plans to address, the team members left with significant personal insights about how they operated, how they differed from others and what they could do differently to make the job easier for themselves and their colleagues.

It had been a powerful couple of hours. As the MD put it to me afterwards, 'That's the most important and valuable piece of business education I've had in my entire career.' ▲

TOOLS
– *for* –

PRIORITY
conversations

The priority matrix

? Why you need it

Because of the positions they hold, their expertise and their personality types, most Leadership Team members hold strong views about what should happen within their organisations.

When they come together to talk about priorities, they are often so keen to articulate their own viewpoints that opposing views collide head on, little listening takes place and constructive exploration of issues and solutions is stifled.

Teams often get bogged down in heated discussions about a few controversial topics, at the expense of a full exploration of the important issues that must be balanced and traded off to arrive at the right answers.

The Priority Matrix is a tool for teams that need to:

▲ Fully understand the full range of issues that need to be balanced and traded off.
▲ Find a way to compare very different types of issues and work.
▲ Work through the total picture of existing and potential work and reduce

it to a deliverable set of priorities for the organisation.

🔧 The tool

The Priority Matrix is a tool that quickly makes everyone's views about priorities – and all the relevant wisdom, knowledge and insight within the team – visible and explicit.

This tool doesn't necessarily call for the involvement of an expert facilitator, but it does require facilitation. It's particularly important that the facilitator is seen as neutral – and free of any preconceived views about priorities.

It uses a two-by-two matrix to separate and make explicit the impact of a possible action and the ease with which it could be implemented.

👉 How to use it

STAGE 1
Making individuals' priorities visible

Initially, team members are asked to think about their top priorities – their view of the most important things that must be worked

The Priority Matrix is a tool that quickly makes everyone's views about priorities — and all the relevant wisdom, knowledge and insight within the team — visible and explicit.

The Priority Matrix

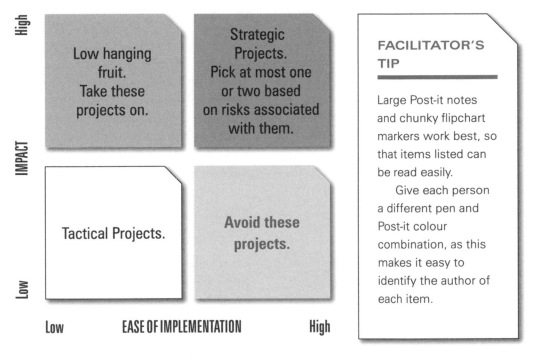

High

Low hanging fruit.
Take these projects on.

Strategic Projects.
Pick at most one or two based on risks associated with them.

IMPACT

Tactical Projects.

Avoid these projects.

Low

Low   EASE OF IMPLEMENTATION   High

FACILITATOR'S TIP

Large Post-it notes and chunky flipchart markers work best, so that items listed can be read easily.

Give each person a different pen and Post-it colour combination, as this makes it easy to identify the author of each item.

on if the team is to deliver on its ambition.

To ensure breadth of thinking, they are encouraged to consider these priority items in terms of Finance, Customers, Processes and People (the categories used in the Balanced Scorecard).

People are given marker pens and large Post-it pads and asked to write down their priorities, one per Post-it note, written in capital letters.

Each participant then sticks his or her Post-its on a wall, reading each one out aloud as it is added. They are asked to do this quickly, without elaboration, and other participants are asked to hold back their questions until everyone has posted their entire list.

When everyone's ideas have been added to the wall, the team is invited to stand up and group all the Post-its into relevant clusters, and to create a new Post-it with an umbrella title for each group.

When the groups are clear, the team is encouraged to reflect on the total picture that has taken shape.

▲ Is anything surprising?
▲ How much agreement is there?
▲ What important differences have emerged?
▲ How similar is this list to the current plan?
▲ How different is it from what the team currently spends its time on?

STAGE 2
Sorting and slotting

The facilitator then draws up a two-by-two matrix on a flipchart and asks team members to decide where each of the priority groupings should be positioned on the matrix. What would have the greatest impact? What would be easiest to deliver?

At this point, however much agreement there has been within the team so far, differences of opinion and emphasis always emerge.

The facilitator helps team members recognise and explore these different perspectives, working towards a final agreed position in the matrix for each priority.

The facilitator should help the team arrive at an approximate 'consensus placing' for each group. Only where there is a serious or profound disagreement about positioning should the facilitator help explore this difference of opinion to discover what's behind it.

STAGE 3
Coming to decisions

Once matrix positions have been plotted for all the priority groups, the facilitator leads the team into a conversation about what the team wants to do. It's often helpful to encourage team members to think in terms of three categories:

▲ Drive actively (invest in and accelerate)
▲ Maintain progress (refine current approach and work more efficiently)
▲ Defer for action later (still important, but needing to make way for proper investment in the other two)

STAGE 4
Consequences

It's important for the team to discuss, agree and assign actions and owners for what will change as a result of this prioritisation.

▲ Who will own and drive each priority area (for all three categories)?
▲ What will each owner do to clarify and check his or her understanding of the actions and next steps for each priority group?
▲ When will the board next review progress on the list and the actions that have been agreed for each of the priorities?
▲ What needs to change on board agendas?
▲ Who else needs to be communicated with about the outcomes?

✔ The benefits

The Priority Matrix is a powerful tool that often sparks rapid progress and much closer alignment, simply by making sure that everything important is made visible and given proper consideration.

By highlighting areas of alignment, it makes it easier to hold more constructive conversations and to focus the team's time on discussing areas of particular complexity or where there are genuinely differing views.

Using the Priority Matrix enables Leadership Teams to arrive relatively quickly at a short list of priorities. Although it is a relatively brief and simple process, it often suggests a quite different set of focus areas for the Leadership Team – and, critically, a new definition of what the Leadership Team needs to work on together and why.

The results are often surprising – not least because there is typically a lot more alignment around what the important issues are than most team members would have guessed.

Most Leadership Teams would admit that time constraints and crowded agendas mean there is little opportunity to have quality conversations in which everything important is seen, explored and put into its broader context. The Priority Matrix addresses this problem directly, producing realistic results and important strategic insights. ▲

The priority matrix

CASE STUDY

Highlighting the expertise gap

A joint venture between two High Street retailers was losing money and seemed to be on its last legs. Everything seemed to be going wrong. Everything seemed to need to be fixed. The merger had created a new entity with a wide variety of problems on top of all the usual integration challenges.

In addition to a range of internal issues, the overriding challenge was the cut-throat market the new company had to succeed in. Competition was fierce, especially from some other, much larger players. What the Leadership Team needed most urgently was an understanding of what must be done first.

When the team ran a Priority Matrix exercise as part of its strategy process, it was soon clear that there were two big new priorities that had not been seen as areas of great focus in either of the parent organisations.

One Priority Matrix grouping concerned the expertise within the organisation – and even in the Leadership Team. A second group of Post-it notes highlighted the need to create a genuinely differentiated position for the company.

The Leadership Team was desperately short of practical knowhow. Team members knew a lot about retailing in general terms, but they had very little detailed knowledge about the products the joint venture company had been set up to sell. This was a serious problem in the boardroom.

> *What the Leadership Team needed most urgently was an understanding of what must be done first.*

What made it worse was the fact that the pattern was repeated right down to shop floor level. For a business operating in such a ferociously competitive marketplace, it was a potentially fatal flaw.

They quickly decided that the company couldn't differentiate itself in terms of locations, pricing or range, as the larger competitors already had a stronger ➤

position in all of these. It could, however, focus on developing real hands-on expertise at all levels of the organisation, so that customers would know they could rely on getting good advice and professional support alongside the product sales.

The Priority Matrix showed the team the areas it needed to work on. But it was obvious the changes would be difficult to achieve, especially under the time pressures imposed by the company's recent poor performance. The other side of the coin, however, was that it would be equally difficult for the firm's competitors to raise their game and match these new levels of product expertise. Handled correctly, the new approach offered the chance to build a genuinely sustainable source of competitive advantage.

The Leadership Team moved fast and created a new academy, with intensive training programmes for directors, senior managers and store staff. Plans were drawn up to ensure that every single member of staff would go through the programme within two years. As an organising principle, product expertise also began to inform every other aspect of the company's activity – from store design to marketing communications. But the market wouldn't wait, and there were many anxious moments before the first signs of a revival began to appear.

First there were scraps of anecdotal evidence – a few good-natured remarks on Twitter about the company's improving customer service. Then the tone of mainstream media comment started to shift from withering to neutral or mildly positive. Slowly the supertanker turned around.

> *Handled correctly, the new approach offered the chance to build a genuinely sustainable source of competitive advantage.*

It took nine months for the changes to start showing up in customer surveys, but then satisfaction ratings began to improve, rising by more than 15 per cent, and sales started to pick up rapidly.

Within two years, the company was not just out of the woods but enjoying real success. Focusing on one crucial priority – the right priority – had saved the day, and the insights gained from using the Priority Matrix had played a critical part in making it happen. ▲

TOOLS
– for –

PRIORITY
conversations

The rapid sort

❓ Why you need it

Strong-minded leaders get so used to articulating their views strongly that they often fail to recognise where alignment within the Leadership Team already exists.

There is a cost to this, as it may mean they do not get round to focusing on areas that need more discussion or exploring the full range of possibilities.

Like the Priority Matrix, the Rapid Sort is a tool for teams that need to:

▲ Fully understand the full range of issues that need to be balanced and traded off.
▲ Find a way to compare the very different types of issues and work.
▲ Work through the total picture of existing and potential work and reduce it to a deliverable set of priorities for the organisation.

🔧 The tool

The Rapid Sort is a simple voting approach for bringing together everyone's perspectives on priorities, so that these can be considered by the whole team. In particular, it highlights the strength of feeling associated with groups of priorities, helping to create a clear focus for the ensuing conversation.

It creates a quick and comprehensive visual map of how all the knowledge and experience in the room rates the relative importance of a wide range of ideas.

👉 How to use it

The Rapid Sort does not require an expert facilitator, but it does require the facilitator to be perceived as neutral.

It can be used on any list of priorities – or as an alternative to Stages 2 and 3 of the Priority Matrix process. In this case, the first step is performed exactly as it would be in a Priority Matrix exercise, with team members writing down their own priorities on Post-it notes, sticking them on the wall and then grouping them under suitable umbrella headings.

This time, however, the idea is to distil a large initial number of priorities into a smaller number of options for prioritisation, rather than positioning them on the matrix.

Once the groupings are identified on the wall, each member of the team is

The Rapid Sort will deliver a clear, visible map of all the views in the room. They tap into the collective knowledge, experience and expertise of all present.

given a pen and asked to cast votes, by marking the appropriate groups, for the priorities he or she sees as the most important. The facilitator reminds everyone to think about priorities from the point of view of both importance and urgency.

Each team member has a budget of seven votes to distribute. Team members can divide their votes however they like, including giving a group more than one vote.

Once everyone has voted, a straight count of the votes marked on each priority note quickly reveals which priorities the team, as a whole, believes are most important – and which it does not rank so highly.

As this is a relatively crude assessment, the facilitator should open up a discussion to test the validity of the conclusions:

▲ Which priorities should be taken forward? (It's sometimes unclear where in the voting list the line should be drawn.)
▲ Is the team comfortable with what has emerged?
▲ Are there any outliers that, despite

receiving few votes, require discussion before they are discarded?
▲ What should happen to those issues not selected? Should they be deprioritised completely, modified or deferred temporarily?

The facilitator can then lead a conversation about what needs to happen next.

As with the Priority Matrix, the team then needs to discuss, agree and assign actions and owners who will be responsible for making changes as a result of this prioritisation.

▲ Who will own and drive each priority area (in all three categories)?
▲ What will these owners do to clarify and check their understanding of actions and next steps for each priority group?
▲ When will the board next review progress on the list and actions agreed for all the priorities?
▲ What needs to change on board agendas?
▲ Who else needs to be communicated with about the outcomes?

PRIORITY *conversations*

The rapid sort

✔ The benefits

There are some obvious similarities between the Rapid Sort and the Priority Matrix tool. But the two techniques also differ in some important respects.

The Priority Matrix gives more structure and objectivity – but takes a little more time and debate. The Rapid Sort is quicker and more decisive, but should be treated as a 'first pass' technique, with conclusions that need to be tested more rigorously.

Both approaches will deliver a clear, visible map of all the views in the room. They tap into the collective knowledge, experience and expertise of all present to focus discussion and effort on those issues that will make the greatest difference to the organisation's future. ▲

CASE STUDY

Best foot forward

A company that supplied orthopaedic shoes and other orthotic devices for people with walking and posture problems had decided to expand its business and begin selling directly to the public through concessions in high street stores.

As the change was being implemented, the Leadership Team found that it had to deal with a degree of scepticism from senior managers in the parent organisation, which had no previous experience or expertise in retailing. There was an urgent need to decide what would matter most and work best in the new business environment.

The CEO chose to use the Rapid Sort to quickly identify the priorities for success in the new shops. Many potential priorities were proposed, but the tool helped the Leadership Team whittle the list down to the one with the greatest potential impact.

After a lively conversation, team members found themselves agreeing that the key to retail success in this field was the quality of the customer interaction with staff in the stores.

They knew that customers with walking and posture problems could not ➤

just be sold one-size-fits-all solutions. They needed shop staff to act as informed advisers, able to talk authoritatively about the alternatives and, where necessary, offer diagnostic services, such as slow-motion video analysis of an individual's gait.

They now realised, however, that this wasn't enough in itself and that customers' experience of the service – from initial contact, through multiple visits for diagnosis and through to fitting and aftersales – would be critical in drawing them away from buying in clinics. Central to this would be the recruitment of store staff who could quickly build relationships with customers and give them the confidence to purchase in this new environment.

There had been a tacit understanding that this would be important, but the issue had never been seen as a clear strategic priority – or given explicit Leadership Team attention. Shifting the company from its historic focus only on manufacturing and distributing products to a future as a service-based sales organisation was a profound change. Amid all the complicated programmes for leasing, fitting out and opening stores, staff recruitment had been a necessary activity. But its key strategic importance had been missed. Now it became the Number One priority.

Armed with this new clarity, the Leadership Team developed a strategy built around attracting, training, and keeping a different type of sales staff.

There had been a tacit understanding that this would be important, but the issue had never been seen as a clear strategic priority

Recruiting and retaining staff with empathy and warmth became an explicit focus, and, indeed, became the organising priority for the entire retailing strategy.

The profound shift of emphasis was a key reason behind the parent company's decision to separate the retailing arm into a separate company with its own Leadership Team and organisation within the group.

Today, the direct-to-customer retailing business has boosted the group's overall turnover by more than 20 per cent. Apart from the additional retail sales, the new shops have given the company more visibility and increased brand awareness, leading to strong sales growth in the core product business. ▲

PRIORITY
conversations

Challenging big rocks

？ Why you need it

The leaders I meet know that by trying to do so much, they achieve less. Almost all their important initiatives are compromised by inadequate resources, and none of them seem to make as much difference as they should.

In most cases, delivery is delayed. Some important initiatives never reach fruition at all, as the business need moves on before they can deliver.

To get beyond this and successfully prioritise, the thinking needs to be clear and realistic – in four important ways:

▲ You must have a strategy with clear organisational priorities.
▲ You must consider the demands of the new priorities alongside everything else that's already in progress.
▲ You must understand that, at some point, you will have to bite the bullet and stop, or delay, some activity.
▲ You must consider the bottlenecks caused by key individuals' capacity limits.

It is fairly common for teams tackling prioritisation issues to take the first three

of these elements into account. The last one is usually neglected.

As ever, it's the human dimension that's central to cracking the problem – and it is typically overlooked. Every organisation I work with has its rate of progress limited by the inability of a small group of key people to take on any more work. This usually includes most of the top team and a handful of other senior people outside it.

These people are the nexus – the place where strategy meets implementation, the point at which thinking becomes doing. Ideas can only be translated into action as fast as these few individuals can handle the work. They are almost always both productive and highly motivated.

But those qualities, while desirable, are also a big part of the problem. These key people are usually so productive that there is little more to get from them by being more efficient. They are usually so dedicated that they will keep accepting ever more work, even when to do so compromises what they are already committed to.

The Big Rocks tool embeds and makes real the work the team does on strategy and organisational priorities.

This tool is for teams who:

▲ Know that key initiatives aren't getting the leadership time and focus to deliver as effectively and quickly as needed.
▲ Have a heavy dependency on a few overloaded key individuals for success.
▲ Have tried prioritising, but found that change on the ground isn't matching the prioritisation that was done on paper.

🔧 The tool

Prioritising properly means dealing with the work that's on the desk of these few leaders. It means looking again at the organisational agenda through the lens of their capacity. Since most of them are in the Leadership Team, this is the best place to start.

The name of this tool comes from the story on page 120, the moral of the story being that if you don't put the 'Big Rocks' in the bucket first, you'll never be able to fit them in after all the sand and pebbles.

The principle is to rigorously test that the issues prioritised by the team, the 'Big Rocks', are adequately prioritised and resourced by every team member.

👉 How to use it

The facilitator tells the Big Rocks story and explains the importance of translating the organisation and team priorities into individual priorities. Some may feel this is obvious, but the facilitator should point out that new or clarified priorities at the collective level are often just added to the existing list of work for each team member – so that proper focus, on both the new items and the existing agenda, is diluted. Team members will usually readily recognise this.

Each team member is given 20–30 minutes to prepare a list of the main things he or she will be spending their time on over the next six months. The list should be written on a flipchart page with the 'Big Rocks' (team priorities) clearly identified.

As a guideline, less than seven items probably means too great a degree of aggregation. More than twelve means that too much detail is appearing on the list.

The team members stand up in turn and talk their colleagues through their

Challenging big rocks

lists. The whole team is then asked to assess what it feels about each list:

▲ Is the list manageable?
▲ Does it represent sufficient focus to guarantee delivery of the team's Big Rocks?
▲ Is all other work properly represented?

Usually the answer to at least one of these questions is 'no'.

Team members are then invited to offer ideas and suggestions about how the list could be modified to get it to a manageable level, with sufficient focus on the key priorities. It's helpful to post a list of areas to consider. See ideas below.

The discussion continues, with the team member making changes to the flipchart list as ideas are agreed. When it seems to have reached a conclusion, the individual is asked how he or she feels about the list that remains. When both the individual and the rest of the team are happy with the outcome, someone else stands up and presents the next list.

The amount of time to reach agreement on a list varies from person to person, but is usually between 20 minutes and an hour. It may well be, therefore, that not all team members' lists can be processed in a single meeting.

While it's tempting to try to find a full day to do this exercise, its unfamiliarity

---

ALTERNATIVE WAYS TO REDUCE OR MODIFY WORK

▲ Stop an activity completely
▲ Defer or reschedule it
▲ Reduce its scope
▲ Change the approach to it
▲ Delegate it
▲ Transfer it to another area or team member
▲ Accelerate it to get it out of the way quickly
▲ Add or move people to support it
▲ Outsource it
▲ Use a technology solution

means that some team members may be reluctant to dedicate a whole day to it before they have seen the process in action. We find the best results come from going through it with two or three team members as part of another meeting. Once team members have experienced the tool's power, there's always a strong appetite to find the time to process the rest of the team.

It's important to record the conclusion of each discussion. The team should then hold reviews to check that the agreed changes have been followed through. The first review should be no more than six weeks after the Big Rocks session, and this should be repeated until all the actions are complete.

✔ The benefits

The Big Rocks tool embeds and makes real the work the team does on strategy and organisational priorities. It turns what are often little more than attractive PowerPoint documents into real change – starting with the work of the members of the Leadership Team.

It also provides a big boost to relationships and team functioning. It's easy to lose sight of the pressures on others when you're struggling yourself. Understanding the other team members' challenges helps each team member become better at supporting the others and to be more empathetic towards their circumstances.

Finally, team members get a big shot in the arm. They walk away with a workload that is more manageable and will allow them to make more of the difference they want to achieve. They also feel a stronger sense of support from their colleagues. These factors combine to lift both their motivation and their productivity. ▲

PRIORITY *conversations*

Challenging big rocks

Sharing the load to ease the pain

I was concerned. I'd been working with a client for some months, but I'd been hearing worrying things in the run-up to the latest meeting. We'd made some great progress with helping the team work together, but behaviours had begun to deteriorate. Tensions were high and a number of big issues were coming to a head. When I spoke to members of the team, they were all struggling with their workloads and the mood seemed very low.

The pressures on the organisation and team were high. Their market was falling and their numbers were following suit. There was a huge amount going on and they were all working incredibly long hours to fight fires, while also trying to advance the big change initiatives that were needed to find a way out of their situation.

> *The sense of relief was palpable. Anxiety had been replaced by optimism. There was still a lot to do. But it was now doable.*

The organisation had a strategy and, some months before, we'd sorted through the new strategic initiatives alongside all of the existing activity to come up with six major priorities. This had been helpful for a time, but the Leadership Team members were now starting to buckle again under the pressure of work. They knew they needed to stop some things – but every attempt to do this had failed.

We did something different. Rather than reprise the strategy or look again at activity across the organisation, we looked at the workloads of the team members.

They each listed the biggest things that they were wrestling with – both from the strategy and also within their own area. Long lists were generated on flipcharts and the details were explained. After a couple of hours, we all ➤

understood the full picture across the team. What it was trying to tackle was plainly unachievable.

We had to think again. I asked the team members to spend some time alone, revisiting their own lists – but this time in the knowledge of everything they knew about the loads everyone else was grappling with. After this, they were to propose a revised list that they could be confident of delivering. They were invited to be creative and consider any and every way to reduce their own lists.

Each then came back with a new list. And, without exception, they were all still too long.

The other members of the team were briefed to help. They were told not to accept any list that didn't look credible – and to help with ideas for how a feasible list could be achieved.

We worked through each list in turn, and the conversations were tough, but supportive. A wide range of solutions were generated. Interdependencies were understood and worked through. Individuals let go of their personal priorities in the pursuit of achievable workloads for others within the total picture. It was hard work, but, by the end of it, many important decisions had been made. We finally had a set of lists that looked achievable and that would deliver what the business needed.

Afterwards, the sense of relief was palpable. Anxiety had been replaced by optimism. There was still a lot to do. But it was now doable. People took me aside to say how pleased they were with the outcome.

Quite apart from the new lists of work, relationships in the team were better than ever. People had come to appreciate the pressures on each other more fully than ever before. They'd forgiven each other for their past responses to those pressures and felt the real support of every one of their colleagues in the effort to get to a manageable agenda.

Within two months, the performance numbers were showing a dramatic upturn. It would be naive to think that this was the product of a single meeting. But it's also extremely unlikely that the emergence of a group of happier, more focused, less stressed leaders, with enough time to move the key initiatives forward, had nothing to do with it. ▲

TOOLS
— *for* —
ACCOUNTABILITY
conversations

The Ladder of Ownership

❓ Why you need it

Making and implementing decisions is one of the central functions of any Leadership Team. Paradoxically, however, most teams don't think very much about their decision-making processes. They think even less about the quality of the decisions they make.

The Ladder of Ownership is for teams who find that:

▲ Discussions can get circular and carry on a long time without a resolution.

▲ Team members leave the room with different interpretations of what has been decided – or even whether a decision has or hasn't been made.

▲ One or more team members aren't really signed up to the decisions that have been made, or may even show unspoken disagreement.

▲ Decisions that seem to be made are revisited repeatedly. Individuals seek to reopen decisions with a view to modifying or reversing them.

This tool will ensure that the team consistently leaves the room with clear and shared commitment to the success of every decision.

🔧 The tool

There are three elements which underpin this tool. All are based on Miles Kierson's work. Expert facilitation is not essential, but it is certainly helpful in managing the discussion and ensuring that the ideas underpinning the models are fully explored.

The first is a model which identifies the different modes of decision-making.

The facilitator introduces the model. We tend to write it on a flipchart rather than use a slide or circulate paper copies as this focuses everyone's attention in one place and is more conversational than a PowerPoint slide.

The facilitator then opens the conversation by inviting views and questions from the team on its mode of decision-making:

▲ Which of these modes does the team tend to default to? Is this appropriate?

▲ Are there any of them that aren't used? Should that be so?

This tool will ensure that the team consistently leaves the room with clear and shared commitment to the success of every decision.

▲ When the team makes its best decisions, which mode does it tend to be using?
▲ When it makes sub-optimal decisions, which approach is most commonly involved?

The second element is another model, the Ladder of Ownership (overleaf). Again, the facilitator introduces the model, writing it up on a flipchart.

The facilitator then opens the conversation by inviting views and questions from the team on its mode of decision-making:

▲ How do you see the distinctions between the different levels?
▲ How often do you see each of the levels in this team? Can you give examples?
▲ How often does the team get to the optimum level on the ladder?

Most teams will quickly get involved in a conversation about the distinction between 'Buy-in' and 'Alignment'. When this happens, the facilitator should introduce the third element, the ➤

MODES OF DECISION-MAKING

Directive – The leader makes the decision and informs the group.

Testing – The leader makes a tentative decision and tests it with others, and is willing to modify based on feedback.

Consulting – The leader presents a problem/situation and asks the group for recommendations. The leader reviews input and makes final decisions.

Delegation – The leader (or the team) sets some boundaries and delegates the decision to others (an individual or a task team).

Voting – Majority quorum, etc…

Consensus – Seeks the agreement of most participants, and the resolution or mitigation of minority objections. ▲

The Ladder of Ownership

The Ladder of Ownership

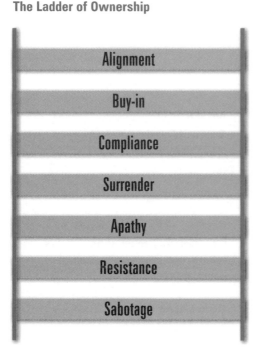

- ▲ Making sure you gain a shared understanding when you don't have one.
- ▲ Making sure you are fully informed.
- ▲ Avoiding the temptation to second-guess others' actions or thoughts.
- ▲ Ensuring you leave the room willing and able to speak sincerely and powerfully in support of the decision – even to the most sceptical audiences.

The facilitator should draw the conversation to a conclusion by inviting team members to discuss and agree how they will ensure that the level of agreement they seek on the Ladder of Ownership is clarified for each decision – and how they will check that it has been reached in each case.

✔ The benefits

'Responsibility for Alignment' summary (opposite).

To be aligned and stay aligned, you will do whatever you need to do to get into alignment. This may include:

- ▲ Speaking out when you don't understand something or when you are not ready to be aligned.
- ▲ Being watchful of yourself and others in relation to what is said and what's done after the decision is made.

A key benefit of this tool is awareness for each person of the decision-making process and the individual's own responsibility in it. Simply knowing that it's their own responsibility to do what's needed to get aligned helps team members articulate their views more often, ask more questions and be more explicit about their level of agreement or otherwise.

Above this, though, is a language for the team to be able to discuss the quality

INDIVIDUAL RESPONSIBILITY FOR TRUE ALIGNMENT MEANS...

Getting yourself to the position where you will fully commit to making the decision a success, whether or not it is the one you would have made.

Doing whatever is needed to be ready to speak in support of a team decision, to potentially sceptical audiences, even if you have significant concerns about it.

'Contributing doubt' by speaking out when you don't understand something or when you are not ready to be aligned.

Being watchful of yourself and others in what you say and what you do after the decision is made.

Making sure you gain a shared understanding when you don't have one. ▲

of any decision. Having labels to describe how team members feel about a decision or their perception of the positions of others in the team allows important issues to be surfaced and discussed:

▲ How aligned are we now?
(Where on the ladder are we?)

▲ How aligned do we need to be?
(Not every decision requires full alignment.)

▲ What do we need to do to get to the level of alignment we need?

Answering these questions allows the team to get to the right level of agreement more quickly. It will help the team keep working on any decision that requires greater alignment until it reaches the point required to ensure successful implementation.

The Collective Decision-making tool described on page 290 provides another method for the next stage, for actually making the decision, swiftly and efficiently.

CASE STUDY

Aligning for survival

In 2010 the economic crisis, and swingeing cuts in UK public spending, proved almost terminal for one company I worked with. Revenue plummeted – almost halved in just six months. It was a devastating blow, with brutal consequences.

Survival was the first priority, and that meant taking some dramatic and difficult decisions about redundancies and cost-cutting. The company was in lockdown mode, with only enough cash to keep running for a few months. The mood in the Leadership Team was bleak.

The team had generated a plan to reduce the company's dependency on government contracts and expand the share of revenue coming from private clients, but it was proving difficult to get all the team members to commit wholeheartedly to the new vision. People were feeling battered and insecure. They had seen colleagues lose their jobs and the company brought to its knees. They were afraid of committing, because they might fail and find themselves being blamed for not delivering against the new goals.

Given the pressures he was under, I was surprised and flattered to get the call from the managing director at this point. We decided to use the Ladder of Ownership to discuss accountability in the team. In the session that followed, there was a lively discussion of how often the levels appeared in the team. What emerged was a general recognition that the default mode within the team was no better than 'Buy-in'.

The CEO then stood up and showed the slides summarising the recovery plan. His message was simple and powerful: 'Delivering this will be tough. Buying in will not be enough. Either we get to full alignment, or we tear this up and come up with another plan. I'm happy to take as long as we need. What is missing for each of us to be able to get fully aligned?'

Everyone spoke. A wide range of questions and concerns were raised. Each was written up on a flipchart. When we had them all, we started to work down the list. ➤

It was a long and challenging day. On some of the issues, the team had some control.

It was clear, however, that a number of elements of the Ambition and Priorities were anything but controllable. They required an absolute commitment to even have a chance of success. The risks were all too clear. Failure could certainly mean the loss of a lot more jobs – and quite possibly the viability of the company.

The mood in the room was solemn, and the CEO spelled out what everyone was thinking.

'I don't know if we can do this,' he said. 'I believe we can, but I can't be sure. We've done what we can to mitigate the risks and satisfy our concerns. Now we have to choose. We have to decide if this is a plan we can all fully commit to. If you can't, I'll understand. We all will. I need absolute honesty from each of you. I have a view, but our decision will have to depend on what we all think. I'd like to hear from each of you whether you can be fully aligned?'

There was a long and thoughtful silence before one of the less dynamic team members – the last person you'd have thought would take the lead – looked around the team and simply said 'I'm in.' This was powerful, as his responsibility was for a part of the plan where the team had tried and failed before.

In response to his quiet but resolute commitment, the mood in the room began to change. One by one, team members confirmed their agreement.

The CEO was the last to speak. 'Thank you. I'm in, too. We're in for a tough ride, but I can't think of a better team to do it with. This just might be the most important day in our history. The hard work starts tomorrow. For now, I hope you'll join me for a glass or two of wine in the bar…'

Almost immediately, this company began to make positive progress, especially in the target sectors. Within three years, over 70 per cent of the business's revenue was coming from a range of private sector clients. The company has reduced its exposure and vulnerability to government contracts and policies and positioned itself well for growth. Revenues have been growing steadily ever since, despite challenging market conditions. The company survived the darkest moment in its history and is gradually growing its way back to a strong and robust position. ▲

Collective decision-making

❓ Why you need it

In every Leadership Team discussion there comes a point where a decision has to be made.

Getting the timing for this moment right has to be a matter of balance. There needs to be sufficient exploration of the situation, goals and options and a full understanding of the relevant knowledge, experience and perspectives of team members. There will also, however, be many other things to talk about. The team will often have to make decisions with incomplete information, so the discussion should not extend any longer than is necessary.

The team needs to find the point where team members' concerns, reservations and needs have been sufficiently addressed. This point will depend on the quality of the decision required, and specifically where on the Ladder of Ownership the team feels it needs to be (see previous tool).

Very few teams, in our experience, are consistently able to strike this balance well. A big part of this is because they don't have a practical mechanism for making a decision in a group.

Collective Decision-making is an invaluable tool for any team that regularly:

▲ Reaches decisions too quickly, with insufficient exploration, or leaves some team members without enough agreement for effective implementation.
▲ Finds itself with doubts or disagreements after a meeting about whether a decision has been made or what exactly the decision was.
▲ Struggles or takes too long to bring discussions to a clear conclusion.

🔧 The tool

The Collective Decision-making tool is simple and does not require expert facilitation. It involves two steps.

STEP 1 The first step begins at the point where any member feels the team may be ready for a decision to be made. The team member initiates the process by saying: 'I have a proposal…' and goes on to articulate a proposed decision as briefly and succinctly as possible.

Few teams have a mechanism for making a decision in a group. Collective Decision-making provides a simple way of doing this which will increase both the speed and quality of it's decisions.

STEP 2 Once one team member has done this, the second step is to ask each member of the team, in turn, for an explicit response. Only two responses are permissible.

Team members can each agree, and they do so by simply saying 'I agree'.

This is all they should say – elaborating on their agreement simply consumes time without adding any benefit.

The only alternative to agreement is to disagree. If this is the case, team members must explain briefly and succinctly why they feel unable to agree and put forward a new or modified proposal.

If there is a counterproposal, all the team members are asked again which of the two proposals (or more, if more than two emerge) they favour.

The decision is made when every member of the team has agreed.

If agreement can't be reached, or there is a split between two alternative proposals, it's almost always because some aspect of the situation, goals or options has been insufficiently explored. In this case, the team will need to cycle back to the relevant issues and talk about them

again until someone feels that the team is ready to decide and makes a new proposal.

Once everyone has agreed, the decision is clearly recorded.

It's important to note that it doesn't have to be the team leader who proposes a decision. Indeed, it's helpful if everyone involved takes on responsibility for trying to identify a possible decision and articulate it as a proposal. This is often a role which is easiest for members of the team who are less directly involved with the content.

✔ The benefits

This is a simple tool with potentially profound benefits.

Every Leadership Team wants to make the best possible decisions. Checking with all the team members whether they agree, or can be fully aligned, ensures that all the expertise, experience and knowledge in the team is fully incorporated.

Requiring every team member to be explicit about his or her agreement also ensures that reservations and questions are fully explored in the room, removing the risk of the decision being second-guessed or undermined after the meeting has finished.

While this might seem like a recipe for interminable discussions before agreement can be reached, our experience is that it almost always saves substantial amounts of time. Getting to a proposal quickly often avoids teams wasting time by 'agreeing violently', and at length. Even when agreement is hard to reach, the process quickly highlights the key issues that need to be addressed, allowing the team to focus in on them and find solutions.

The final benefit is a subtle but important one. Frustration with the team's ability to get to – and stick to – decisions is one of the most common complaints we encounter. As the team becomes better at getting to high quality decisions quickly, confidence – in one another and in the team – grows rapidly.

As well as making team meetings more enjoyable and fulfilling, this growing confidence means that teams can often square up to some of the more contentious issues that they have been circling for a while. The impact of getting these tabled, and finding resolutions, is profound for the organisation, as well as the team. ▲

Setting fire to £11m

The best Leadership Team I ever worked in was an eclectic mix of very different personalities and styles. The MD, Mike, had spent some time assembling it and it was full of big personalities with strong views.

The business we were leading was in trouble. Our market was not growing, competition was fierce and the inevitable effect on the profitability of our products was negative. Both we and our competitors had sales forces that were busily engaging in a race to the bottom, offering services to everyone else's customers at lower and lower prices. Our parent company saw little future for the business and was actively thinking of selling it. Prospects were bleak.

As well as the usual avalanche of day-to-day operational decisions, we had a number of huge calls to make. These ranged from whether to launch internationally, how to make big cuts in costs, how to deliver a complete corporate rebrand in the marketplace, and how to approach an ambitious business transformation agenda.

At first we found decision-making difficult. Mike had a reflective and thoughtful style and leaned strongly towards consensus as an approach to decision-making. While this undoubtedly gave the best chance for us to access all the expertise in the team, it made for very long meetings. We would talk and talk, even sometimes when we were all but agreed. Mike began to attract criticism, from both inside and outside the team, about the speed of his, and our, decision-making.

As part of our team development, we were introduced to the Collective Decision-making tool. As with anything new, it made us feel awkward and self-conscious at first. But we soon got used to it – and it transformed our meetings.

I remember one decision in particular. We'd been working through a major IT project for some years, but it seemed to be going nowhere. We were in a familiar pattern. A paper would be put before us, explaining the latest set of setbacks ➤

Collective decision-making

and problems and putting the go-live date back, sometimes for a few weeks, sometimes for months.

We'd discuss what had gone wrong at length, trying to understand the problems. We'd talk about the new launch date and try to muster confidence that we would meet it. The team would be sent away to carry on. Our MD would have to report the delay (and additional costs) to the main board. And sure enough, a few weeks later, a new paper would come before us. It always started the same: 'Unfortunately…' And so we went on.

Then, one meeting, it all changed. We were going through the same familiar process of trying to understand, and failing as usual, when the IT director, of all people, said:

'I have a proposal to make… We've been circling this project for months, if not years. We have been completely unable to bring it to a conclusion. Every month it's burning tens, even hundreds of thousands, of pounds.

> *Sure enough, a few weeks later, a new paper would come before us. It always started the same: 'Unfortunately…'. And so we went on.*

'We all know that we'd choose a different solution if we were to start it again today. I propose that we cancel the project. We need to explore the implications more fully, so I further propose that we should suspend all spending on it today until we can understand fully what a cancellation would mean. What do you think?'

There was a stunned silence. We'd already sunk over £11m into the project – and the latest launch date was only six months away. Could we really countenance just cancelling it? What would the board say? What would our people make of it?

When people started to respond, we surprised ourselves. Some were ready to agree straight away. Others modified the proposal by adding in things that we'd need to address during the moratorium period, before a final decision could be made.

We did stop the spend that day. And we did subsequently cancel the project. In the end, we got credit from our people for taking such a brave decision. Even the main board recognised how tough a call it had been to make and praised our courage for grasping the nettle.   ➤

Once we'd made the decision, a number of things fell into place. Another project was expanded to pick up some of the scope. Makeshift processes that had been cobbled together to get us by until the new system arrived, and that had been allowed to remain in place for far too long, were properly redesigned. The people who had been tied up on it were redeployed to other, more productive, work.

For the team, letting the project go was a huge release. It had been a millstone round our necks. We must have spent many days debating it. That one intervention by the IT director allowed us to cut all of that wasted time. That one decision transformed our confidence and changed how we saw our role. Suddenly, no decision was too big for us. No issue was too thorny, no view too controversial.

As a Leadership Team, we transformed the company. From this point on, we were able to deliver several successive years of double-digit profit growth. Given our marketplace, this was a feat so amazing to others in the group that we were described as 'defying gravity'. All talk of selling us disappeared.

> *Suddenly, no decision was too big for us. No issue was too thorny, no view too controversial.*

There was obviously far more to our success than one meeting process. But we started getting our big decisions right far more often than we got them wrong – and always left the room with enough clarity and alignment to deliver what we'd agreed. ▲

TOOLS
for
DELIVERY
conversations

The project charter and PINS

❓ Why you need it

One of the most common issues with projects in organisations is a lack of genuine alignment about what a project is supposed to achieve and deliver. Time pressures often mean that the project is defined too vaguely. Misunderstandings and differences from the original brief are then magnified as it works its way through implementation.

Alternatively, where teams do have a clear approach to projects, they are often so cumbersome and bureaucratic that there is a disincentive to use them and the value these disciplines can offer is not realised.

The Project Charter and PINS will allow the team to:

▲ Get alignment on all of the key aspects of a project at its inception.
▲ Empower the leader and project team by giving them a clear brief and parameters within which to operate.
▲ Manage project updates quickly and succinctly – in ways that are most supportive and helpful to the project team.
▲ Do all of this with the minimum of paperwork and bureaucracy.

🔧 The tool

Neither part of this tool requires an expert facilitator.

The Project Charter is a one-page summary of the critical aspects of any project, under six headings: objectives, deliverables, timings, risks and mitigations, team resources, and stakeholders.

The PINS document complements the Project Charter and provides a snapshot of a project's current status in terms of three factors – Progress, Issues and Next Steps.

👉 How to use it

There are a number of ways of creating a Project Charter. The most effective is to follow on from a Priority Conversation. The Leadership Team works together or breaks into small groups to develop a draft charter for each piece of work. This establishes broad parameters for each project and ensures alignment in the team at the next level of detail.

A leader for the project is then nominated and he or she works outside the meeting with the team that will be responsible for delivering it to refine the draft. Once this has been done, the final

Generating clarity and alignment right at the beginning of the most important projects is critical. This tool allows this to be done rigorously and concisely.

Sample Project Charter

Project rationale — why has the project been commissioned, in this way, at this time?

Objectives

What are the desired outcomes/results?

Key deliverables

What will the project produce or deliver and by when?

What quick wins will it produce?

Measures and targets

How will success be measured?

What are the specific targets?

Risks and dependencies

What might impede or derail the project?

How will we mitigate each risk?

Resources

Who should be the project leader?

Who should be in the team?

What other resources are required?

Stakeholders and needs

Who else needs to be involved or informed? How? How often?

RACI (who should be Responsible, Accountable, Consulted and Informed?)

The project charter and PINS

version is brought to the Leadership Team for approval and sign-off.

Most teams find the Project Charter deceptively simple. They start with the expectation that completing it will be rapid and straightforward, but soon discover that it provides a surprising level of rigour.

When the Leadership Team needs to be updated on each project's status, the project leader circulates a one-page PINS document at least forty-eight hours before the meeting. The document summarises project status under three headings:

> **P**rogress
> **I**ssues
> **N**ext **S**teps
> (including requests for support)

If necessary, this can be backed up with other documents that provide more detail. But the PINS summary itself should draw specific attention to the elements of the supporting information Leadership Team members need to focus on.

Everyone in the team is required to properly read the papers before the meeting and to identify any questions or needs that need discussion.

At the meeting, the Project Leader starts by summarising what is needed from the conversation. The people around the table are then asked in turn what questions or needs they would like to address.

The presenter notes all of these and then decides on a logical order to work through the list, ensuring that the most important issues are given the most time by being dealt with first. He or she then manages the discussion, ticking off each issue or query as it is dealt with.

✔ The benefits

Generating clarity and alignment right at the beginning of the most important projects is critical. This tool allows this to be done rigorously and concisely. It makes good project discipline simple and accessible and thus makes it far easier to embed and sustain good practice.

By setting projects up well, the Leadership Team empowers and motivates the leader and the project team charged with implementation.

The PINS process reduces the amount of Leadership Team time required to manage the project by focusing on only those aspects that require their attention or support.

In this way, the Leadership Team can make the transition from managing a collection of projects to managing the overall programme of organisational change needed to reach the ambition.

By keeping themselves updated quickly and succinctly on updates for all major ongoing projects, the Leadership Team members become capable of effectively managing more important projects at one time and achieving better results. ▲

Big rocks first

A Leadership Team of an engineering business we worked with had become stale. Results were good enough to keep the parent company happy but the company was treading water, making only small annual gains, while competitors were steadily eroding its position in two of its key markets.

The team had fallen into the habit of having long-winded meetings that lasted for hours. People rambled and the team frequently didn't get to everything on the agenda. Delayed finishes, running well into the evening, were the norm.

The catalyst came in the form of an employee survey which revealed, among other things, that the Leadership Team's reputation within the organisation had hit an all-time low.

Members of the team often came unprepared. When project leaders presented an update, they ended up wasting time ensuring everyone was familiar with the background before they could even start to address their projects' status or needs. Project managers often left meetings feeling frustrated because they hadn't got the engagement or support they required. ➤

The project charter and PINS

While there were many signs that dramatic changes were needed, the catalyst came in the form of an employee survey which revealed, among other things, that the Leadership Team's reputation within the organisation had hit an all-time low.

When the CEO decided to involve us, we quickly saw that it was going to be essential to engage the wider leadership group much earlier in the process than usual as an important first step on the road to rebuilding the relationships between the Leadership Team and the rest of the organisation.

We gathered all the key leaders in the business, about sixty people, in a room. We used a large group version of a Priority Conversation to gather and sort their views on the biggest issues facing the organisation.

Within a few hours, the group settled on eight key priorities, ranging from a product repositioning to a new approach to customer management and from an operational process redesign to a leadership development programme for first-level line managers.

A certain amount of work was already underway on some of the eight projects, but others needed to be started from scratch. Even those where work had begun were not well defined, overlapped in places and needed much more clarity and focus.

> *Within a few hours, the group settled on eight key priorities.*

Everyone in the room elected themselves to various groups, each working on one of the eight issues. Each group had the task of drafting a Project Charter for its project. These were posted around the room as they were completed, so that, by the end of the day, everyone had had a chance to see, and add comments to, all eight charters.

Team leaders then took these drafts away, assembled teams and refined the charters before they were signed off by the Leadership Team. It was decided that each project would update the Leadership Team every other month and the structure of team meetings was redesigned to make these updates a central part of their agenda.

➤

The PINS approach was adopted for updating at team meetings and the team made big changes very quickly. The reports were brief and everyone read them when they were pre-circulated. Because they knew that they would be asked for their specific questions, they made notes before meetings. Updates were shorter, but the key issues that arose were consistently addressed.

Soon the process had reached the stage where project managers actively looked forward to their sessions with the Leadership Team. They left each meeting having benefited from constructive challenge, help where it was needed and encouragement that they were on the right track.

Meetings became shorter and more focused. The Leadership Team was able to get through agendas faster and more efficiently, and project results improved rapidly.

A team that had been languishing and ineffective had become a role model that even the global board wanted to learn from.

The projects themselves soon began to bear fruit. Results began to improve markedly.

By the time the next staff survey came around, the change for the better was so striking that the previously uninterested parent company convened a shared board meeting to learn more about how they had turned things around so quickly. A team that had been languishing and ineffective had become a role model that even the global board wanted to learn from. ▲

TOOLS
– for –

DELIVERY
conversations

The leadership audit

❓ Why you need it

All MDs and CEOs are constantly wrestling with one key question – do I have the right people on my team to succeed?

Too often, though, this judgement is dominated by the individual's perspective on team members' ability to deliver within their own areas. While this is obviously important, it is not enough to guarantee success in building and realising the benefits of a powerful Leadership Team.

There is, for example a strong correlation between team performance and the number of team members who demonstrate high levels of empathy – and an even higher correlation with the number of members who have the courage to challenge one another's behaviour (Hay Group, 2001).

Most teams will include some people who are already strong team players, others who can be shifted to contribute strongly and often at least one member who is disruptive to the functioning of the team.

Being able to distinguish between these types, and dealing with each of them appropriately, is critical to delivering the potential of the Leadership Team and the results the organisation needs.

The Leadership Audit allows the MD or CEO to:

▲ Assess team members on the basis of what they deliver and how they do it.
▲ Separate those who are, or can be, team players from those who are likely to have a negative effect on the team's functioning.
▲ Decide who to persevere with and support – and those for whom a more direct and decisive solution is required.

🔧 The tool

This tool does not require an expert facilitator.

The Performance-Behaviour Matrix (sometimes known as the GE matrix, as it was championed by Jack Welch at General Electric) separates and makes explicit two separate dimensions of leadership effectiveness.

Results delivery is an assessment of how effective the individual is at producing the job outputs required – in financial or other terms.

The Leadership Audit allows the MD or CEO to decide who to persevere with and support – and those for whom a more direct and decisive solution is required.

The Performance-Behaviour Matrix

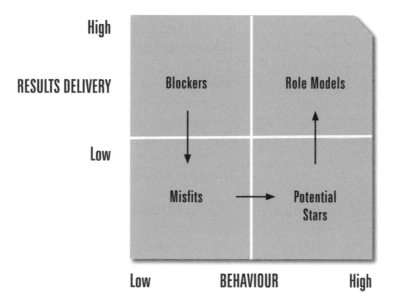

Behaviour is an assessment of how the person does the job (the inputs, if you like), and how aligned this is with the culture and behaviours the team and organisation need to promote for success.

The matrix therefore separates people into four categories:

Role models, who demonstrate both strong performance and good behaviours.

Potential stars, who aren't generating the performance they could be, but whose behaviours are good.

Misfits, whose performance and behaviour are both weak.

Blockers, who perform well but display the wrong behaviours in doing so.

The leadership audit

👉 How to use it

To use this tool for your team, simply place the initials of each team member in the position on the grid that best reflects the person's level of delivery and behaviour. This can be made as scientific as you like, using performance management data and other sources, but a quick and subjective first pass will often provide some good insight. Positioning everyone on the same matrix also enables easy comparisons between individuals in both dimensions.

The approach to the team members in each quadrant is then different.

Role models

The people in the top right-hand quadrant are the strongest members of your team. They are getting great results and doing it in ways that set the right example and get the most from those around them.

The biggest issue is managing the risk of losing them, as they are often overworked and can feel unappreciated or that others aren't pulling their weight.

The focus for this group, therefore, is on making them feel valued and deploying them where they can make the most difference.

Potential stars

Those in the bottom right quadrant are doing things the right way, but are not getting the results they should be capable of.

When we look at them more closely, we usually discover that some relatively small changes will improve their results and shift them up into the top right-hand quadrant. This can usually be achieved fairly easily with the right coaching, support and development.

Misfits

People in the bottom left are clearly in a bad situation – for themselves and for the organisation. They are generally easy to identify, as they aren't getting results and they aren't behaving as they should.

These situations need to be tackled head-on. A discussion is required, both to understand the situation and look at the alternative options that are available. They may need to be moved to new roles within the organisation that are a better fit for their skills, or have their existing roles reshaped to create a better fit. They may even need to leave to find a new challenge elsewhere.

If these situations aren't being confronted, it's usually due to a noble but misguided desire not to put the individuals in a difficult or upsetting position. By failing to take action in relation to anyone in this situation, you are playing a part in perpetuating an even more uncomfortable position in which neither party will be happy.

Blockers

The hardest people to deal with are those who appear in the upper left-hand quadrant. They are getting good results for the organisation, which makes them valuable, but they set a bad example by the way they operate. Most leaders I speak to know instantly and instinctively which individuals in their team or organisation fall into this category.

Because they are getting good results, blockers are likely to have been positively rewarded for undesirable behaviour, both financially and also in other ways. This will have reinforced their behaviour, usually over a long period of time.

These people can sometimes improve, but it will take a great deal of time and effort and, crucially, they must have the desire to make the change.

There are several reasons why getting these people to change behaviour and move to the top right is likely to be a long process, at least, and often an impossible one:

▲ They hardly ever 'jump across' straight to the upper right quadrant. The arrows on the diagram show the normal path individuals follow when developing. So these people need to start by changing their behaviours, develop and embed the new behaviours and then, gradually, learn how to perform and get results in a different way.

▲ This means that their performance actually worsens in the short term, so they move down, then right and then up. This is hard for both the organisation and the individual and it's very easy for the person to regress to old, more comfortable ways.

▲ Having been rewarded for a long time for doing things the way they do, they will usually find that mustering the motivation for change, and the sustained effort to make it happen is difficult.

▲ Because results tend to suffer in the short term when they change their behaviour, and they are used to success, the process of change is particularly stressful and difficult.

▲ Those around them will expect the person in question to behave in their usual ways and treat them accordingly, which has the effect of making changes even more challenging.

If you've read this far, you'll know that creating a powerful Leadership Team is incredibly valuable but also requires time and hard work.

The leadership audit

Trying to build a strong team without addressing the blockers will, at best, greatly slow progress. At worst, it can stop it completely. Leaving blockers in place will always limit the team's ability to realise its potential.

Confronting blockers is a crucial component of creating a great team – and doing it requires leaders to be brave and decisive. Dealing with these individuals is particularly challenging because their positive value is all too easy to quantify.

The alternative, however, is worse. Leaving blockers in place creates big problems. The costs are often far greater, but they are less visible and much harder to quantify.

People in every organisation watch movements among senior personnel closely. David Nadler calls this 'Kremlin watching' (Nadler and Spencer, 1998). Who is promoted or rewarded and who is moved aside are critical signals with the power to create both positive and negative impacts.

Messages from the top about appropriate behaviour are undermined by blockers. They seem to their colleagues to do the opposite of what is being asked for, and yet they appear to be rewarded for this. Employees often conclude that the Leadership Team isn't serious about setting behavioural standards – or even that its messages are hypocritical.

Conversely, removing people who are consistently giving the wrong message, even though they are delivering well, sends a strong signal to the whole organisation that behaviour is important and that everyone is expected to make the requisite effort and changes.

In addition to the impact on organisational culture, problems are frequently caused by the blockers' behaviour, within their own teams and with customers and other stakeholders. These problems are often hidden from view, so their scale and severity may only become apparent when the blockers have left.

Few organisations we have ever encountered have been doing enough to address their blockers, either inside or outside the Leadership Team. It's not easy or cheap, but failing to tackle this problem head-on is ultimately even more difficult and costly.

Auditing your wider leadership group

One of the most common causes of complaints from Leadership Teams I work with is the weakness of the wider leadership group. This usually manifests itself most in the shortage of good people to take on important new projects or initiatives. Teams find they are constantly having to turn to the same small group of key people. As a result, these people become overloaded, don't have the capacity for new things and can become disillusioned.

This tool can also, therefore, be used by the Leadership Team to audit the next tier of leaders. The team will need to set aside the time needed to assess each person in the next-tier management level – bearing in mind that this could easily involve sixty or seventy people in a large organisation.

If you spend five minutes on each of them, that's five solid hours of Leadership Team time. And is five minutes each really going to be enough? Probably not. But if a lack of resources at this level is hampering delivery of the biggest, most important changes the organisation needs to make, failure to take on this commitment has serious consequences.

✔ The benefits

By clearly identifying those whose behaviour is damaging the organisation, as well as those who need more support in delivering the desired behaviour and results, the Leadership Team will set a clear and unambiguous example. People watch what leaders do, not what they say, so a pattern of strong and consistent behaviour in senior leaders will be multiplied many times over by their followers.

Removing those people whose behaviour is inconsistent with the company's goals, even though they are achieving good results, communicates a clear message about what is and what is not acceptable, both to the Leadership Team and to the organisation as a whole.

Painful as this process may be, it does create an opportunity to introduce fresh blood, new ideas and a new style. This might involve bringing in an external recruit with valuable knowledge and experience from elsewhere, or it might be a chance to promote someone internally who has much to contribute but hasn't yet had the platform to allow this. ▲

CASE STUDY

The case of the profitable blocker

A firm of accountants we worked with had a problem with the director of one of their departments. He had had difficulties in dealing with clients. He caused friction when dealing with other members of staff. There had been many cases where his management of client funds, files and legal compliance had not been carried out according to the firm's policies.

Nothing had ever been serious enough to warrant disciplinary action, but there was a steady stream of problems. While most of these were small in themselves, taken together they formed a worrying picture. The senior partner knew that something wasn't right. He was so worried that he told me he'd been losing sleep about what he would do when the inevitable happened and one of these minor issues turned out to be more serious.

> *This department director was, however, one of the best fee earners in the business, and had been for a number of years. Because of this, and because he genuinely wanted to give him a chance to change, the senior partner had been reluctant to face up to the issue.*

This department director was, however, one of the best fee earners in the business, and had been for a number of years. Because of this, and because he genuinely wanted to give him a chance to change, the senior partner had been reluctant to face up to the issue.

Time and again, he had held tough conversations with the department director in an effort to address the issues of behaviour. Each time, things would improve for a while, but he soon fell back into his old ways.

When I discussed it with the senior partner he asked me for advice about what he should do with this errant individual. When I showed him the ➤

Performance-Behaviour Matrix and explained it to him, he instantly recognised that he was dealing with a classic blocker.

I explained why it had been so difficult to shift this individual's behaviour and the senior partner quickly concluded that the firm needed to move him on.

The first step was a direct conversation. It was tough, of course, for both parties, but the department director was less surprised and less difficult than the senior partner had expected. After a few weeks, an exit was agreed and the individual left.

Only then, as is usual in these situations, did the full extent of the problems become apparent. Once he was gone, people felt free to speak out about the problems he had caused. With access to the files he had managed, the Leadership Team found twelve potentially serious breaches of the rules in the way he had dealt with complaints from clients and in matters of legal compliance.

> *Time and again, he had held tough conversations with the department director in an effort to address the issues of behaviour. Each time, things would improve for a while, but he soon fell back into his old ways.*

At the time of writing, the Leadership Team is still repairing some of the damage he had caused. However, the firm has now found a replacement who (to everyone's surprise) is already more than matching the fee generation levels of her predecessor – and in a way that is consistent with the firm's brand and its values.

The department is now back on track, fees are improving and the firm has been seen to have dealt strongly but sensitively with an issue that everyone had been avoiding.

The senior partner was pleased with all these outcomes, but told me that the biggest change for him, personally, was not waking up every morning worrying about the possibility of an imminent disaster. ▲

TOOLS
– for –

DELIVERY
conversations

Contracting for cultural leadership

❓ Why you need it

The behaviours modelled by the leaders of an organisation have an enormous impact on how everybody works.

Contracting for Cultural Leadership is for teams that want to:

▲ Set the tone for the culture they want to see in the organisation and lead the change by example.
▲ Improve the behaviours in, and functioning of, the Leadership Team.
▲ Learn by personal experience what it takes to change behaviour – and what is, therefore, needed to support and accelerate it in others.

🔧 The tool

This tool doesn't require, but will benefit from, an expert facilitator.

It draws on the pool of knowledge and experience across the team about the best examples of leadership its members have encountered. From this, it builds a set of descriptions of the leadership behaviour that is most important to what the organisation needs to deliver.

The tool also ensures that each person is both supported in making personal changes and held accountable for making them. In this way, every member of the team will do things differently, which will have its own impact. Each individual also learns more about the process of making such changes, which is helpful when it comes to supporting behavioural and cultural change in those outside the Leadership Team.

It is energising, empowering and affirming.

👉 How to use it

Members of the team are divided into pairs (there may be a group of three). The pairs interview one another for 15 minutes each way on:

▲ What most attracted you to seek, and accept, a leadership role?
▲ Which leader has been most influential on your understanding of what great leadership looks like? What, specifically, did they do that demonstrated that leadership?
▲ What's the most positive example of leadership you have seen in our

Contracting for cultural leadership ensures that each person is both supported in making personal changes and held accountable for making them.

organisation (or industry, if the person joined recently)? What, specifically did the person do?

▲ When do you think you have been at your best in leadership? What did you do and why?

▲ What are your highest hopes for leadership in this organisation? What exactly would we see people doing if they were leading this way?

When asking the questions, the pairs should be asked to listen intently to the answers that emerge. These questions reveal a lot about leadership, but also uncover what matters most to the person responding.

When we brief people for the exercise, we ask them to listen as though it was one of their children telling them about the child's first day at school or their best friend describing his or her wedding day. As in these situations, listening of the highest order is required. The listener must focus on fully understanding the answers, and resist the temptation to add his or her own perspectives.

When responding, team members are asked to describe their examples as fully

and richly as they can, with particular emphasis on what people actually did. They are asked to respond with stories that are as full and complete as possible. What was the situation? What happened? What behaviours did the leader show – and how was this done? What were the results?

After the exercise is complete, the team members, in turn, report back on the key themes and stories they heard from their colleagues. As the team does, so the facilitator asks people to write down key themes, points and stories on large Post-it notes. These are stuck on a wall, as they arise, until the team feels that all the important ideas have been listed.

Together, the team then sorts the Post-it notes into groups, retaining all of the elements for each group to avoid losing the detail and colour from each Post-it.

Later, all the Post-it notes can be assembled into a set of headlines and behavioural descriptions. This needs to include rich descriptions of behaviour that people can recognise in others and emulate themselves, as in the example overleaf.

Contracting for cultural leadership

Stepping up to cultural leadership

Team members are then asked, in turn, to make a formal commitment to the rest of the team at least one change that they are prepared to commit to – effectively a contract to deliver – and to ask for the help and support they would like from the others to help them make and sustain the change.

For the next three months, there is a short session at the end of each team meeting in which all the team members report on how their commitments are going, and what further support would be helpful to them. Others in the team are invited to provide feedback on what they have seen, to offer support where they have seen changes made and to suggest other ideas that might help them.

✔ The benefits

The written output from this exercise is a summary of the cultural and leadership qualities that will be necessary for the organisation to succeed.

Rather than just rehearsing the noble, but vague and unactionable, statements usually found in such lists, this summary contains rich and colourful descriptions of behaviour that people can recognise in others and follow themselves (see Figure 27 on page 303).

The benefits of this exercise aren't only the insights that appear in the document.

Team members will have started on their own journey to step up their leadership contributions. By making a public commitment, they take on the challenges of changing behaviour – and know that they have the support and help of the other team members in doing it.

As they wrestle with making these personal changes, they learn more about what helps them, which provides invaluable insight when it comes to supporting others in their teams to make similar changes.

Because the source of the ideas and actions is rooted in each person's own experience, and in many cases their own leadership, team members' confidence in their ability to achieve them is much greater. If something has been done before in the organisation, or indeed if you've done it yourself in the past, it's only natural that you will feel more confident that you will be able to deliver it.

There is yet another valuable benefit, too, which is not immediately apparent. Using the questions to really understand what leadership means to each person provides a powerful insight into their values and motivations. We always introduce the exercise by saying that it will profoundly deepen and strengthen the relationships in the team. Team members usually dismiss this as hype at the outset – but never by the time they have been through the process. ▲

Example of cultural and behavioural descriptors

Fast and effective decision-making:

Working with urgency, involving the right people and making good decisions even with ambiguous or incomplete information.

We often have to take decisions with incomplete information — and on issues that will have implications for colleagues across the company. Making decisions calls for trade-offs between involvement and speed, and between certainty and risk.

We must all take responsibility for making decisions, rather than looking to others to make them for us. We must judge how to make the best decisions possible, as quickly as possible and with the right level of input from relevant colleagues. Where our input is sought in relation to a decision, we play our part by responding quickly and constructively.

As leaders, we recognise that each situation requires its own approach. Both consensual and directive decisions are appropriate at times. We will challenge ourselves and one another to improve decision-making processes so that sound decisions are made and communicated quickly.

Why am I waiting for someone else to decide, when I could take more responsibility?

Who is waiting for input from me to make a decision?

Who can I publicly celebrate for taking a brave decision?

What decision processes can I improve?

Which decision facing me requires a different approach?

Contracting for cultural leadership

Game-changing leadership on the pitch

A close friend and colleague of mine, Don, sent out a few speculative letters to businesses when he started his own leadership consultancy.

One of these was sent to the manager of the Premier League football club he had supported since he was a boy, and Don couldn't resist mentioning that he was a huge fan. At the time, the club was having a disastrous season and was right at the bottom of the league table, with a pitiful points tally. Most observers had already written the club off as doomed to relegation.

Don didn't really expect to hear back, so he was taken completely by surprise that afternoon when the phone rang in his car and he found himself talking to the team's manager.

The manager thanked him for his letter and told him that he was just calling to 'keep up with my PR obligations'. They started to chat.

After a while, Don asked, 'Do you mind if I tell you what I think is missing in the team at the minute?'

> *The club was having a disastrous season and was right at the bottom of the league table, with a pitiful points tally. Most observers had already written the club off as doomed to relegation.*

'You might as well,' the manager said. 'Everyone else has.'

'I think you don't have enough leaders on the pitch.'

This seemed to hit a nerve, and the manager embarked on a long, expletive-filled rant. Eventually, though, as the manager calmed down, he asked what Don thought could be done about it. They discussed a few options, but it was clear that a further conversation was needed.

'Well,' said the manager, 'we've got a training session tomorrow. Could you come and see me this evening?' ➤

Despite the four-hour drive involved, Don agreed, turned the car round and drove straight there, full of excitement and trepidation. Could this really be happening?

The manager welcomed him into his home and, while his wife entertained guests in the living room, the two men sat in the kitchen and drew up a plan.

The very next day, after the morning training session, Don found himself in a room, sitting in a circle with the entire first team squad – of his own team, his football heroes. It was an unreal moment.

The work, however, was simple. He broke the players up into groups of three and asked them to think about the best leader they had ever played with and exactly what he had done. Some of the names he recognised; others were more obscure. Most of the leadership examples that were mentioned were simple and powerful.

After the discussion about the leaders and their qualities, each person in the group of three made a commitment to his two colleagues. They helped him refine it and agreed what they would do to support him, and to remind him of it in the game on Sunday. When they had all done this, every player repeated his commitments to the whole group.

Sunday's game was an away match against one of the big clubs, a team that was doing well and pushing for a Champions League place. No-one expected anything other than an easy home win. They were wrong. Don's

> *No-one expected anything other than an easy home win. They were wrong.*

team produced its best performance of the season and won two-nil.

In the TV studios, the pundits were at a loss to explain the underdogs' transformation. No doubt, the home dressing room was an uncomfortable place to be, but the mood on the away team's bus was ecstatic.

At home, in his armchair in front of the TV, Don allowed himself a contented smile and treated himself to a celebratory glass of red wine. Survival for his club and a good start for his business were beginning to look rather more likely. ▲

TOOLS
for

LEARNING
conversations

Stuctured dialogue

? Why you need it

The Structured Dialogue tool is for Leadership Teams that need to:

▲ Develop a deeper, more complete and more insightful understanding of issues, find better solutions and decisions and improve their results.
▲ See the big picture, taking full advantage of the range of their experience, knowledge and insight to understand and respond to complex issues.
▲ Have meetings that build shared meaning, rather than descending into clashes of opinion that foster disagreement, frustration and confusion.

⚒ The tool

Structured Dialogue is unlikely to deliver its full value without the initial guidance of an expert facilitator. It is a very different way of interacting and facilitation is useful to coach and support the team while it is learning these new skills.

Real dialogue – the sort of dialogue that builds understanding, trust, insight and ambition – does not just happen. Productive dialogue can be separated into four components (see page 319):

▲ **Framing** explains the background and thinking behind a contribution.
▲ **Advocacy** involves making a proposal or proposition.
▲ **Illustration** provides examples to support the advocacy.
▲ **Inquiry** asks open questions that invite others to contribute their input and interpretations.

Ensuring that each contribution and interaction includes all four elements creates better conversation and better outcomes. The Structured Dialogue tool builds awareness of the four elements and helps teams practise incorporating them as they work on the real issues of the day.

☞ How to use it

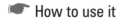

STEP ONE
Introduce the concept of dialogue

The facilitator starts by explaining the difference between discussion and

Teams who use Structured Dialogue see the big picture, taking full advantage of the range of their experience, knowledge and insight to understand and respond to complex issues

dialogue and invites the team to share views about their experiences of both.

There's a useful list of these differences, compiled a few years ago by personal development trainer Barry Winbolt, which I have adapted for use with Leadership Teams (see overleaf):

The facilitator should then explore with the team:

▲ How often have they experienced each mode?
▲ How do the results of each mode differ?
▲ Are the different modes better suited to particular subjects or types of conversation?
▲ What would be the benefits if more dialogue could be introduced where appropriate?

STEP TWO
Introducing the model

The facilitator next describes the four components (Framing, Advocacy, Inquiry and Illustration) and invites an exploration of the team's usual ways of interacting;

▲ Which elements are usually present and which are missing in the team's interactions?
▲ Is the present mix getting the best results?
▲ What would need to change for conversations to be more productive?

STEP THREE
Use the model to reflect on a working session

The team should now move on to a working session on a subject that needs to be addressed. At the end of the session, the facilitator invites the team members to reflect on where the interaction went well and where they got stuck.

▲ What was the balance between dialogue and discussion?
▲ Was the balance different with the Structured Dialogue model in mind?
▲ Where all the elements were present, did it improve the conversation?
▲ Where the conversation faltered, what element might have been missing?

Structured dialogue

Discussion vs Dialogue: The Seven Key Differences

Discussion	Dialogue
Adversarial: trying to prove the other side wrong	Collaborative: working together to find a shared view and a common understanding
About winning: the assumption is that there is a right answer and that this is it	About exploring: the assumption is that there are various pieces to an answer that need sharing
A closed-minded attitude, coupled with a dogmatic determination to be right	An open-minded attitude: based on openness to change and to the possibility of being wrong
Listening for flaws: focusing on differences and making counter-arguments	Listening to understand: making links and discovering shared views
Defending assumptions as unchangeable 'truths'	Uncovering assumptions for discussion and evaluation
Criticising the other side's position and defending one's own views	Re-examining every position and accepting that others' views might improve one's own
Affirming one's own point of view	Enlarging and even changing the views of both sides

TORBERT'S MODEL FOR PRODUCTIVE DIALOGUE

Torbert's 2004 *Action Inquiry: The Secret of Timely and Transforming Leadership* identifies four elements that, together, form the basis for productive dialogue.

Framing

Refers to explicitly stating what the purpose is for the present occasion.

For example, 'We're about halfway through this course and I'm not at all sure that many of the participants have enough of a grasp of the material to pass the exam. I'm very concerned that people aren't understanding but also aren't asking questions or participating in the discussion.'

A frame is usually an expanded description of the dilemma you are trying to resolve, including being explicit about the assumptions you believe you or others may be making. This is the element that is most often missing from conversations and meetings, as people often assume that everyone shares the same understanding of the current situation.

Advocating

Refers to explicitly asserting an option, perception, feeling or proposal for action.

For example, 'We've got to do something about class participation. We should raise our concerns with the group.'

Illustrating

Involves telling a story or giving a concrete example that puts meat on the bone of the advocacy and orients and motivates people more clearly.

For example, 'I'm thinking that we might open the next session with a question for everyone to answer, such as "How confident do you feel about the material?" Or perhaps we should ask small groups to discuss and recommend what we need to do to increase participation.'

Inquiring

Involves questioning others, in order to learn something from them.

For example, 'How well do you think the participants have understood the content so far?', 'Why do you think participation is low?' and 'Do you have any ideas for how to address this?' ▲

Structured dialogue

While the team members are getting used to the new approach, it's helpful to continue to reflect regularly on where the four elements are present or absent and what effect this is having on the quality of the team's interactions.

✔ The benefits

Even the first experiments with Structured Dialogue can have an immediate impact on the Leadership Team's interactions, as team members experience a different way of working together. Knowing the difference between dialogue and discussion, they can make conscious choices about the best way to work for the tasks in hand and the results they need.

Because dialogue is collaborative, it enables team members to glimpse and use the power that can be generated when the team brings its collective intelligence, insight, experience and knowledge to bear on the issues that really matter.

Remember the tale of the five blind sages describing the elephant that I mentioned in the chapter on Learning Conversations? By failing to pool their observations, the five blind men came up with some very odd ideas about what sort of animal they were exploring.

Real dialogue lets teams combine their intelligence and data points to see the whole elephant. It gives them access to more options for tackling problems and creating better solutions. And, of course, by removing the destructive combative, competitive and confrontational elements from the interactions, it makes meetings more enjoyable, as well as more productive. ▲

A new way to talk creates a better way to work

The new managing director of a food chain had inherited an executive board that included some individuals who were highly talented but had little experience of working together as a Leadership Team. The directors were split into several factions, each with very different views of the business, and conversations often quickly descended into debates between these camps.

Every time this polarisation arose, it either rumbled on unchecked or was resolved unsatisfactorily by the managing director, who would have to step in and take decisions. Team members on the losing side of a decision were often unaligned with the outcome and didn't go on to support it fully. Sometimes they even deliberately undermined it.

'If I'm going to have to decide everything that comes up, I might as well not have a Leadership Team,' the new MD told me. 'And, unlike some of them, I don't always think I know best.'

I could hear the frustration in his voice, and I suggested the use of Structured Dialogue at the next team awayday to introduce the team to the benefits of seeing more and different points of view. He was unsure, but attracted by the idea of finding solutions that incorporated everyone's ideas and insights instead of binary decisions that supported one point of view, but almost always had downsides because of a failure to address some of the issues raised by others.

> *'If I'm going to have to decide everything that comes up, I might as well not have a Leadership Team.'*

At the following team event, we started by talking about the structure of good conversations. We analysed the difference between dialogue and discussion and looked at the four components of good dialogue – Framing, Advocacy, Illustration and Inquiry – before going on to discuss a major issue facing the business.   ➤

Structured dialogue

The company was under a lot of financial pressure and the annual store managers' meeting had come under close scrutiny because of the high costs involved. Hundreds of managers were traditionally brought in from around the country by air or train, put up in good hotels for two nights, fed and watered generously and given a range of attractive performance awards alongside messages and incentives for the forthcoming year.

The Leadership Team was divided on this issue. One faction insisted that the store managers' meeting was an essential part of the company's culture. The other said that, given the need to cut costs, it was important to send a message to the organisation that management was avoiding unnecessary and extravagant expenditure.

Both views were put across forcefully and the group began to polarise around the two viewpoints. The polarisation deepened as more team members joined the argument on both sides. Frustration grew, and the discussion became increasingly loud and fractious.

I was on the point of intervening when the operations director, who had been silent so far, broke the pattern. He told a story of a high-performing group of store managers from one region at last year's event.

He framed the conversation by saying how much these people had looked forward to the annual event and how much it meant to them to be recognised with awards for their hard work. One store manager, he said, had been on the verge of tears when he received an award. This man had taken the award back to his team and used it as part of a motivational meeting aimed at inspiring great performance in the following year.

The operations director's advocacy was that the cultural significance of the event was only part of its value and that there was lots of evidence that the celebration, recognition of exceptional results and sharing of best practice had a big impact on performance. He illustrated this by pointing out how well a number of specific stores and areas had performed and how they'd used the conference to help motivate their people. Finally, he asked his colleagues if there might be a way to retain the valuable impact on morale and performance without sending the wrong messages on cost. ➤

The shift was immediate. The conversation quickly evolved into a creative exploration of how the Leadership Team could hold the event at a realistic cost – and use it to communicate how seriously they took both the cost and performance agendas.

The team found ways to cut the cost of the annual store managers' meeting by half, while preserving most of the cultural and morale benefits that made it important in the company's calendar. The event was to be shortened so that delegates were only in hotels for one night, and session times would be adjusted so people could travel on off-peak fares. Accommodation costs could be reduced by striking exclusive deals with a single hotel chain. Various other ideas were put forward and it quickly became clear that team members were relishing this new way of working.

The session review that followed was illuminating. The operations director had not consciously used the model to inform his contribution. And none of the rest of the team had recognised it either – until it was pointed out. Everyone realised, however, that his intervention had shifted the conversation from an unproductive and destructive pattern to one which generated a great outcome.

> *It was apparent from the very next session that they were all thinking more carefully about the content of their contribution.*

The Leadership Team members had glimpsed the power of incorporating all the four elements, and it was apparent from the very next session that they were all thinking more carefully about the content of their contribution. It took a few sessions for this to begin to feel natural, but their slightly faltering first efforts steadily became more assured. The more they used the Structured Dialogue model, the more often they had positive and productive conversations.

I recently had cause to sit in on a team meeting. Even after over a year, it was noticeable how many times the four elements were explicitly referred to. Even more striking, though, was the complete absence of any of the factions or tensions that had so characterised their working before they learned the skills of talking by using dialogue as well as discussion. ▲

TOOLS
– for –

LEARNING
conversations

Good, tricky, do differently

❓ Why you need it

Good, Tricky, Do Differently (GTDD) can be used to review anything from individual performance to project status and from documents to discussions. The application of it here, though, is as a tool for improving how the Leadership Team works together.

Most leaders are strong advocates, at least in theory, of the importance of continuous improvement and learning. But this is rarely applied to the arena of Leadership Team interactions. This is, as we have seen, an area of huge cost, many missed opportunities and considerable frustration for most organisations.

GTDD is for teams that need:

▲ A quick and systematic way to reflect on and continually improve the way they work together.
▲ To lead by example by consistently seeking to learn and improve.
▲ A review tool with a wide variety of applications that can be used to get better results on a range of issues.

🔧 The tool

GTDD is a straightforward, practical way of reviewing the team's work that can be used to assess almost any aspect of team function. Best of all, it takes just a few minutes.

If I could choose just one change, and embed it deeply in the working practices of every Leadership Team we try to help, it would be to make Good, Tricky, Do Differently part of the team's routine behaviour.

GTDD is easy to remember and easy to use.

Once people are familiar with it, it doesn't require expert facilitation, though using a facilitator initially will make it easier and quicker to get to a point where the team can use it without help. It's not complicated but, like all new techniques, it can feel awkward to use at first and can easily fall into disuse if benefits aren't seen and experienced quickly.

The tool asks three simple but powerful questions.

▲ What was Good about [the subject we are reviewing]?
▲ What was Tricky about [it]?

GTDD is a straightforward, practical way of reviewing the team's work that can be used to assess almost any aspect of team function. Best of all, it takes just a few minutes.

▲ What could we Do Differently next time to improve [it]?

So far, so simple. But look more closely. The exact wording of these questions is enormously important.

What was Good about [the subject we are reviewing]?

This elicits clear statements of judgement. It generates learning by focusing on and affirming the positive aspects of what has been done, which are all too often overlooked as a source of ideas and information. The affirmative nature of the question helps to defuse any defensiveness.

What was Tricky about [it]?

This involves providing data about personal experience – which can't be disputed. If you found something tricky, no-one else can insist that it wasn't. The wording avoids judgemental or threatening language and reduces the likelihood of defensive reactions.

What could we Do Differently next time to improve [it]?

The final question is future-focused. It invites people to look for options and explore different answers, encouraging constructive dialogue and creative thinking. It involves building on the 'Goods', as well as changing things that were 'Tricky', and it produces constructive discussions on what can be improved beyond either of those areas.

☞ How to use it

Thirty minutes needs to be set aside at the end of the session for a meeting review.

The facilitator begins by explaining the importance of the tool and relating it to the need to continually improve all aspects of the organisation's functioning – with the effectiveness of Leadership Team meetings being an important element in that.

The tool is then introduced and the nuances of the language are explained.

Each team member is then invited to reflect on the meeting under each of the three headings. It often helps to give people a minute or two to gather their thoughts.

Good, tricky, do differently

The facilitator asks everyone to hold questions and comments until all the team members have shared their thoughts, and each person then gives his or her answers to each three of the questions.

Once everyone has spoken, the facilitator stimulates a discussion:

▲ What questions do we have about what we heard?

▲ Were there any surprises in what we heard?

▲ From the Do Differently answers, what will we change for our next meeting?

After this first experience, and while people are getting used to the process, it's best to use it to review longer team meetings, of half a day or more, where time is easier to find. Set aside 15 minutes to review subsequent meetings by following the process from the first meeting.

After two or three meetings, when team members have become easy and natural with it, open a discussion about other areas of team activity where GTDD might be best applied.

▲ Other than team meetings, where would the team most like to improve?

▲ What isn't working well and would benefit from some reflection and changes?

▲ How and when could the team best apply GTDD to those issues?

✔ The benefits

Used systematically, GTDD will radically alter the effectiveness of a Leadership Team and, by extension, the organisation as a whole. It's a powerful way for the Leadership Team to show by example how people can work together and to turn the theoretical concept of 'continuous improvement' into something real and practical.

By using this simple tool consistently and well, the team will develop a culture of feedback and a way of working that is always looking at how it can improve. New improvements follow each review. Some are big and some are small, but the cumulative effect is huge.

GTDD can also be used in many other ways. Wherever it's introduced, GTDD reliably leads to a set of constructive discussions about what could change and how. Because everyone is directly involved, people typically feel a high level of commitment to the suggestions that emerge.

Using this tool will generate new ideas and agreements about how to improve, which will lead directly to better performance. Used well it will always improve things – and remarkably rapidly.

We have successfully used GTDD as a tool to improve everything from relationships, team interaction in meetings and meeting outcomes to decisions, project delivery and individual performance. ▲

CASE STUDY

From a simple tool to a way to run the business

The Leadership Team of a plastics company had fallen into a pattern of working that was so destructive that the whole organisation was suffering. Team meetings were an ordeal to be endured. They had become a succession of updates. Every time the team got together at least one unlucky person would be caught in the spotlight as everyone else took the opportunity to jump in, criticise and offer 'advice'.

Team members' personal priorities revolved around making sure that they were not going to be singled out as this week's victim. The rest of each Monday afternoon, after the weekly meeting, was filled with team members talking in small groups and in one another's offices about the ineffectiveness of the latest session, the way someone or other had been unjustly picked on and the frustrations of never seeing the real issues confronted. Meanwhile, results were suffering.

When the new chief executive took over, she knew this must not continue. But she didn't know how to shake things up without inducing yet more defensiveness. She felt she had little to lose, however, so I suggested a thorough review of the way the team functioned, using the GTDD tool.

We decided to do this at the next management meeting. I set it up and everyone was invited to think about: ➤

- ▲ What is *good* about how we're working together?
- ▲ What is *tricky* about how we're working together?
- ▲ What could we *do differently*?

The CEO went first, setting the tone for the degree of honesty and directness that she knew was essential. She was clear and candid and didn't mince her words as she named a number of 'elephants in the room'. While some of her critique was uncomfortable, she adhered strictly to the three questions. She also made a number of positive observations, supplemented with some concrete proposals about how things could be improved.

What was meant to be a half-hour session turned into a conversation that lasted all morning. While there had been many 'water cooler' conversations between team members, it was the first time they had all talked together about the way the team worked. Because all the team members were invited to talk about their perspectives and experience, in a way that felt safe and not threatening, some big issues were raised. Unsurprisingly, many of these were shared concerns.

In the discussion that followed, the team focused on three themes:

- ▲ Within the group, things were often left unsaid that would have been better aired openly, and there were several relationships that were difficult and sometimes antagonistic.
- ▲ Meetings were unproductive. The team wasn't achieving its goals, despite spending many hours around the boardroom table.
- ▲ The team had allowed a toxic culture to develop within the organisation, and macho, coercive behaviour was tolerated. Behaviour within the team was reinforcing this, as the more assertive members tried to bully others into seeing things their way.

The team members agreed that these problems could no longer be tolerated and created a plan to work on improving each issue – starting with their own meetings.

➤

As the changes began to take effect, these meetings became very different. Instead of forceful behaviour being the norm, the team found it was increasingly able to examine all the issues on the table in a way that welcomed diverse points of view, encouraged exploration and steered the conversation towards clear, shared decisions.

From then on, the Leadership Team made a point of asking the three GTDD questions at the end of every meeting. Now they are fluent, these reviews take little time. Even after good meetings, further opportunities to improve are almost always identified.

> *GTDD became part of the culture and language, and a standard way of reviewing activity. It is now the natural way for people at the company to talk about how anything is going.*

Although we hadn't discussed this, some team members also began to adopt the same approach in their own departments, using it as a basis for both individual performance assessments and project reviews.

The questions were repeated so often that they became embedded in the organisation's culture, with every employee understanding that this was how he or she was supposed to look at progress and outcomes. GTDD became part of the culture and language, and a standard way of reviewing activity. It is now the natural way for people at the company to talk about how anything is going.

Consistently using GTDD questions in the Leadership Team and across the organisation produced impressive results. People at all levels engaged actively with the review process and found clear, intelligent and focused ways to work with the outcomes.

Within two years, the organisation had reversed a long decline and begun producing much improved results. When reviewing the company's turnaround (using the GTDD format as a structure, of course) the CEO specifically named the GTDD approach (it was no longer thought of as just a tool) as one of the key 'Goods' that had underpinned the transformation. ▲

Separating your Leadership Team meetings

? Why you need it

Leadership Teams have to be extraordinarily agile in how they think and operate. They may need to switch abruptly from high-level strategic thinking to managing the details of urgent crises. At the same time, they have to keep abreast of many legal and compliance requirements.

Leadership Teams often try to discuss everything in a single regular session. But this is not always the best way. The different requirements of each type of activity make it hard to deal effectively with long-range planning and then move seamlessly into a different mode to tackle governance issues or operational firefighting.

The result is usually sub-optimal discussions of all types and an inevitable domination of the agenda by issues that are urgent as well as important. Issues like strategy, which is always important but rarely urgent, often suffer (Taylor and Haneberg, 2011).

Separating these very different categories of work into different sessions allows the team to:

▲ Prevent the tyranny of the urgent from swamping important strategic and other discussions that require more time.
▲ Ensure that operational issues receive prompt and decisive attention.
▲ Give governance issues proper time and quality discussion.
▲ Make faster and more efficient progress in every area.

🔧 The tool

This tool does not require an expert facilitator.

There are three broad categories of Leadership Team discussion:

Strategic

Strategic conversations tend to involve exploring a relatively small number of wide-ranging, complex issues. There are multiple 'right' answers to most of the questions and these may differ widely from one another.

Strategic conversations usually have an agenda with a relatively small number of items, each of which needs deep exploration. They demand a mode of

Leadership Teams often try to discuss everything in a single regular session. The different requirements of each type of activity make it hard to deal effectively with long-range planning and then move seamlessly into a different mode to tackle governance issues or operational firefighting.

thinking and talking that is broad, exploratory and creative.

Operational

Teams need to discuss what has happened in the last week or month, what the current problems are, and what needs attention. This type of content is often detailed and urgent and the discussion needs to be decision-oriented. Potential solutions are usually less diverse but will need to be based on a good understanding and a clear fact base.

Operational conversations usually have a longer list of short items, all requiring crisp discussion and quick decisions. These issues call for a mode of thinking and talking that is focused, brisk and efficient.

Governance

Leadership Teams must also deal with statutory and other prescribed issues, including risk, health and safety, quality and other areas of compliance.

The focus is on ensuring that the organisation follows what are usually quite prescriptive processes and that members of the team understand and are committed to the actions that are needed from them to meet the requirements.

Governance conversations are often guided by expert input and require a mode of thinking and talking which is disciplined and thorough, and which engages members in what can be quite dry content.

These different types of content require such diverse modes of thinking and talking that they benefit from different approaches. Each requires a particular style of chairmanship or facilitation and each needs a different type of participation from Leadership Team members.

☛ How to use it

Teams get better results when they discuss different categories of issue separately. Each type of conversation should ideally have its own meeting – or, at the very least, a certain amount of prescribed time set aside within a longer event.

The frequency with which these separate meetings are held varies from one organisation to another. Typically, operations meetings will be held weekly or monthly, strategy meetings will take place

Separating your Leadership Team meetings

offsite every two or three months and governance meetings will be organised less frequently.

The first task, therefore is to identify which subjects fall into each of the three categories. The easiest starting point is the last few months' team meeting agendas, but it's often the case that some issues are clearly not getting enough attention, so there are likely to be other topics that need to be added to each of the categories.

Once this list is agreed, a meeting calendar can be drawn up that clarifies the standing agenda items for each meeting and is co-ordinated with the other timetabled reporting cycles. It is also important to leave some unallocated free time for the new issues that will inevitably arise.

✔ The benefits

Grouping the similar types of content together allows team members to tune in to the right mode of operation for each category. This alone makes for more effective and productive meetings.

Each of the three types of content also benefits in different ways.

Strategic issues benefit from having protected time. Because these issues are always important but rarely urgent, they are often compromised by being squeezed onto agendas full of immediate and pressing operational issues. The extra time allows for more exploration, better understanding and higher quality thinking in strategic discussions. More and better options become available.

Operations meetings will see more progress and quicker decision-making. The narrower focus on the current issues requiring the attention of the Leadership Team often reduces the amount of time that needs to be spent on them – and in some cases also means that not all team members need to be present.

Governance meetings are many team members' least favourite chore, and are often squeezed in around everything else. Separating dedicated time for them makes these important issues more manageable and helps ensure that they are given proper time and consideration. ▲

Making time for strategy

I was part of the Leadership Team at a branded goods business which started out as the offshoot of a bigger parent and grew rapidly in its early years. Growth began to level off just when the parent company was expecting the business to start repaying the huge investments it had made.

The company was headed by a successful and charismatic managing director whose style was flexible and opportunistic rather than structured and disciplined.

This had been helpful in the early years, when the agility of the business allowed it to make rapid gains on the competition. As the company grew, however, it became clear that leaders across the organisation needed a clearer framework to make local decisions, rather than always having to seek direction from the managing director and the Leadership Team.

The problem was that our Leadership Team meetings were always dominated by operational issues. The rapid growth of the company meant that there were many teething problems, practical decisions, activities and projects that required active management.

Amid all this, there was never time to engage with some of the broader issues – or to articulate a strategy to help others make some of the decisions that were percolating up to the Leadership Team.

Amid all this, there was never time to engage with some of the broader issues – or to articulate a strategy to help others make some of the decisions that were percolating up to the Leadership Team. The CEO's reactive style meant that he was quite comfortable with this mode of working and meetings became longer and longer as the list of issues to address grew inexorably bigger.

We knew that we needed a clear, communicable strategy to help devolve ➤

Separating your Leadership Team meetings

more decisions deeper into the organisation, and I was tasked with helping the team to articulate it.

I quickly realised that the team would need some dedicated time to work through the strategy and how to communicate it – and that this wasn't going to be possible within existing meetings.

I sat down with the CEO and we made a start by sorting out the issues and agenda items under the three headings. Once we could see the whole picture, we drew up a new meetings calendar to ensure that attention was given to one category at a time, and that everything important was covered.

The strategy meetings took the form of a series of awaydays. At first there was some resistance to the idea of spending time away looking only at strategy when everyone's diaries were already full. Initially just two of these events were put in the diary, in short succession, to get the process moving.

It became apparent early in the first strategy meeting that there was a huge amount to discuss. The discussions that took place on the first two strategy days were so obviously valuable that, even after the new strategy had been clarified and communicated, there was a continuing appetite across the team for protecting time to continue the discussions and the team decided to organise regular quarterly awaydays.

The strategy rollout, meanwhile, was a big success. It allowed the individual product categories and geographies to focus their efforts. A side effect was to increase the number of decisions that were made below board level, allowing the operational board meetings to be focused on a smaller range of more important issues.

Most importantly, though, the organisation went from a situation in which growth had plateaued to almost doubling its revenues in two years. ▲

Resolving conflict

❓ Why you need it

As discussed on page 50, Leadership Teams have more conflict than other working groups. It is both inevitable and necessary. The issue is how that conflict is channelled and managed so that it is generative and productive.

In the Thomas-Kilmann model (see diagram on page 51), this is described as collaborative. It's a type of conflict that expands the range of options available to the team and helps achieve win-win outcomes. This type of conflict always focuses on the issue and never on personal antagonism. As one client of mine puts it: 'We play the ball, not the man.'

Every one of the Six Conversations will play a part in ensuring that the team consistently achieves genuinely collaborative and constructive conflict. But destructive conflict does sometimes erupt, and it must be dealt with quickly.

The Resolving Conflict tool is for teams that:

▲ Suffer from serious, destructive conflicts which impede the ability of the team to operate effectively.

▲ Can't afford to wait for the effects of a team development programme or work on the Six Conversations to resolve the problem.

▲ Feel that destructive conflict needs to be addressed to open the way for the team development programme to work its magic.

🔧 The tool

The tool is based on two concepts. The first is the Conflict Iceberg, which shows how the hidden dimensions of any conflict need to be understood before it can be resolved. The second is the key role of the CEO in both sustaining and resolving the conflict.

It has three phases. Since Phase Two is explicitly concerned with the role of the CEO, a facilitator is required. The best results will be obtained by using someone with broad experience of coaching and conflict resolution. It is essential that whoever is chosen is outside both the team and the situation in question.

Every one of the Six Conversations will play a part in ensuring that the team consistently achieves genuinely collaborative and constructive conflict. But destructive conflict does sometimes erupt, and it must be dealt with quickly.

☛ How to use it

PHASE ONE
Understanding the iceberg

Most personal conflicts come to a head in the form of a defining event. But they can almost always be traced back to a number of previous instances of poor behaviour on the part of those involved. Underlying these behaviours are the emotions and beliefs that colour the thoughts and reactions of these individuals.

Phase One of the tool involves talking to each of the parties to ensure an explicit understanding of all four layers of the Conflict Iceberg.

In order to investigate what lies below the waterline, in particular, the facilitator will usually want to spend time with each of those involved. There may appear to be two apparent protagonists, but it's very common for the facilitator to discover that other people are also involved. It is also valuable to get a wider perspective, so we always recommend talking to all members of the Leadership Team.

By now, the facilitator will have developed a broad, deep understanding of the issue from the perspective of the team

as a whole. The last part of the process will be to explore the same questions with the CEO or MD and look at the leader's role in the conflict as it stands and in potentially resolving it.

PHASE TWO
Understanding the role of the CEO

There are a number of ways a CEO can approach a conflict within the Leadership Team, and most will have one or two ➤

The Conflict Iceberg

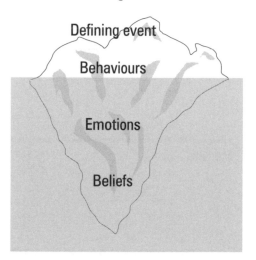

for the TOOLBOX

Resolving conflict

CEO options for dealing with conflict

CEO Option	CEO Response to Conflict
Delegate	Count on team members to work out the conflict.
Conclude	Resolve the conflict by removing either the person or the situation.
Direct	Instruct protagonists to resolve the problem themselves.
Support	Work with each of the protagonists individually to help them find a solution.
Arbitrate	Ask both teams to present their arguments and decide between them.
Mediate	Facilitate process and discussion to achieve resolution.

Adapted from Nadler and Spencer (1998).

Advantages

Promotes individual responsibility and empowers the people involved.
Allows for different management styles.

Direct intervention will change the conflict.
Appealing speed and simplicity.

Sends a clear expectation about resolution.
Empowers the individuals.

Can strengthen relationships.
Keeps ownership with team members, and develops their ability to resolve the problem.

More efficient use of CEO's time.
Pushes responsibility for clearly articulating positions to those involved.

Both empowering and supportive.
Develops individuals' competence.
Builds relationships between protagonists and the CEO.

Disadvantages

May be a form of avoiding conflict and abdicating responsibility.
Can allow conflict to fester.

Can be extreme.
Does not allow others the opportunity to resolve the conflict.
May 'train' others to depend on the CEO.

May be a form of avoiding involvement.
Protagonists may not have the skills to resolve the issue.

Requires strong relationships and a high level of skill.
Can get CEO mired in details and absorb a lot of time.

Can 'train' team to depend on the CEO.
Decision may please one person and alienate the other – making future conflict more likely.

Can absorb a lot of the CEO's time.
Tempting to revert to a less empowering option if agreement is not found quickly.

default modes for addressing these problems. CEOs will often have only a partial awareness of the full range of options open to them and the part they may be playing in creating or sustaining the present situation through their present stance towards it.

The facilitator should discuss the range of options available, summarised in the table on pages 338-9, with the CEO and explore:

▲ Which role is the CEO presently taking on the conflict in question?
▲ Which other approaches (if any) has the CEO tried?
▲ What impact is this choice making on maintaining or resolving the situation? (The facilitator is likely to have collected useful data here from interviews with the protagonists and others in the team.)
▲ Which role or roles offer the best prospects for resolving the conflict?
▲ How comfortable does the CEO feel about adopting a different role?
▲ What support might the CEO need?

PHASE THREE
Choosing an intervention

Once the perspectives of the whole team about the issue, and the CEO's preferred role for dealing with it, have been investigated,

an option can be chosen and an intervention designed to resolve the conflict.

It's not possible to prescribe a single intervention that's suitable for every situation but, in general terms, we have found variants on the tools for Relationship Conversations, especially Speed Feedback (page 256), and the tools for Learning Conversations, particularly 'Good, Tricky, Do Differently' (page 324), provide a good basis on which to build.

Whichever intervention is chosen, it will need to explicitly address a number of key stages:

▲ Mode – the whole team, or just part of it? Should the CEO be present?
▲ Time and place – where and when should action be taken to give the best chance of success?
▲ Signing up those who need to be involved – what's in it for them?
▲ Clarify steps and boundaries – how will the process move to a conclusion?
▲ Sharing perspectives – how to ensure that all are heard and all get to understand the whole picture?
▲ Reflection – what questions do people have about the new information?
▲ Actions – what is each person prepared to commit to towards a resolution?
▲ Sustainability – how and when will progress be reviewed and sustained? ▲

From conflict to breakthrough

Graham and Neville's company was a classic technology start-up. They had met at university, developed their product as part of their final year studies and gone on to create a large and profitable business that made them both very wealthy.

Where they had been smarter than most, though, was to realise when the company had become too big for them to manage. They had brought in an external CEO and each then continued to work in the business as the director responsible for the area he had made his own – sales and marketing for Graham and product development and technology for Neville.

Anne, the new CEO, had done a great job. The company had continued its meteoric rise and she had recruited other directors to create a strong team.

A conversation about sales of one of the new products erupted into a violent argument.

Over the previous year, however, the core product seemed to have reached sales maturity and growth had all but stalled. Other products had been developed, but none were achieving the sales volumes needed to balance the portfolio or grow the business.

Worse still, competitors were advancing and showing signs of taking market share.

The pressure to rediscover growth had increased tensions that had been building up between the two founding directors. Each blamed the other for the slowdown in sales. Graham would say both publicly and privately that the lack of significant new products was the problem. The clear implication, though it was never said, was that this was Neville's fault. Neville was less vocal, but no less clear, about his view that sales had been riding too long on a product which ➤

Resolving conflict

had sold itself and that, now things were a bit tougher, the people in the sales team had 'failed to up their game'.

The tension was constantly simmering below the surface. It was proving harder and harder for Anne to get the team working effectively on even basic decisions and some of the newer directors were privately thinking about moving on.

The defining moment came in an otherwise ordinary board meeting, when a conversation about sales of one of the new products erupted into a violent argument. The other directors drew away and Anne tried, without success, to mediate. She ended up calling an end to the meeting and keeping the two founders behind.

What they didn't know was that Anne had seen this coming. She and I had already been discussing how and when to tackle it. The row provided the perfect opportunity.

She told the two of them about the corrosive effect their relationship was having on the team and organisation. She explained that she had been

> *The defining moment came in an otherwise ordinary board meeting, when a conversation about sales of one of the new products erupted into a violent argument.*

delegating the resolution to them but that this had clearly not worked, and that she was going to work with them both to solve the problems. She gave each of them a list of questions, based on the Conflict Iceberg, to take away and reflect on. The questions explored how they felt about their own and one another's behaviour, how they felt about the situation and what they thought was the underlying problem.

The next day she met with each of the founders to discuss these questions. As we had expected, the initial answers were relatively superficial and tended to focus on blaming one another. By probing more deeply, particularly into the part that was being played by their own feelings and beliefs, she helped each of them begin to recognise and acknowledge his own role in the unsatisfactory state of affairs.

When she brought them both together, the temperature was already much lower. They talked about what was going on for each of them and why they felt ➤

things had simmered and escalated as they had. It wasn't an easy conversation, but it became easier as their understanding increased.

They all agreed that both product development and sales needed some profound changes. Graham also revealed that he had been feeling increasingly uncomfortable with his sales and marketing role. He had taken it on in the first place because he was clearly better suited to it than Neville, but, as the company had grown, the skills needed to drive sales had changed. Neville, in turn, was finding that his expertise was becoming more and more thinly spread as he grappled with the demands of leading a large team and driving an increasingly large portfolio of development projects.

The breakthrough was Graham's suggestion that he might return to work in product development alongside Neville.

> *The breakthrough was Graham's suggestion that he might return to work in product development alongside Neville.*

This would allow the recruitment of an experienced sales director but also, critically, make it possible for the two original partners to work together again on product development. In particular, it would allow the two of them to work on innovations to revitalise the core product, re-differentiate it from the emerging 'me-too' competitors and generate new revenue streams from the company's large installed base. They quickly agreed on the principle and the conversation rapidly turned to ideas for extending the core product.

It took a while to see the organisational changes through, but the tension and conflict subsided immediately and the change was noticed both inside and outside the boardroom. At the time of writing, it's too early to say whether growth has returned, but the company now has a number of innovations approaching launch and everyone is very excited about the future. Equally importantly, Anne has a strong, well-functioning Leadership Team, working together to drive the company forward. ▲

TABLE OF FIGURES

LIST OF TOOLS

INDEX OF CASE STUDIES

Priority Conversations

Relationship Conversations

Other

BIBLIOGRAPHY

Allan, D., Kingdon, M., Murrin, K., and Rudkin, D. (2002). *Sticky Wisdom: How to Start a Creative Revolution at Work*. Oxford: Capstone.

Argyris, C. (1983). Action science and intervention. *The Journal of Applied Behavioral Science, 19*(2), 115-135.

Argyris, C. (1990). *Overcoming Organizational Defenses: Facilitating Organizational Learning*. Needham, Mass.: Allyn and Bacon.

Argyris, C. (1991, May-June). *Teaching Smart People How to Learn*. Harvard Business Review, 69(3) pp. 99-109.

Beisser, A. (1970). *The Paradoxical Theory of Change*. In J. Fagan, and I. Shepard., Gestalt Therapy Now: Theory, Techniques, and Applications (pp. 77-80). Palo Alto, CA: Science and Behavior Books.

Bohm, D. (1996). *On Dialogue*. London New York: Routledge.

Charan, R., and Colvin, G. (1999). *Why CEOs Fail*. Fortune.

Cohen, S. G., and Bailey, D. E. (1997). *What Makes Teams Work: Group Effectiveness Research from the Shop Floor to the Executive Suite*. Journal of Management, Vol 23, No. 3, 239-290.

Covey, S. R. (1990). *The Seven Habits of Highly Effective People: Restoring the Character Ethic*. New York: Fireside.

Deutschman, A. (2007). *Change or Die: The Three Keys to Change at Work and in Life*. New York: HarperCollins.

Eisenhardt, K. M., Kahwajy, J. L., and Bourgeois, L. I. (1997). *How Management Teams Can Have a Good Fight*. Harvard Business Review July-August 1997, 77-85.

Ernst and Young. (1998). *Measures that Matter: An Exploratory Investigation of Investors' Information Needs and Value Priorities*. Ernst and Young Centre for Business Innovation and Organisation for Economic Co-operation and Development.

➤

Goffee, R., and Jones, G. (1998). *The Character of a Corporation*. New York: HarperCollins.

Goffee, R., and Jones, G. (2009). *Clever: Leading Your Smartest, Most Creative People*. Boston, Mass: Harvard Business Press.

Greenleaf, R. K. (1991). *Servant Leadership: A Journey into the Nature of Legitimate Power and Greatness*. New York: Paulist.

Hambrick, D. (1995). *Fragmentation and the Other Problems CEOs Have With Their Top Management Teams*. California Management Review 37(3), 110-127.

Hambrick, D. C. (1997). *Corporate coherence and the top management team*. Strategy & Leadership, 25(5), 24-29.

Harrison, R. (1971). *Role Negotiation: A Tough Minded Approach to Team Development*. Development Research Associates.

Harvard Business Review. (2011). *Building Better Teams*. Boston, Mass: Harvard Business Review Press.

Hawkins, P. (2011). *Leadership Team Coaching: Developing Collective Transformational Learning*. London; Philadelphia, PA: Kogan Page.

Hay Group. (2001). *Top Teams: Why Some Work and Some Do Not*.

Kaplan, R. S., and Norton, D. P. (1996). *The Balanced Scorecard: Translating Strategy into Action*. Boston: Harvard Business Review Press.

Katzenbach, J. R. (1998). *Teams at the Top: Unleashing the Potential of Both Teams and Individual Leaders*. Boston, Mass: Harvard Business School Press.

Katzenbach, J. R., and Smith, D. (1993). *The Wisdom of Team: Creating the High Performance Organization*. Boston, MA: Harvard Business School Press.

Kierson, M. (2009). *The Transformational Power of Executive Team Alignment: Organizational Success Beyond Your Wildest Dreams*. Charleston, S.C.: Advantage.

Katzenbach, J. R. (1998). *Teams at the Top: Unleashing the Potential of Both Teams and Individual Leaders.* Harvard Business School Press.

Kotter, J. (2008). *A Sense of Urgency.* Harvard Business School Press.

Lencioni, P. (2002). *The Five Dysfunctions of a Team.* San Francisco: Jossey-Bass Publishers.

Levin, L. S. (2011). *Top Teaming: A Roadmap for Teams Navigating the Now, the New, and the Next.* Bloomington: iUniverse Inc.

Nadler, D. A., and Spencer, J. L. (1998). *Executive Teams.* San Francisco: Jossey-Bass Publishers.

Nicholson, N. (1997). *Evolutionary Psychology: Toward a New View of Human Nature and Organisational Society.* Human Relations, 50, pp. 1053-1078.

Nicholson, N. (2005). *Meeting the Maasai: Messages for Management.* Journal of Management Enquiry, September 2005; 14 (3) pp. 255-267.

Oncken, W., and Wass, D. (1974, Nov.-Dec.). *Management Time: Who's Got the Monkey?* Harvard Business Review, 52(6) pp. 75.

Oshry, B. (2007). *Seeing Systems: Unlocking the Mysteries of Organizational Life.* San Francisco: Berrett-Koehler Publishers.

Raes, A. M. (2011). *Top Management Teams: How to Be Effective Inside and Outside the Boardroom.* New York: Business Expert Press.

Raes, A., Glunk, U., Heijltjes, M., and Roe, R. (2007). *Top Management Team and Middle Managers: Making Sense of Leadership.* Small Group Leadership, 38(3), 360-386.

Raes, A., Heijltjes, M., Glunk, U., and Roe, R. (2011). *The Interface of the Top Management Team and Middle Managers.* 36(1), 102-126.

Senge, P. M. (2006). *The Fifth Discipline: The Art and Practice of the Learning Organization.* New York: Doubleday/Currency.

➤

Senge, P. M. (2006). *The Fifth Discipline: The Art and Practice of the Learning Organization.* Broadway Business.

Sheard, G., Kakabadse, A., and Kakabadse, N. (2009). *Leadership Teams: Developing and Sustaining High Performance.* Basingstoke: Palgrave Macmillan.

Shiffrin, R., and Nosofsky, R. (1994, April). *Seven Plus or Minus Two: A Commentary on Capacity Limitations.* Psychological Review, 101(2), pp. 357-361.

Smith, et al. (1994). *Top Management Team Demography and Process.* The Role of Social Integration and Communication. 39, 412-438.

Taylor, J., and Haneberg, L. (2011). *Connecting Top Managers: Developing Executive Teams for Business Success.* Upper Saddle River, N.J.: FT Press.

The Power of Positive Deviance: How Unlikely Innovators Solve the World's Toughest Problems, June 16, 2010, Harvard Business Review Press by Richard Pascale, Jerry Sternin, Monique Sternin.

The Sage Handbook of Methods in Social Psychology, Carol Sansone, Carolyn C Morf, A. T. Panter, SAGE Publications, 2004.

Thomas, K. W. (2002). *Thomas-Kilmann Conflict Mode Instrument.* CPP.

Torbert, B. (2004). *Action Inquiry: The Secret of Timely and Transforming Leadership.* Berrett-Koehler.

Wageman, R., Nunes, D. A., Burruss, J. A., and Hackman, J. R. (2008). *Senior Leadership Teams.* Boston, Mass: Harvard Business School Press.

Weick, K. E. (1979). *The Social Psychology of Organizing.* McGraw-Hill.

Whitmore, J. (2002). *Coaching for Performance: Growing People, Performance and Purpose.* London Naperville, IL: Nicholas Brealey.

Zeidner, M., Matthews, G., and Roberts, R. D. (2004). *Emotional Intelligence in the Workplace: A Critical Review.* Applied Psychology: An International Review, pp. 371-399.

FURTHER READING

Barner, R. W. (2000). *Executive Resource Management*. Davies Black Publishing.

Bobinski, D. (2009). *Creating Passion-Driven Teams*. Career Press.

Bossidy, L. and Charan, R. (2011). *Execution – The Discipline of Getting Things Done*. Random House Business Books.

Bungay, S. (2011). *The Art of Action*. Nicholas Brealey Publishing.

Carpenter, M. A. (2011). *The Handbook of Research on Top Management Teams*. Edward Elgar Publishing Ltd.

Champy, J. and Nohria, N. (2000). *The Arc of Ambition*. John Wiley and Sons Ltd.

Elliott, C. (1999). *Locating the Energy for Change: An Introduction to Appreciative Inquiry*. International Institute for Sustainable Development.

Flood, P., MacCurtain, S. and West, M. (2001). *Effective Top Management Teams*. Blackhall Publishing.

Goffee, R. and Jones, G. (2006). *Why Should Anyone be Led by You?* Harvard Business School Press.

Pearce, T. (2003). *Leading Out Loud*. Jossey-Bass.

Prinzessin zu Waldeck, T. (2007). *The Effect of Team Composition on Strategic Sensemaking*. Deutscher Universitats-Verlag.

Stober, D. R. and Grant A. M. (2006). *Evidence Based Coaching Handbook*. John Wiley and Sons Ltd.

Taylor, J. and Haneberg, L. (2011). *Connecting Top Managers*. FT Press.

Watzlawick, P., Weakland J. and Fisch, R. (1974). *Change - Principles of Problem Formation and Problem Resolution*. W. W. Norton and Company.

INDEX

Numbers in **bold** indicate a table
or illustration